D0887760

The Ivory Trade

THE IVORY

Joseph Horowitz

Music adviser to Northeastern University Press
GUNTHER SCHULLER

TRADE

Piano Competitions
and the Business of Music

Northeastern University Press
BOSTON

Copyright 1990 by Joseph Horowitz

First published 1990 by Summit Books, a division of Simon & Schuster. Reprinted 1991 by Northeastern University Press by agreement with Summit Books.

All rights reserved. Except for the quotation of short passages for the purposes of criticism and review, no part of this book may be reproduced in any form or by any means, electronic or mechanical, including photocopying, recording, or any information storage and retrieval system now known or to be invented, without written permission of the publisher.

Library of Congress Cataloging-in-Publication Data
Horowitz, Joseph, 1948–
    The ivory trade : piano competitions and the business of
music / Joseph Horowitz.
      p. cm.
    Reprint. Originally published: New York : Summit Books, c1990.
    Includes bibliographical references and index.
    ISBN 1-55553-117-2
    1. Van Cliburn International Piano Competition. 2. Music—
Competitions—Texas—Fort Worth. I. Title.
ML76.V23H7   1991
786.2'079'7645315—dc20   91-19290

Designed by Carla Weise/Levavi & Levavi
Printed and bound by Edwards Brothers, Inc., Ann Arbor, Michigan. The paper is Glatfelter Offset, an acid-free sheet.

MANUFACTURED IN THE UNITED STATES OF AMERICA

96 95 94 93 92 91   5 4 3 2 1

PERMISSIONS ACKNOWLEDGMENTS
Doubleday: Extracts from *The Super-Americans* by John Bainbridge © copyright 1961 by John Bainbridge. Reprinted by permission of William Morris Agency, Inc., on behalf of the author. Extract from *The American Orchestra and Theodore Thomas* by Charles Edward Russell © copyright 1927 by Doubleday, a division of Bantam, Doubleday, Dell, Incorporated. Farrar, Straus and Giroux, Inc.: Excerpt from *Less than One*, by Joseph Brodsky. Copyright © 1986 by Joseph Brodsky. Reprinted by permission of Farrar, Straus and Giroux, Inc. *Guitar Review*: Excerpt from "To Seek Together," by Eliot Fisk, published Spring 1989. *Musical America*: Excerpt from "The 8th International Tchaikovsky Piano Competition," by Daniel Pollack, published March 1987. *The New York Times*: Excerpts from "Russians Cheer U.S. Pianist, 23," by Max Frankel, April 12, 1958; "U.S. Pianist, 23, Wins Soviet Contest," by Max Frankel, April 12, 1958; "Moscow Rolls Out Red Carpet," by Mark Schubart, April 20, 1958; "A Winner on His Merits," by Howard Taubman, April 20, 1958; "Triumphs and Turmoil at the Cliburn Competition," by John Ardoin, October 9, 1977; "Piano: De Groote Gives Concert," by Harold C. Schonberg, December 13, 1977; "André-Michel Schub May Be Emerging from the Shadows," by Joseph Horowitz, July 29, 1979. Copyright © 1958/77/79 by the New York Times Company. Reprinted by permission. Princeton University Press: Excerpt from Elliot Forbes (ed.), *Thayer's Life of Beethoven* (1949); Pantheon Books: Excerpt from Felix Mendelssohn's Letters, as edited by G. Selden-Goth (1945). Summit Books: Excerpt from *Reflections from the Keyboard*, by David Dubal (1984). *Time*: Excerpt from "The All-American Virtuoso," May 19, 1958. Copyright 1958 Time Inc. Reprinted by permission.

For Agnes and Bernie

Acknowledgments

SIX DAYS BEFORE THE START OF THE EIGHTH VAN CLIBURN INTERNA-
tional Piano Competition, the *Fort Worth Star-Telegram* identified
me as a visiting New York author "viewed by some as a harsh
critic" of piano competitions. And yet, with rare exceptions, the
natives—even those who suspected I was up to no good—
maintained their Texas hospitality. I especially remember the warm
welcomes of Faye and Leon Brachman, and of Renie and Sterling
Steves. Susan Tilley, Denise Chupp, and Beth Wareham of the
Cliburn Foundation were unusually helpful. So was Nancy Shear,
the Cliburn competition's national press representative.

I am indebted, as well, to the counsel and assistance of Grant Johannesen, chairman of Cleveland's Casadesus competition; Sey-
mour Lipkin and George Moquin, artistic director and executive
director of the University of Maryland's William Kapell competition; Lucy and Robert Mann, who oversee New York City's Walter
Naumburg competition; and Paul Pollei, founder and director of the
Gina Bachauer competition of Salt Lake City (where my hosts were
John Walker and family). Ellen Highstein of the Concert Artists
Guild, Dorothy Jaroschy of Pro Musicis, and Susan Wadsworth of
Young Concert Artists eagerly welcomed my attendance at their re-
spective auditions. T. Roland Berner kindly lent me his scrapbooks

from the Leventritt competition. Eileen Cline graciously invited me to make use of her doctoral dissertation on piano competitions. Jack Pfeiffer enabled me to assemble a comprehensive collection of Van Cliburn recordings and tapes.

As this is a book about pianists, I must have spoken to at least a hundred of them in the course of writing it. Seven, in particular, unstintingly shared their thoughts and experiences; these were the late Steven De Groote, José Feghali, Jeffrey Kahane, Santiago Rodriguez, André-Michel Schub, Alexander Toradze, and William Wolfram. At the 1989 Cliburn competition, Pedro Burmester and Jean-Efflam Bavouzet were particularly tolerant of my interrogations. Van Cliburn and Martha Hyder made me feel welcome in their homes.

My manuscript was read by Emanuel Ax, Agnes Bruneau, Robert Cornfield, Dr. Jacob Horowitz, Kathleen Hulser, and David Schiff, all of whom had interesting things to say about it. Walter Frisch helped me come up with a title in a moment of terminal despair.

An author of my acquaintance describes writing a book as a "pathology." Only writers and their families know that this is no exaggeration. My wife, Agnes, and two-year-old son, Bernard, tolerated my too frequent absences and were invaluably supportive in their different ways. Robert Cornfield, my agent, also pacified and advised me. Ileene Smith, my editor at Summit Books, prodded me toward several vital revisions. Her assistant, Alane Mason, was a model of competence and care. I even liked working with my excellent copy editor, Marge Horvitz—which was quite an accomplishment on her part.

Contents

Introduction

"MUSIC COMPETITIONS TODAY DON'T HAVE ONE PURPOSE," SAYS AN-drew Raeburn. "That cannot happen anymore. Whether you like it or not, putting on a major competition costs a lot of money. Social purposes intrude. Civic purposes are served. The pressures from all sides are very great." The Van Cliburn International Piano Com-petition, which Raeburn administered in 1985, is a signature event for the city of Fort Worth, Texas, as germane to its identity as any physical landmark, local industry, or college football team. It lures visitors, businesses, and new residents. It fosters friendships, din-ner parties, and community pride. It sells T-shirts, earrings, and classical music. Combining the repertoire of maximum popularity with the drama and human interest of the Olympic Games, its sixteen days of Bach and Beethoven, Chopin and Liszt, attain some-thing like mass appeal.

For its 1989 competition, the Cliburn Foundation raised over $2.8 million and sold 36,000 tickets. Salt Lake City's Gina Bachauer International Piano Competition and Festival lasts nearly four weeks, during which over one hundred pianists perform twice daily in local banks, schools, and malls; the Bachauer takes partial credit for Salt Lake City's unsurpassed per capita ratio of piano teachers and students. At the University of Maryland's nine-day International Piano Festival and William Kapell Competition, recitals and talks by famous jurors attract half the audience that attends competitive minirecitals by obscure twenty-year-olds. Multipurpose music competitions have entered the popular consciousness as television shows that double as advertisements for competing competitions. There is even a Hollywood movie, *The Competition*, in which Richard Dreyfuss and Amy Irving pit Beethoven's *Emperor* Concerto against the Prokofiev Third—and also fall in love. The Russian contestant is an automaton whose teacher suddenly defects. The winner is coached by a foul-mouthed pedagogue who preaches "competitive edge." Music diffuses through a mélange of soap opera, romance, and sports.

With their big, democratized audiences, their overcirculated sonatas and concertos, and their ballyhooed winners, music competitions are a microcosm, an exemplary lesson in what transforms and perplexes Western high culture in the late twentieth century: its popularization.

As their popularity grows and their purposes multiply, music competitions themselves proliferate. According to one survey, there are more than twice as many international piano competitions today as in 1970, more than ten times as many as in 1950. As recently as the mid-fifties, piano students at the leading American conservatories were likely never to compete. As of 1990, the *Musical America International Directory of the Performing Arts* shows more than five dozen competitions for pianists in the United States alone—and this exhausting list is far from being exhaustive.

Anybody with enough money can start an international piano competition. The Owensboro (Kentucky) Symphony has one. Miami hosts a *two*-piano competition. The Palm Beach International Piano Competition, "the fastest rising in the world," is by invitation only; one recent contestant calls it "a kind of paid vacation." A singular competition spinoff is Indianapolis's Festival of Champions, featuring major competition winners in "the most beloved music in the repertoire." Also peripheral to the competitive mainstream are low-profile "auditions"—Young Concert Artists and Affiliate Artists are the best-known—whose prizes are in-house concert management for groups of unranked winners. And then there are the conservatory competitions, the winners of which receive scholarships or coveted dates with the school orchestra.

The larger artistic goal of all these events—actually or ostensibly—is to create performance opportunities for young mu-

sicians. No longer is a New York debut recitalist reasonably assured of obtaining a review; no longer is a good review reasonable
assurance of obtaining management. Private auditions and behind-
the-scenes networking, too, are less efficacious than before. The
music business's preferred winnowing procedure is one that guar-
antees applause and publicity, often concerts and recordings; one
that assumes the burden of choosing which youngsters to back.
Only a handful make headway without competitions. Usually,
these exceptions prove the rule. Ivo Pogorelich did not win the 1980
Chopin competition—but in losing it, he became a cause célèbre.
András Schiff placed only third in Leeds in 1975—but Charles
Rosen, on the jury, helped him secure major American manage-
ment. Vladimir Feltsman—whose first prize in the 1971 Long-
Thibaud competition is irrelevant to his current stardom—is a
publicized refugee. Yefim Bronfman is looked after by Isaac Stern.
Peter Serkin is Rudolf's son.

For the overwhelming majority of aspiring young solo performers, competitions are ubiquitous and incessant: a fact of life.

Piano competitions proliferate; so—even more—do pianists. As
many as *eight thousand* of them graduate every year from America's
professional music schools. The 1990 *Musical America* directory—sometimes called "the world's greatest collection of people
who don't work"—lists 572 solo pianists available for booking, from
Achucarro to Zuponcic; twenty years ago, the number was
199.

Richard Probst, until 1989 the director of concerts and artists for
Steinway & Sons, once tabulated the frequency with which pianists were engaged and found "that half or more than half the
annual opportunities to be employed by North American orchestras, major and minor, went to ten pianists, who were getting, on
average, fifteen concerto jobs each—which of course could mean
many more than fifteen performances. And there were somewhere
between 125 and 150 getting one or two opportunities each. So you
had ten pianists getting virtually all the repeat business."

Meanwhile, the number of recital opportunities is dwindling.
Presenters now prefer group attractions: choruses and brass quintets, foreign dance companies and chamber orchestras whose fees
are state subsidized. Even without growing overpopulation, this
would be a period of diminishing opportunity.

*   *   *

Music competitions have always been controversial. Felix Mendelssohn wrote in 1840:

> Today I made a resolution over which I am as happy as a bird, and that is never again to participate in any way in the awarding of prizes at a musical competition. Several proposals of this kind were made to me and I did not know why I was so annoyed, until it became clear to me that fundamentally it would be sheer arrogance on my part, which I would not tolerate in others. I should therefore be the last person to set myself up as a criterion and my taste as incontrovertible, and, in an idle hour passing in review all the assembled competitors, criticizing them, and—God knows—possibly being guilty of the most glaring injustice toward them.

When in 1884 Claude Debussy won a composition contest, he nevertheless complained: "The contestants are trained like racehorses for the Grand Prix. . . . If you are not in form that particular month, so much the worse for you. It is a purely arbitrary affair. . . . Possibly, the institution derives its strength from the fact that it has attained, in certain circles, the status of a superstition. To have won settles the question of whether one does or does not have talent. If it is not absolutely certain, it is at least convenient and provides public opinion with a sort of ready reckoner." Béla Bartók said: "Competitions are for horses, not artists." Joseph Szigeti said: "It seems to me that the effect of inexplicable failures, with their attendant damage to the young performer's morale, more than outweighs the success of the few." Gregor Piatigorsky called competitions "absurd": "I suffer agony to see young artists go through the humiliation of a competition. . . . The joy of those who succeed is spoiled by the sorrow of those who have been hurt. . . . It cannot be useful to discourage a hundred merely to encourage one."

More recent complaints about music competitions have kept pace with the excess of the events themselves. The late Glenn Gould claimed they inflict "spiritual lobotomy." The pianist and pedagogue Russell Sherman christens them "the anti-Christ." A young pianist of my acquaintance, once a mainstay of the competition circuit, calls piano jurors "criminals." According to conventional wisdom, juries gravitate toward bland, "consensus" candidates at the expense of more controversial, more original talent. Competitions are said to turn innocent young artists into hard-bitten road warriors. They allegedly transform guileless masterworks into gauntlets.

But conventional wisdom also maintains that competitions launch

careers, teach discipline, and provide necessary performance experience. The prevalent view, held even by most who administer,
adjudicate, and win, is that they are the worst method except for
every other one. They are a "necessary evil."

Competition-bashing is such an easy sport that it becomes hard
to stop. Harder still is the effort to understand. Good or bad, right
or wrong, they are here. They are less a cause than a symptom—of
what? Study them and you can find out how careers in performance
are made. How classical music is perceived and marketed. How it
interfaces with commerce, with the media, with the culture at
large.

My study is of the quintessential music competition: the type for
pianists; of the quintessential American piano competition: the Van
Cliburn; of the quintessential piano-competition winner: Van
Cliburn himself. Though much of what I have to say pertains
globally, my explicit scope is American and includes competitions
and auditions of all shapes and sizes. I begin with Van Cliburn
winning the 1958 Tchaikovsky competition: the quintessential
piano-competition victory. I end with his 1989 "comeback," plus—
in this paperback edition—a 1991 Afterword. In between, I take
up the history of music competitions, with particular emphasis
on the Cliburn and its most significant American predecessor:
the Leventritt, which began in 1940 and ended in 1976. Next,
chronicling the recent history of the Cliburn competition, I adopt
the viewpoints of six who took part between 1976 and 1985. Alexander Toradze, André-Michel Schub, Jeffrey Kahane, José
Feghali, William Wolfram, and the late Steven De Groote are not
famous pianists; rather, they are pianists of talent whose futures,
save De Groote's, are unknowable. I portray each not as a contestant but as a person. That is: these portraits are purposely digres-
sive. They show something of the life of the concert pianist and
also illustrate other generic themes. The portrait of De Groote
partly documents the perils of instant celebrity. The portraits of
Toradze and Wolfram partly contrast integrated Soviet training
with the laissez-faire American variety. The portraits of Schub and
Feghali partly contemplate the impact of television. The portait of
Kahane partly considers the role of family and management. This
survey of six pianists, while of course not comprehensive, point-
edly includes a range of types: the heroic pianist, the versatile
pianist, the pianist who is fortunate in his career development, the
pianist who is a perennial competition loser. My six portraits also

survey a gamut of responses to the piano's diminishing centrality as a Romantic icon. Toradze, at one extreme, is a throwback to the tormented virtuoso; Kahane plays chamber music, contemporary music, even popular music. The portraits are 1988 snapshots preceding the 1989 Cliburn competition, which becomes the subject of the third section of my book. May 1991, the month of the first Gilmore International Keyboard Festival, concludes my narrative—all of which unfolds, in the present tense, as a four-year diary of events and observations. (My first, 1988, impressions of Steven De Groote therefore do not acknowledge his death on May 22, 1989—which I ponder in due course.)

Competitions claim "objectivity." I do not. If certain pianists are my friends, I feel richer, not poorer. At the 1989 Cliburn competition, Jean-Efflam Bavouzet was my Ping-Pong partner. Rather than attempting to neutralize this intervention, I let him win a few games just before the chamber music round, in which he excelled. My formal relationship to the competition was that of a typical journalist—the tickets and social invitations were complimentary; I paid my own transportation and hotel expenses.

Like my *Understanding Toscanini*, in which I addressed "How He Became an American Culture-God and Helped Create a New Audience for Old Music," *The Ivory Trade* will disappoint readers looking for solutions. The popularization of high culture is a central theme of our day, not a problem awaiting a remedy. I share George Steiner's conviction that "it is enormously interesting to be alive at this cruel, late stage in Western affairs." I try my best to side with de Tocqueville, who was more intrigued than dismayed, and who observed: "It is . . . not true to assert that men living in democratic times are naturally indifferent to science, literature, and the arts; only it must be acknowledged that they cultivate them after their own fashion. . . ."

PRELUDE: THE VAN CLIBURN STORY

THE YEARS OF COLD WAR BETWEEN THE SOVIET UNION AND THE UNITED States were also years of cultural war. Music sometimes amplified, sometimes soothed, political and economic tensions between the two "superpowers." An early musical forum for rivalry and concord was the Queen Elisabeth competition in Brussels. The Russians had dominated it before World War II; David Oistrakh, in 1937, and Emil Gilels, in 1938, were the first winners. When the Queen Elisabeth resumed in 1951, a violin year, Russians finished first (Leonid Kogan), second, fifth, and seventh. Americans finished ninth and eleventh. As Howard Taubman wrote in the *New York Times*: "These new Russian successes caused government officials and interested private citizens to wonder whether we were meeting this challenge on the cultural front with our strongest resources." At the suggestion of the State Department, a committee was formed to select a team of American pianists to compete in Brussels in 1952. The Ford Foundation would pay their travel expenses. Eight pianists were chosen; one, Leon Fleisher, accepted—and won. The *Times*'s senior music critic, Olin Downes, reported: "The cheering was long and loud, and the throat tightened, in these days of insanity and international suspicions and rumors and alarums of war, to feel that in the domain of art all the hearts present beat as one, and rejoiced in a talent come into its own." *Time* magazine likened Fleisher's victory to winning Wimbledon. And yet, as it happened, no Russian pianists had competed that year. Taubman and others remained concerned that America was unequipped to defeat Soviet musicians, whose training and selection were supervised and subsidized by the state. In 1955, America (the violinist Berl Senofsky) beat Russia (Julian Sitkovietsky) in Brussels. In 1956, Russia (the pianist Vladimir Ashkenazy) barely beat America (John Browning). Americans also placed high in piano competitions in Bolzano, Vercelli, and Rio de Janeiro. Meanwhile, in 1955, Oistrakh and Gilels had performed for the first time in the United States—to high acclaim. Two years later, Canada's Glenn Gould became the first North American classical musician to play in cold war Russia—and was at least as enthusiastically received as Oistrakh and Gilels had been in New York. Silencing these musical exchanges, however, were the screaming headlines of October 5, 1957: SIGHT RED BABY MOON OVER US. SOVIET LAUNCHES FIRST MOON. SOVIET FIRES EARTH SATELLITE INTO SPACE.

"A great victory over the United States," crowed the Soviet press. "A triumph of the Soviet regime." "A first step to the moon." American scientists said they needed at least four more tests before trying to hurl a much lighter satellite into orbit. And Russia, unlike the United States, had successfully fired an intercontinental ballistic missile. Congress reacted with alarm, consternation, and shame. Would Khrushchev be able to drop atomic and hydrogen bombs from space? Could he target New York and Los Angeles with his long-range weapons? What were the unaligned nations of Africa and Asia thinking? A *New York Times* editorial asked: "Why did not our policy makers realize the tremendous prestige, propaganda, and political gains likely to accrue to the Soviet Union if it was the first to send up a space satellite?"

This was the context in which Moscow, some two months later, invited American participation in the new Tchaikovsky International Competition. Dmitri Shostakovich, the leading Soviet composer, was chairman of the organizing committee. The jurors included the great names of Russian pianism: Gilels, Alexander Goldenweiser, Heinrich Neuhaus, Sviatoslav Richter. Of course, the Soviets were expected to win. The repertoire was weighted in favor of Russian music. The jury was dominated by Soviet-bloc nations. And everything in Khrushchev's Russia was political.

Entering the Tchaikovsky competition was not Van Cliburn's idea. It may have originated with Rosina Lhévinne, Cliburn's seventy-eight-year-old teacher at the Juilliard School, herself a distinguished graduate of the Kiev Conservatory. She enlisted the support of Juilliard's dean, Mark Schubart, and its president, William Schuman. Steinway's Alexander Greiner also helped prevail on Cliburn to go to Moscow. The thinking was not only that Cliburn was an outstanding young American pianist but that he excelled in the Russian Romantic literature the new competition would stress. According to an irresistible story told by the pianist Olegna Fuschi, at that time a Lhévinne pupil: "Madame read the [Tchaikovsky] brochure, then, holding it in her hand, she went to the window and looked out, staring. Suddenly I heard her say very softly, half to herself, 'Van.' "

In fact, at the age of twenty-three, Van Cliburn had already committed his soul to Russia. Years later he recalled: "I was immediately taken with the idea of going to Moscow because I had always wanted to see the Church of St. Basil. That had been a . . . dream of mine since I was six years old, when my parents had given me a child's picture history book of the world. I remember this so well, as if it were yesterday." When he landed in Moscow in April 1958 and was met by a representative of the Ministry of Culture, he asked first to be driven to the Church of St. Basil. Standing in snowy Red Square late at night, he thought his heart would stop. He identified the Moscow Conservatory, where the competition was held, with his hero Rachmaninoff, who had graduated with a gold medal in 1892. When he visited Tchaikovsky's grave in Leningrad, he took away some Russian earth to replant at Rachmaninoff's grave in New York. He called the Russians "my people" and said, "I've never felt so at home anywhere in my life."

Cliburn's adoration was returned. His lanky six feet four inches, his blue eyes and mop of frizzy blond hair, were recognized everywhere. People hugged and kissed him on the street, calling him "Vanya" and "Vanyushka." He was showered with flowers and personal mementos. Women wept when he played, and students shouted "First prize!" Outside the conservatory, militiamen were used to maintain order. His pandemonious victory, announced April 14, confirmed the popular verdict of days before.

The Cliburn furor was of unprecedented, unrepeatable, incomprehensible proportions. Caged, cut off, Russians craved warming contact with the dreamed-of West. Van Cliburn, the mythic American, dreamed of Russia. Living a dream, he moved with charming innocence, with a clairvoyant sureness, touching outstretched hands, pledging friendship between nations. Speaking from the stage, he told people what it meant to him to perform where Tchaikovsky had taught and Rachmaninoff had studied. At a Kremlin reception, he tried unsuccessfully to refuse champagne, which he was unaccustomed to drinking. When the irrepressible Nikita Khrushchev threw his arms around the Cliburn beanpole and asked why he was so tall, Cliburn grinned: "Because I'm from Texas." He addressed the dour Nikolai Bulganin with grave courtesy as "Mr. Molotov." When he left Moscow he backed toward his airplane waving to well-wishers, tears streaming down his cheeks. In both the Soviet Union and the United States, he was inevitably called "the American Sputnik."

Moscow's competition might have escaped immediate notice in the United States—even the American ambassador at first paid little attention to it—but for Max Frankel, a *New York Times* Moscow correspondent, who had been advised by Mark Schubart that a great scoop awaited him at the Moscow Conservatory. Two Frankel reports made page one. RUSSIANS CHEER U.S. PIANIST, 23—a three-column headline over a two-column photograph of Cliburn at the keyboard—appeared April 12; the story began: "A boyish-looking, curly-haired young man from Kilgore, Tex., took musical Moscow by storm tonight." Two days later, Frankel's page-one story carried a three-column photograph and a four-column headline: U.S. PIANIST, 23, WINS SOVIET CONTEST. As Frankel was a foreign correspondent, not a music critic, the focus of his reportage was not Cliburn's playing but its reception. He described Cliburn as "the rage of the town. Nothing has been so scarce here in a long time as a ticket to his performance. . . . The competition is not just another cultural event here. It has gripped the city as the baseball world series captivates Americans."

When Cliburn won, the *Times* also carried stories by Mark Schubart (writing from Moscow) and Howard Taubman (writing in New York). Schubart said:

> From the Tchaikovsky competition itself we can learn a great deal. In the United States competitions as they exist elsewhere are little understood. We have a number of them, of course, but they are little publicized. They are usually conducted in private and only the results become public property. . . .
>
> The entire [Tchaikovsky] contest took place in the large and beautiful concert hall of the Tchaikovsky Conservatory, and except for the preliminaries, all performances were open to the public. And what a public! Every seat was taken for every performance and by the time the final round was reached tickets were not to be found even, according to

rumor, by V.I.P.'s in the party. More impressive than the size of the audiences, though, was their attitude. For the Russians love their virtuosos the way the Italians love their opera singers. And when the big pieces of the Russian literature were being played, every flubbed passage was greeted with audible sighs of dismay, always regretful, never contemptuous. And it was probably this wildly demonstrative audience that brought the competition to an almost unbearable pitch of emotional tension and made of the whole project not only a contest to decide a victory, but also a musical event of first importance.

Taubman added:

> There are some . . . cold truths that need consideration. . . . The Russians made their Tchaikovsky contest almost an occasion of national celebration. The highest authorities took time out to pay their respects to competitors and winners. In other countries where competitions take place the situation is similar. . . .
>
> It is an open question whether we should plunge into the big-competition field. There is no question about our high competence in performance and creation. All we need is the wisdom to recognize and respond to it.

In the short run, the United States did "respond to it." Van Cliburn was a national hero overnight. New York gave him a ticker-tape parade. Cliburn stood in an open car, waving and blowing kisses. The "Van Cliburn Day" marchers included three high school bands, Boy and Girl Scouts, and more than a thousand elementary school students. In Philadelphia a few days later, a screaming crowd tore the handles off his limousine. Not to be outdone by Khrushchev (although he was), President Eisenhower received Cliburn and his parents at the White House. Cliburn played the finale of the Tchaikovsky First Concerto on the "Steve Allen Show" (which outmaneuvered Ed Sullivan); Jack Gould, the *Times* television critic, found "his tolerance of the little jokes peculiar to video variety shows" to be "most disarming." "Person to Person" with Edward R. Murrow followed, and the quiz show "What's My Line?"

Cliburn's concert calendar suddenly showed dozens of dates for the summer and coming season, including engagements with the major orchestras. His fee, according to a *Time* cover story, had jumped from $1,000 to $2,500 and more "within hours," after which he struck a deal entitling him to 60 percent of box office receipts; one date, with the Dallas Symphony, was likely to earn him $9,000 ("We want to be the first to pay him his biggest fee," said the orchestra's president). RCA Victor signed Cliburn to "one of the fattest contracts ever offered a young artist." His first recording, of the Tchaikovsky First, topped the LP charts along with Johnny Mathis and *South Pacific* (and eventually became the first classical recording to sell more than a million copies). Previous pianists—Liszt, to begin with—had received comparably frenzied acclaim. But none had achieved such lightning and pervasive stardom.

One new factor, of course, was global and electronic media: the *Times*'s instantaneous transcontinental reportage; the TV shows; the Tchaikovsky recording. And new media had created a new audience—initially a twentieth-century American phenomenon, dating from the advent of radio in 1920 and tutored by the interwar "music appreciation" movement. Arturo Toscanini, the first new-audience superstar, was said by *Life* magazine to be as well known to Americans as Joe DiMaggio. *Variety* likened Cliburn's fame to Lindbergh's when he crossed the Atlantic—a feat more celebrated than anything DiMaggio did. When Cliburn first played in Carnegie Hall after returning from Russia, a veteran doorman described the standing-room-only crowd as atypical: "It's not the regulars—there are a lot more people here out of curiosity than out of interest in music." The Grant Park audience in Chicago, which pushed and elbowed toward Cliburn's dressing room, the girls shrieking and pulling their hair, was compared by a writer in *Family Weekly* to an Elvis Presley crowd—which was prophetic, because the city's Elvis Presley Fan Club changed its name to the Van Cliburn Fan Club.

Cliburn was tall and good-looking. He did not smoke or drink. He was so patriotic that he began his recitals with "The Star-Spangled Banner." He was so religious that he once sang in Billy Graham's choir at Madison Square Garden. He was born Harvey Lavan Cliburn, Jr., in Shreveport, Louisiana. His father was a minor oil company executive. His mother, born Rildia Bee O'Bryan, was a piano teacher who had studied in New York with Arthur Friedheim, a pupil of Liszt. An only child, Van took lessons with her from the age of three. He played with the Houston Symphony at twelve. He went to high school in Kilgore, Texas, to which the family had moved when he was six. From there he went to New York, where he allegedly presented himself to Rosina Lhévinne with the much-quoted announcement: "Honey, ah'm goin' to study with you."

According to innumerable graphic yet unreliable second- and

third-hand 1958 accounts, he was wholesome, friendly, and unpretentious. In high school he had been a "good, solid boy" who went to parties and liked to dance. With his height and coordination, he ostensibly could have become "a great athlete." He was at one time engaged to a "tall, lissome brunette" but broke it off because he was "not yet ready to reconcile marriage with a career." Unspoiled by success, he remained devoted to his family and "disarmingly untemperamental." He still spoke in an easy drawl, crooned "Blue Moon" and "Embraceable You," and turned a compliment "so deftly that the happy recipient could go on basking for days in its rosey afterglow." He adored "sitting behind the wheel of a big, smooth car." His natural affection for people predisposed him to giving unexpected gifts—as when he returned from Russia with seven suitcases of presents and packages. He was, *Time* summarized, "Horowitz, Liberace, and Presley rolled into one."

Writing of the "genius act," the social critic Dwight Macdonald once observed: "The masses put an absurdly high value on the personal genius, the charisma, of the performer, but they also demand a secret rebate: he must play the game—*their* game—must distort his personality to suit their taste." For classical musicians, the preferred personality is the antithesis of "longhair snob"; even Toscanini and Vladimir Horowitz were redrawn to seem regular guys.* And so was Van Cliburn redrawn—as if every Texas boy spends hours a day at the piano, is tall and awkward, writes old-fashioned poetry, and must be excused from gym for fear of injuring his hands. Cliburn once characterized his childhood experiences outside the family as "a living hell" (or so one reads). His Juilliard classmates remember him as intellectually innocent and endearingly gracious—and yet undeniably eccentric. His Southern charm was uncalculated—but he was not insensitive to its effect. I have never met a Cliburn acquaintance who considered him an uncomplicated man.

Few, in the heady days of Cliburn's Sputnik launch, stopped to ponder whether he was being propelled too high too fast. His manager, William Judd of Columbia Artists, certainly did not.

---

*According to *Life* magazine, Toscanini was "a simple, affectionate man, who works hard, [and] is unbelievably modest. . . . Soup is his favorite food. If he has no rehearsal in the afternoon, he goes for a long fast auto ride." According to the *New York Times*, Horowitz was "more like a man of affairs than the conventional figure of the musician." He had "a reputation for aloofness" but was "really shy." "Like his father-in-law [i.e., Toscanini], he has a charming simplicity in his relations with ordinary people." He was full of admiration for the United States, preferring "eager, open-minded Americans" to "patronizing and snobbish" Europeans.

Cliburn repeated what Columbia termed his "prize-winning program"—the Tchaikovsky First Concerto and Rachmaninoff's Third—four times in seven days upon returning home. And these were the works he continued to feature for months to come. Faintly audible amid the adulatory din was the dissenting voice of Paul Henry Lang, music critic of the *New York Herald Tribune*. Like the caustic Virgil Thomson, whose job he had inherited, Lang knew no sacred cows, and mistrusted war-horses. He warned that Cliburn risked becoming a "flesh and blood jukebox" and suffering "permanent intellectual disability," unless he took time off to pursue "a more catholic study of music":

> The hullaballoo raised by Columbia Concerts and the public about Mr. Cliburn is not the way to foster a brilliant young artist's career. Is this young man going to be exploited mercilessly while the going is good? They can easily ruin him, for after the prize-winning contest has been pounded out a few dozen times the world may look upon Mr. Cliburn as our champion musical athlete.

Even in the mainstream *New York Times Magazine*, the pianist and radio personality Abram Chasins wrote an article, "Will Success Spoil Van Cliburn?," in which he worried that "his meteoric success has plunged him into a killing pace that no man can sustain for long." Cliburn was "too keyed up" to sleep soundly, Chasins reported. He was burdened with business meetings and speaking engagements. He could not even go shopping without creating a "mob scene."

But his fans seized on Cliburn's high earnings and hectic pace as signatures of his success. And if he always played the Tchaikovsky First and Rachmaninoff Third—they, too, were Cliburn signatures.

It was merely predictable that the Cliburn craze fixated on personality, not music. In fact, Cliburn was already well known to the musical community. In 1954, he had won the Leventritt competition, America's most important for pianists. It was presumably the Leventritt that Mark Schubart had in mind when he wrote of "little publicized" events "conducted in private," in contradistinction to the Tchaikovsky, Queen Elisabeth, and Chopin competitions. Cliburn's Leventritt victory had been announced to the world in three tiny *New York Times* paragraphs. In 1955–56, he had played with the New York Philharmonic and the orchestras of Buffalo, Cleveland, Denver, and Pittsburgh, among others. After that, this modest beginning trailed off.* Some American commentators were insulted when, days after the Tchaikovsky verdict, Dmitri Shostakovich stated: "We, for our part, are extremely happy that this outstanding young American artist earned his first wide and entirely deserved recognition among us here in Moscow." Yet Shostakovich was essentially correct. However unwittingly, headlines like SET THE REDS ON THEIR EARS! and TEXAS PIANIST WINS IN MOSCOW OVER REDS signified that the Reds had not only immeasurably enhanced but actually validated Van Cliburn's United States career.

Validated, but not explained. Even Cliburn's fans—who celebrated his success, not his playing—wondered why he had won. Howard Taubman noticed, and wrote: "Over and over again the question . . . has been: 'Is this Van Cliburn really that good?' " According to one widespread rumor, the Russians had engineered an American triumph as a grand propaganda gesture. After all, Cliburn in America had never known anything like the acclaim he received in Russia.

The Soviet jurors, on the other hand, had had no trouble determining how good Van Cliburn was. Even if, as has been credibly reported, they had been instructed to vote for a Russian (Lev Vlasenko) and had sought and received the personal approval of Khrushchev before crowning Cliburn, their preference was never in doubt. Gilels, the jury chairman, had embraced Cliburn backstage after his Rachmaninoff Third. Goldenweiser had said he had not heard the concerto better played since Rachmaninoff himself performed it. The composer Aram Khachaturian had called Cliburn's performance "*better* than Rachmaninoff's; you find a virtuoso like this once or twice in a century." Richter had called Cliburn "a genius—a word I do not use lightly." Both he and Neuhaus had joined in the final ovation.

How good was Van Cliburn? His RCA recording of the Rachmaninoff Third provides further evidence. Made in concert in Carnegie Hall on May 19, 1958, it is as unforgettable as the furor it documents. Americans associated this big, densely embroidered concerto with Vladimir Horowitz, for whom it showcased his febrile, piledriving virtuosity. Cliburn's treatment is majestically ex-

---

*Post-Moscow, Cliburn's earlier neglect by American audiences and presenters was exaggerated by *Time* and in *The Van Cliburn Legend* by Abram Chasins and Villa Stiles. It is true that his earnings diminished after 1955–56 and that he returned to Kilgore partly to teach his mother's pupils. But his mother had been incapacitated by a back injury. And Cliburn had cut down on potential engagements because he expected to be inducted into the army. As it happened, he received a 4-F deferment.

pansive, never hectic or distorted. Horowitz is the more brilliant colorist; his blinding speed and mercurial nuance evoke Rachmaninoff himself. And Horowitz conveys—exaggerates—Rachmaninoff's nervous instability. But the interpretation as a whole, with its superabundant surface detail, is emotionally unfocused. Cliburn's fingers never brag. His tone is not kaleidoscopically varied but invariably round, burnished, unforced. The long lines he intuits sing beautifully of sadness and nostalgia. His course is steady and farsighted. Its current heaves upward in great concentrated waves, slowing the pace, weighting the climaxes. The first-movement cadenza, the concerto's central storm point, an upheaval of expanding force and sonority, builds with utter sureness; Cliburn simply lets it come. The tidal altitude and breadth of its crest are dizzying. The long descent is equally thorough; to begin the coda, the first theme returns dazed and spent.

In America, critics and audiences lacked confidence that Cliburn was everything he seemed. In Russia, what Cliburn seemed cannot be compassed. As in America, there were extramusical inducements: a wholesome young Texan in unsettling times, an image of the "enemy" as reassuring as any pipe dream. Yet in Russia, Cliburn's spiritual innocence registered not only in details of demeanor. Heine summarized Liszt's gift as "divination." Playing Tchaikovsky and Rachmaninoff in Moscow, Cliburn divined another, better world.

The unlikelihood of this achievement, however obvious, bears stressing. Many of Cliburn's important American contemporaries were taut, crew-cut 1950s musical personalities, not in the least Romantic. Cliburn impressed the Russians in their own, Romantic music. A post-competition article in *Sovetskaya Kultura* complained that the Russian contestants, by comparison, lacked "creative individuality."

In a 1988 interview, the conductor Christoph von Dohnányi said: "You shouldn't forget to lead a life. . . . The only thing that is interesting, ultimately, is the personality. Everything else any idiot can learn." This advice to young conductors also pertains to young pianists. Today, when musical careers begin and end too early, we forget how long it took a Rubinstein or Serkin or Arrau to ripen. The very rare instances of precocious originality—the young Glenn Gould, the young Martha Argerich—arise from intuitive powers to which ripeness or "leading a life" are irrelevant; even a young Gould or Argerich cannot have mastered the mature subjective sagas of a Beethoven. Young Van Cliburn was of this type. In Moscow, his

Beethoven was received ambivalently. Rachmaninoff's yearning voice records no seasoned personal confessions.

At twenty-three, Cliburn was not—could not yet be—a complete musician. But he could already surrender himself completely. Few performing artists ever achieve as much.

Cliburn's American popularity tainted his reputation among musical highbrows. Even before he won the Tchaikovsky, they had looked askance at his patriotism and religiosity, his narrow repertoire and resistance to chamber music. By the mid-sixties, he was said mainly to play for ladies with blue hair and fur coats. His RCA albums, with their cover photographs of the dreamy-faced artist, included titles like "My Favorite Chopin" and "My Favorite Encores." He was rarely heard in New York—leading a Manhattan critic to "suspect his manager, the canny Sol Hurok, of trying to conserve the young man's reputation." According to one Texas pianist: "Van's most shocking Dallas performance was of the *Emperor* Concerto in 1969. He sounded more or less lost throughout the last movement. I remember thinking: 'Here's a guy with the highest fees in the business who isn't prepared to play the piece.' Another sobering thing about that concert was the behavior of the Dallas audience—which *adored* Van Cliburn; local women, especially, just doted on him as the very symbol of the artiste. People at first didn't know how to react. They had to sort of *convince* themselves that this really was Van Cliburn. And then they gave him a delayed ovation."

Cliburn watchers say the decline was sporadic, not absolute; that the "jukebox" renditions of Tchaikovsky and Rachmaninoff—and also of the *Appassionata* Sonata, which seemed to turn up on every other recital program—were only part of the picture. Cliburn's recordings add contradictory impressions. He never made another as ardent as his 1958 Rachmaninoff Third—unless it was the Rachmaninoff Second Sonata, also recorded in concert, in Moscow in 1960. In American studios, he recorded sixteen concertos, eleven sonatas, and a variety of shorter solo works. Here, the Cliburn imprint remains sonorous and expansive. He majestically sweeps through his "Favorite Encores"—by Chopin, Scriabin, Rachmaninoff, and Schumann/Liszt—in love with their stormy rhetoric. Elsewhere, the lustrous sheen and monumental architecture attain a sort of embalmed perfection. One close observer has surmised: "It was as if he were trying to compensate for his lackadaisical public performances by being super-fussy. He would want to record the same thing over and over and over. Then he'd go crazy with the editing. And then he might turn the whole thing down. His recordings are like drawings that have been erased too many times; the process was unnatural. And I'm not convinced that he felt prepared to make some of those recordings in the first place."

In 1978, at the age of forty-three, Van Cliburn stopped giving concerts. An orchestral administrator remembers: "Major orchestras were no longer engaging him. The reason wasn't just the wrong notes; they were excused by his ability to make the piano sound beautiful. The reason was that his artistic failings had been unmasked in works like the *Emperor* Concerto and the Brahms D minor." A prominent conductor adds: "I consider him to have been ethically defective as an artist. He never took it seriously that he had a pair of miraculous hands. I think that when his instincts could take him no further, he didn't make the effort to buttress instinct with conscious understanding." From another point of view, Cliburn had shrewdly invested twenty years of high earnings. "In my opinion, Van never believed his own fairy-tale success," says one longtime acquaintance. "He was always afraid the bubble would burst. So he subjected himself to a grueling schedule, playing one hundred concerts and more year after year. Then one day he discovered he was a rich man and could quit." Cliburn himself has commented that he wanted to travel less, to eat dinner at a regular hour, to attend concerts and pursue friendships. "I had planned to stop playing for a long time . . . and I wanted to [do] it while I was young enough to enjoy it."

A period of reduced public prominence followed. Cliburn's father had died in 1974. His vibrant mother (who had toured with her son as his road manager, employed by Hurok, and who knew better than anyone how to counteract his proclivities to tardiness and indecision) lived with him in New York's Salisbury Hotel, where their two-floor suite eventually expanded to fifteen rooms, mainly because Cliburn cannot bear to throw anything away. He was seen at the ballet, at the opera, and at dinner, to all of which he invited young pianists of promise. He had a habit of giving away hundred-dollar bills. He occasionally hinted at plans to return to the stage, or to compose a piano sonata, or to acquire new repertoire by Mozart or Schubert. In a rare 1981 interview, for the *Rochester Sunday Democrat and Chronicle*, he answered questions "with fuzzy, philosophical abstractions." When he was told that his friends "didn't see how Cliburn could be happy unless he returned to the concert stage," he "roared with laughter" and shouted: *"Try me!"*

He asked to choose from the shots a photographer was taking before they were sent to Rochester. "Will they take the lines out of my face?" he asked. "Can they make me look young?"

Five years later, he and Rildia Bee moved from New York to Fort Worth, Texas, where he had purchased an eighteen-acre estate. Just before the following Christmas, they were visited by John Davidson, a writer for *Texas Monthly* magazine, whose May 1987 report is the fullest published account of the Cliburn life-style. At four in the afternoon, the Cliburns are just out of bed. Van, wearing a bathrobe and slippers, looks "far too young to have possibly won the first International Tchaikovsky Competition in Moscow in 1958." Rildia Bee, now ninety, is lunching in a quilted robe and pink nightcap. A close companion of the Cliburns, Tom Zaremba, is also still in his bathrobe; he teaches mortuary arts at Wayne State University in Detroit, to which he commutes. The house's vast living room accommodates six or seven Christmas trees. For a trip to the dentist in his new Lincoln Continental, Cliburn changes into a three-piece suit and a cashmere topcoat. On the way home, he empties a florist's showroom, filling the car's back seat and open trunk with reindeer-shaped baskets of poinsettias. He writes a check for $1,000 and tells the florist: "If that's not enough, send me the bill." To John Davidson he says: "You know, I've always loved flowers. When I had my first little apartment, in New York, there was a florist's shop on the ground floor of my building, and a lot of times I would spend my lunch money on flowers. But the odd thing about me is that I enjoy flowers as much when they get old and dried out as when they were fresh. I don't know—I just look at those flowers, and in my mind, I still see the beauty they once had. I never threw any of them away." Back home, Rildia Bee is now attired in a knit suit, high heels, and a sable hat and coat. She is urged to play the piano and complies with an English folk song with the chorus: "What good is water when you're dry, dry, dry?" Cliburn tells Davidson: "I always said that I was going to work at the beginning of my life and at the end of it, but that I was going to take the middle off. And I must say I'm enjoying it. When I wake up, I feel like I did when I was eighteen. In fact, I feel better. . . . I practice, and I'll start performing again soon." The Cliburns dine with friends in a small restaurant and return after 1:00 A.M. Rildia Bee now begins opening the mail. Van sits in the living room with Tom Zaremba and Susan Tilley, chairman of the Van Cliburn Foundation, who frequently visits him around this hour.

If the Cliburns' nocturnal cocoon seems decadent in Davidson's account, it is also wonderfully benign. "I had no sense of him as a

troubled artist casting about for new meaning," Davidson concludes. "He seemed happy and confident." In fact, Fort Worth—
where Cliburn was never envied or disdained, and where his
celebrity never ended—has clearly proved restorative. At concerts
and at parties, he attracts knots of admirers, among whom he
swoops and plunges with eager gregarious instincts, kissing ladies
on the cheek, patting gentlemen on the back. He regularly attends
the Broadway Baptist Church, whose concerts and choral-
orchestral services he encourages. He quietly and generously supports other local causes, including Fort Worth's Van Cliburn piano
competition. He returns the pride the community takes in him.

Perhaps Susan Tilley's devotion to Cliburn and his better future
takes up where Rildia Bee left off. In any event, less than two years
after leaving New York, Cliburn performed in public for the first
time in a decade: at a December 1987 White House reception for
Mikhail and Raisa Gorbachev. Following selections by Brahms,
Rachmaninoff, Schumann, and Debussy, and kisses from Mrs.
Gorbachev, Cliburn sang and played the popular song "Moscow
Nights." The Gorbachevs sang along; the Reagans watched. A
month later, he performed the Liszt transcription of Schumann's
Widmung at the nationally televised opening of the Bob Hope Cul-
tural Center in Palm Springs. The Reagans again attended, as did
former president Gerald Ford. It was only a matter of time before
Cliburn would announce that his "sabbatical" was over.

My first visit to the Cliburn residence takes place at two in the
morning in September 1988. I am with a group including the pianist Alexander Toradze, who has just performed with the Fort
Worth Chamber Orchestra. Cliburn greets us at the door in his
usual navy blue suit. Susan Tilley, a tall, handsome woman whose
youthful appearance in middle age rivals Cliburn's, is in the living
room. In the dining room, Rildia Bee sits at a table surrounded by
photographs of herself, her husband, and her son. She smiles
broadly, and her eyes dance when she says, her voice firm and
loud, "So *glad* you could come!"

Cliburn, at fifty-four, is a presence. His sonorous bass baritone
precedes him; like his piano tone, it is mellifluously public. It wells
up from a place deep inside, caressing his slow, meaningful Texas
speech. "Very nice to meet *you*." He fixes a stranger's upward gaze
with a welcoming smile and big, worried eyes. His face is a bit
puffy, his hair a bit gray, but there is a coltish vigor to the way he
strides suddenly, chest forward, from room to room, inquiring,

"Does everybody have everything they *want?*" He projects warmth, anxiety, modesty, charm, vulnerability, a lingering shyness. When Toradze proposes that the visitors be shown around the house, he complies instantly. Like the immense living room, the library and the solarium on either side have their own decor and their own Steinway grand. Some birthday decorations are already up for Rildia Bee's ninety-second, next month. The kitchen is as large as a restaurant's; the refrigerator is a walk-in vault. Cliburn even shows us the messy second-floor bedrooms, of which his is the smallest. There are more pianos, and also a Christmas tree. The third floor, which we do not see, reportedly includes a replica of a giant white cake for Rildia Bee's ninetieth birthday, and closets full of unworn clothes. Cliburn also cannot part with his old luggage, which, I am told, occupies two rooms. The upstairs walls are covered with career memorabilia: pictures, posters, newspaper articles. A television in one of the bedrooms plays a *Rambo* video. We also visit four elaborate guest apartments that Cliburn has recently had built over his house-size garage.

When NBC did a "Portrait of Van Cliburn" in 1966, a frustrated reviewer wrote: "He walks, sits, stands within a sheath of reserve so thick you could cut it with a Bowie knife. The dimensions of a television producer's or an interviewer's problem are outlined when he says, in a soft Southern slide, 'I'm a very subjective, *personal* person in what I like and dislike,' and replies to the obvious follow-up question with a gentle, 'Oh, I'm so personal that I would never let anybody know what I like or dislike.' " Today, Cliburn seems a lot more relaxed than when he found himself playing Jack Armstrong, All-American Boy. But according to those who know him, he remains essentially unknowable. The enveloping graciousness of his public persona daunts intimate inquiry. Journalists expect not to interview but to experience him—which he makes not a frustration but a pleasure. I attempt a single question. Both Toradze and John Pfeiffer, Cliburn's record producer in New York, have told me about a remarkable concert performance of the Brahms B-flat Concerto, taped in Moscow with Kirill Kondrashin. Pfeiffer has been urging Cliburn to let RCA release it. Cliburn has been wavering for months. Has he decided? He is, he tells me, still wavering: worrying about wrong notes and slow tempos. "I worry about *everything*," he says in slow, plaintive tones—and I believe him. At the moment, however, he is mainly occupied with a small dog he has recently acquired—a white, fluffy Maltese he cuddles and fondles in his big hands. "Do you think I could take it with me to *Russia?*" he asks. Like such corollary observations as "In *Tex*as, we like to stay *ba*bies," this remark is, I sense, neither misleading nor wholly innocent. When Cliburn says he "refuses to grow up," he both describes and teases himself. Adults who remain children are simple people; Cliburn's trademark sentimentality is complex. When he has the facial creases erased from his recent photographs, there is more than vanity at stake. He seems knowingly, helplessly, to fetishize the past. He hangs on to his youth and to the miracle of 1958, which he can never repeat. He speaks of music as a sacred trust, "eternal," "timeless," "priceless." "Great music," he will say, invoking a favorite metaphor, "is like a great painting that you take into your inner home. It is always valued. If it is a classic, it is always in vogue. It is forever." In another man's mouth, even an artist's, this language would sound platitudinous. But Cliburn, seated in his vast living room at three in the morning, shutting out the daylight of the present, sounds sincere.

"Thank you *so much* for coming," he says as we leave. I try not to feel opportunistic.

Not only Van Cliburn himself but the greater musical arena still registers the shock and aftershock of Moscow 1958. For generations of young pianists, he and his victory were prototypes. It was Cliburn, more than anyone, who proved that Americans could compete as equals on music's home ground in Europe, who demonstrated that fame and potential fulfillment could come heady and fast. It was the 1958 Tchaikovsky competition that caused Mark Schubart to think twice about "little publicized" music contests "conducted in private" and to marvel at the way an ardent and knowledgeable public could help create "a musical event of first importance"; that made Howard Taubman wonder if America should "plunge into the big-competition field." America did take the plunge: in Fort Worth, where the First Van Cliburn International Piano Competition, announced in 1958, took place in 1962.

What is the meaning of the Van Cliburn story? For Abram Chasins, who co-authored *The Van Cliburn Legend* in 1958, Cliburn was "something new on the face of the earth," a classical musician whose appeal was so potent and pervasive it promised "a turning point in our cultural evolution." For Santiago Rodriguez, who twice competed in the Cliburn competition, finishing second in 1981, Cliburn's story is "the central force, the central syndrome. It has inspired careers, and it has destroyed them because of the incredible pressures pianists inflict on themselves. Why has the Rachmaninoff Third become so popular, when thirty years ago nobody played it? Every competitor knows what Van Cliburn played in Moscow. They may not know what their father looked like in 1958, but they will remember Cliburn's winning repertoire. It isn't just the glamour of Van Cliburn that attracts and fascinates; it's his instantaneous success."

What does one make of Van Cliburn the pianist thirty years later? He will give us an opportunity to find out. In January 1989—some four months after my visit to Fort Worth—Cliburn announces that he will end his sabbatical at an outdoor summer concert with the Philadelphia Orchestra. It will take place on June 19, 1989—just eight days after the eighth Van Cliburn competition names its winner.

I

A TEXAS-SIZE PIANO COMPETITION

Where the West Begins

FORT WORTH, AMON CARTER USED TO SAY, IS "WHERE THE WEST begins." To which his friend Will Rogers added that Dallas—only thirty-five miles down the road—is "where the East peters out." Variations on this theme are being written to this day. Fort Worth faces west toward rolling ranchland. Dallas faces flat farmland to the east. Low-slung, hot, prairie-dry, Fort Worth stands for cattle and oil. Dallas, with twice as many people, is banking, real estate, and merchandising, glittery nightlife and chromium skyscrapers. Dallas is Neiman Marcus. Fort Worth is the Cattleman's Steak House. Dallas is business. Fort Worth still calls itself "Cowtown."

Like all Texas cities, Dallas included, Fort Worth is too young to have shaken all the dust off its boots. It takes its name from Camp Worth, built in 1849 to protect settlers from Indians. Within a decade, however, Indian attacks ceased and the fort was abandoned. Fort Worth was incorporated in 1873. Soon after, it became a hub for intersecting cattle drives: the last stop for supplies before heading north; the first good place to raise hell on the way back. Railroads made it richer and less raw; streetcars and gas lamps were added, then electric lights. When the railroad doomed the trail drives, meat packing was the logical, lucrative outcome. West Texas struck oil in 1917; within a year, Fort Worth presided over a spectacular new industry to take the place of cattle. When oil declined, its replacement was aviation and defense. A Fort Worth plant made World War II's B-24s; subsequently, as a division of General Dynamics, it became Tarrant County's biggest employer. Across town, Bell Helicopter builds its Long Rangers. In 1979, American Airlines transferred its corporate headquarters to Fort Worth from New York. Most recently (but not as recent as the resignation of Fort Worth's Jim Wright as Speaker of the House), nearby Waxahachie was selected to become the site of the $4.4 billion "superconductor"—the projected largest and most costly scientific instrument in the world.

In 1989, *Newsweek* listed Fort Worth among America's six "Best Places to Live and Work." With a population of 450,000 and a 1989 unemployment rate of under 7 percent, Fort Worth has weathered the oil crash better than Dallas or Houston. Its cowboy lineage confers identity and style. If the prevalence of bars and of violent crime remembers the frontier, so does the retention of fabulous personal wealth. What other city of under half a million has 19 golf courses or 114 foundations with assets approaching $1 billion?

Downtown Fort Worth presents a confused image of past and present, poverty and wealth. Like other American downtowns, it is visibly unfulfilled. But the image is less one of urban decay than of eerie irrelevance. Two components, old and new, sit in lonely juxtaposition on the prairie flatness, fringed by train tracks and telephone poles, empty sidewalks and elevated highways. The first component is summarized by the vintage Woolworth's, nestled in a nondescript three-story rectangle. The second consists of a modest assortment of generic glass-and-steel skyscrapers, linked by skywalks, flanked by concrete garages. The "new" downtown also includes an ambitious restoration project encompassing the 1895 Tarrant County Courthouse, with its handsome clock tower and red granite facade, and the bars, restaurants, and boutiques, all with turn-of-the-century exteriors, of Sundance Square—so named because Butch Cassidy and the Sundance Kid were the most famous of the many gunslingers, bank robbers, and gamblers who made old Fort Worth their hideout or home. Also "restored" are the flat faces of numerous would-be storefronts, painted to suggest "Famous Shoe Shine," "Corset Shop," "Drugstore," and the like. The oddest piece of restoration, next to the courthouse, is the civil courts building, whose matching "red granite" facade is made of Styrofoam. All this hopeful renewal stems from the initiative and generosity of the leather goods merchant turned Radio Shack tycoon Charles Tandy, who died in 1978, and of the four Bass brothers, heirs to a legendary oil fortune, whose net worth has been estimated at $5 billion.

A second restoration project, to the north, is the Stockyard District, 107 acres of shops, restaurants, and hotels where Swift and Armour once had packing plants, and where the livestock market was once the second largest in the United States. The 1908 Coliseum, built for annual fat stock shows, now hosts the Cowtown Rodeo. The adjoining barns, pens, and auction arenas still get some use. Real cowboys walk the covered wooden sidewalks. City Councilman Steve Murrin, who raises longhorn and bison, explains that more than tourism is at stake: "We've got to keep people with shit on their boots here."

Actually, today's Fort Worth is essentially a city of residential neighborhoods, ranging from Hispanic barrios to millionaires' enclaves where the only Hispanics are gardeners, and some people's yards are big enough to graze horses or cattle. More than Sundance Square or the Stockyards, the city's panoply of huge and distinctive houses is an authentic astonishment. For diversion, wealthy Cowtowners may travel to Manhattan or Mexico or the south of France—or even to Dallas, where they prefer to shop. A local night on the town may mean dinner at the country club, whose chef may be French. There are also four man-made lakes nearby, including one with a world-famous yacht club.

If parts of the downtown and Stockyards are undeniably ersatz, Fort Worth wealth is—by Texas standards, at least—the real McCoy: not flashy, brand-new money but the West Texas legacy of ranchers and oilmen. In his 1961 book about Texas, *The Super-Americans*, John Bainbridge observes:

> visitors often get the impression that people in Fort Worth are indeed as open, direct, and friendly as people in Texas, according to the legend, are supposed to be.
>
> In contrast to Dallas millionaires, who appear frantically determined to prove their sophistication, Fort Worth millionaires seem to take theirs quietly for granted. They act as if they knew and were satisfied with who they are, and consequently they are considerably more relaxed. In fact, they tend to spend part of their time exploring the possibility that there may be something more important, or perhaps just more entertaining, than making a few extra millions or adding another peak with their name on it to the skyline. Not that they lack ambition or community pride; rather, with them ambition is not sleepless and the skyline is not a religion.

Of course, local differences are diminishing as Texas becomes more homogeneously urban and industrial. Even the Dallas–Fort

Worth rivalry is fading. In 1961, representatives of both cities literally buried a hatchet. In 1965, they agreed to share an airport after each had spent millions to maintain one of its own. Fort Worth has actually acquired a Neiman Marcus (significantly, it is located in affluent Ridgelea, not downtown). People, too, become homogenized. The city's First Citizen for more than a quarter of a century, until he died in 1955, was Amon Carter, whose friends included presidents and generals, and about whom Vice President John Nance Garner once said: "That man wants the whole Government of the United States to be run for the exclusive benefit of Fort Worth." A blacksmith's son, Carter eventually owned radio stations, the *Fort Worth Star-Telegram*, and Shady Oak Farm, where he would rouse guests to dinner by galloping astride his palomino while firing a pair of six-shooters. Carter's bosom friend Sid Richardson, a legendary wildcatter, was reputedly the richest man in America. He lived in a three-room apartment at the Fort Worth Club—an indulgence compared to his earlier residence on a rented cot in the Westbrook Hotel. Today's Bass brothers, heirs to great-uncle Sid Richardson's fortune, represent a new breed, quieter than yesteryear's iconoclasts. If they forfeit local color, they retain strong local loyalties; and people appreciate that they spurn New York brusqueness.

In short: with its abortive downtown and its cowboy heritage, Fort Worth is neither urban nor suburban. The natives get a lot done without seeming high-strung or hectic. They tolerate informality and personal eccentricity. Non-Texans who have moved here see darker sides: the unempowered black and Hispanic minorities, constituting 36 percent of the population; the vapidity of the party circuit; the underlying arrogance of friendly folks accustomed to getting their own way. But these are second and third impressions that take first impressions for granted.

Ultimately, Fort Worth fascinates because its very differences seem characteristic of an older America. In a city of 450,000, individual initiatives, especially if accompanied by individual wealth, make a tangible difference. Confidence in the righteous destiny of oneself, one's family, and one's community—attitudes discouraged in more crowded, more confused, more "sophisticated" places— here endures. As John Bainbridge remarks: "In the same way that America stands as the frontier of Europe, so Texas stands in the collective American imagination as the frontier of America— the land of the second chance, the last outpost of individuality, the stage upon which the American drama . . . is being performed . . . as if for the first time."

*   *   *

"The Metropolis swallowed the Frontier like a small snake swallows a large frog: slowly, not without strain, but inexorably," writes the Texas novelist Larry McMurtry. "And if something of the Frontier remains alive in the innards of the Metropolis it is because the process of digestion has only just begun." The Metropolis proposed concerts and plays; the Frontier resisted high culture as sissy stuff—but relented.

At first, it *was* sissy stuff. As late as the 1940s, Texas men played cards or went hunting while Texas women banded together to sponsor music and art. The same thing happened throughout the American heartland, of course, but the Texas example is "Super-American"—larger than life, as exaggerated as the local gender gap. "The basic difficulty," McMurtry suggests, "is that the cowboy lacks a style that would put him at ease with women and women at ease with him. His code has prepared him to think of women not as they are, nor even as they were, but in terms of a vague nineteenth century idealization." In Fort Worth, the story of high-cultural ascent is linked to the decline of specifically masculine diversions. The city's first piano belonged to the wife of Major Ripley Arnold, who founded Camp Worth; she brought it with her from Washington in 1850 and used it to entertain guests. But Fort Worth's dominant entertainments, in what came to be known as "Hell's Half-Acre," were boxing and cockfights, keno and poker, tavern bands and dancing girls.

The public improvements of the 1870s and 1880s, which gave Fort Worth a more finished look, invited more finished, more "feminine" social pleasures. The 1,200-seat Fort Worth Opera House, built in 1883, served a variety of shows and revues, not excluding *Carmen*, *La traviata*, and *Faust*, sometimes with touring stars, sometimes (in fact, surprisingly often) with local soloists. In subsequent decades, the Euterpean Club, the Harmony Club, and the Civic Music Association sponsored visiting singers, violinists, and pianists. In 1920, Enrico Caruso sang for over eight thousand people in the stockyards Coliseum—reputedly his largest tour audience anywhere. Later in the same decade, Amelita Galli-Curci, John McCormack, Ignace Paderewski, Ernestine Schumann-Heink, and the New York Philharmonic all passed through town. A landmark in the institutionalization of refinement was the founding of the Fort Worth Symphony in 1912. But the orchestra's early history was sporadic: it was twice disbanded; its conductor worked without salary; it played in a church and a high school before settling in the huge Will Rogers Auditorium, built in 1936 as part of a complex housing the annual Southwestern Exposition and Fat Stock Show. The Fort Worth Opera Association, begun in 1946, once staged a *Lucia di Lammermoor* marking the retirement of Lily Pons and the first American appearance in a major role of Plácido Domingo.

By the 1960s, many civic leaders had begun to question Fort Worth's reliance on Dallas for consolidated highbrow fare. The turning point, in 1972, was the opening of the Kimbell, widely regarded as one of America's premier art museums. A single local benefactor—Kay Kimbell, who made his fortune in grains—underwrote both its construction and its continued support (the annual acquisitions budget is second only to that of Malibu's Getty Museum). Designed by Louis Kahn as a series of self-supporting cycloidal vaults, the building itself repudiates ostentation. Its wide-ranging permanent collection is both small and remarkably selective. Its location, a few blocks east of the oak-shaded mansions of Rivercrest, falls within a Cultural District also including the important Amon Carter Museum (which emphasizes the American West and was designed by Philip Johnson), the Fort Worth Art Museum (which concentrates on Abstract Expressionism), the Fort Worth Museum of Science and History (the "largest museum in the Southwest"), and the Casa Mañana Theater. Meanwhile, the Fort Worth Symphony has stabilized and grown since 1976, when its nucleus became a chamber orchestra of thirty-two full-time members, mainly financed by the Sid Richardson Foundation. The Bass fortune has been instrumental in establishing the Fort Worth Ballet. Other Fort Worth arts institutions include the nationally known Texas Boys Choir and assorted theater and dance troupes—not to mention the Van Cliburn International Piano Competition, which, like the Fort Worth Symphony, Ballet, and Opera, may eventually relocate to an enlarged version of the Cultural District, already the "third biggest in America."

In other words: Fort Worth's support for the visual and performing arts is remarkable for a city its size, and the people proud of it are not just culture-conscious ladies but their once recalcitrant husbands. This rapprochement is underlined by a recent survey showing that the same Cowtowners enjoy seeing barrel racing and bulldogging at the rodeo, show and cutting horses at the new equestrian center, the great masters at the Kimbell, and the gold medalists at the Cliburn. Their big money has imposed high standards: the Kimbell and the Cliburn, in particular, are "better than Dallas"; prerogatives of wealth decree: If you're going to do it, do it right. But there is also quiet concern that what is right for the Basses may be wrong for the Smiths. Some of Fort Worth's longtime arts patrons worry that the new cultural réclame is overscaled, overpromoted, and overly fashionable. They see the grass roots they once cultivated being trampled by rich folk.

The Cliburn competition encapsulates this ascent to cultural prominence. It was born at a 1958 banquet for Van Cliburn and his mother in Fort Worth. Irl Allison got up and proposed that a piano competition be established in Van Cliburn's name, that it be quadrennial, and that the winner get $10,000—at the time, an unprecedented purse for a music contest. The founder and president of the National Guild of Piano Teachers and former dean of the music department at Hardin-Simmons College in Abilene, Allison was a veteran proponent and organizer of piano competitions. As he later recalled: "Van had just come back from Moscow after winning the Tchaikovsky competition. . . . Mrs. Allison and I . . . were en route to the banquet when the idea occurred to me that the National Guild of Piano Teachers might be able and willing to have a Van Cliburn Competition in America like the Tchaikovsky Competition in Moscow. I didn't even mention it to Mrs. Allison on the way, but when I got up and told about my idea that evening, it really startled everybody." The homespun optimism of Allison's vision was buttressed by other uncomplicated views. Once, when a national magazine asked him whether playing on the "competition circuit" could hurt a young artist's development, Allison had this to say: "Well, I think that every competition entered by any artist adds something toward his or her own development. . . . I groomed my pupils to play competitions; I worked them just like a football coach. But I also think competitions are developing a feeling for music like nothing else in the world is doing. We certainly need every possible way to keep the classics alive. These rock players can draw 50,000 people, but Van is one of the few classical musicians who fills houses everywhere he plays." "Do competitions tend to breed 'competition players' who have great technical finesse but comparatively little creativity?" Allison was asked. "I've never heard that point brought up at all," he replied.

Many assumed that if Allison's Cliburn competition was to materialize at all, it would materialize in New York City. But Grace Ward Lankford, Allison's Fort Worth hostess that banquet night, had other ideas. Mrs. Lankford, who died in 1967, was a cofounder of the Fort Worth Piano Teachers Forum and a friend of Rildia Bee Cliburn. She is remembered as a "won't-take-no-for-an-answer kind of gal." Photographs suggest a matriarch of indomitable will. Tenaciously, resourcefully, she embroidered Allison's proposal until people actually believed that such an event could take place in Fort Worth. She enlisted as sponsors her piano teachers forum, Allison's piano teachers guild, the chamber of commerce, and Fort Worth's Texas Christian University, which agreed to provide its auditorium and practice rooms. She added seven monetary awards to the $10,000 first prize. She met a budget of $70,000. She studied piano competitions in America and abroad, and came up with a set of rules and procedures. The result, in 1962, was the first Van Cliburn International Quadrennial Piano Competition: a mom-and-pop show of international scope, a mélange of amateur and professional, courtesy and bravado, sophistication and innocence.

American-style volunteerism was a distinctive feature from the start. To get things done, Mrs. Lankford relied on hundreds of helpers who served without pay. The forty-six contestants, from sixteen countries, were housed not in a TCU dormitory but in private homes (the four Soviet pianists had expected to stay in a hotel with a bodyguard; Mrs. Lankford made them play by the rules). As in Moscow or Brussels or Warsaw, the contest began with solo rounds and climaxed with concertos. The required repertoire, beginning with Scarlatti and Bach, was broad. Like the Tchaikovsky, Queen Elisabeth, and Chopin competitions, the Cliburn stressed native composers: two American works, including one of Edward MacDowell's sonatas, were mandatory, plus a commissioned work by Lee Hoiby. The jury of eight included judges from Brazil, Mexico, Japan, and the Soviet Union (the eminent Lev Oborin). In addition to his $10,000, donated by Allison's national guild, the winner would get to play concertos with the orchestras of Abilene, Amarillo, Fort Worth, New Orleans, and Roanoke, and with a London orchestra; chamber music with the Paganini Quartet in Santa Barbara; and solo recitals in Grand Rapids and at Carnegie Hall. And he would be managed in North and South America by Cliburn's own impresario, the legendary Sol Hurok.

Mrs. Lankford succeeded in establishing the Cliburn competition as a valued component of Fort Worth's civic identity. The efficiency with which the event was run, the optimism it exuded, the enthusiasm it generated, were acknowledged and admired. But contrary to expectations, its winners did not advance dramatically in their careers, as Cliburn had in 1958. The generous first prize did not provide for engagements with major orchestras or conductors. And Mrs. Lankford and her first successors failed to gauge the potency of the media: there was no validating national coverage on radio or television to sway the music business or the public at large. In fact, a higher profile became overdue. The "Van Cliburn" imprimatur ensured automatic popular appeal. And—thanks partly to Cliburn himself and to Sol Hurok—there were the Russians. No other American music competition had succeeded in attracting contestants and jurors from the Soviet Union, as had the Cliburn in 1962 and 1973. The guaranteed result was a higher level of performance. Moreover, the Russians and Van Cliburn both promised a potential glamour that Irl Allison, Grace Ward Lankford, and other piano teacher types had not even glimpsed.

It fell to Martha Hyder to consummate this potential after 1973. She was no piano teacher but an heiress to oil-related wealth, whose husband, Elton, was a prominent Fort Worth attorney. Mrs. Hyder made the Cliburn competition more sophisticated, more fashionable, more famous, and more expensive. In the process, she became known, according to *Town and Country*, as "one of this country's great ladies of organized charity."

As with concurrent developments in the Cultural District, the Cliburn's new, glossier face alienated some old-timers: piano teachers who felt pushed aside by the rush of high society; former host families supplanted by new hosts with mansions and Mercedeses. Some thought the work of the late Mrs. Lankford was now undervalued and misremembered. And yet the Cliburn's new visibility was crucial. As Martha Hyder was quick to realize, it served high-cultural as well as high-social purposes. The music business itself craved glamour. It assessed market value in terms of past promotion and future promotability. Even if she had transformed only the trappings of the Van Cliburn piano competition, Mrs. Hyder would have transformed the whole.

Hyderization

THE HYDERS' HOME IN FORT WORTH IS A VILLA, THREE QUARTERS OF A century old, on a bluff overlooking a panorama of water and trees stretching to the horizon. No single room inside the house is as readily grasped as this exterior view. Covering every table and shelf and obscuring the walls are such objects as a large wicker Victorian bird cage, an eighteenth-century Italian commode, and collections of Russian icons and African sculpture. Competing for attention on one table—chosen at random, and on a random day—are ornamental ashtrays, miniature boxes and chests, a magnifying glass, and figurines of the following: elephant, bird, monkey, horse, swan, ladybug, angel (a lamp), and Our Lord Jesus Christ. A nearby fireplace is framed by crucifixes and crosses, some of which are Byzantine. The miniature cannon underfoot are from Mr. Hyder's collection. This decorative menagerie is not haphazard but planned. Mrs. Hyder's boldest piece of planning is her stoa: a covered, colonnaded room, open on one side to the garden and extending nearly the length of the house. It was the stoa she transformed into a French café, with costumed waiters and tricolors wrapped about the columns, to entertain the 1977 Cliburn competition jury; and where, only two weeks before that, she hosted a Russian party, for the Kimbell Museum's Hermitage show, using a menu from the wedding breakfast of Nicholas and Alexandra. Even the house's smallest gestures are considered—the hundreds of pillows covered in remnants of antique fabrics and tapestries; the fragments of eighteenth-century iron used to fashion the stoa furniture. Mrs. Hyder once summarized the decor for the *New York Times*: "It's no style. I suppose it does have a sort of European feeling."

Her addiction to excess would make Martha Hyder a cartoon were she not at the same time so intelligent, resourceful, and shrewd. She is no naïf but an eccentric whose unorthodoxies hold naïveté hostage. And her house is not sort of European but essentially American—both for its serene eclecticism and for the can-do spirit with which its mistress has for thirty years exercised her creative willpower upon it. On a trip to Manhattan, it is said, she once fell in love with some Italian marble columns she found holding up a building; these same columns now stand in her living room.

Mrs. Hyder herself—as I discover upon meeting her in 1989— does not dress like her house. I am told that years ago, when she first lobbied Europe for the Cliburn Foundation, "Martha was dripping with gold—she wore so many gold things that it made her shoulders sag." Her style is simpler now: "tailored and understated," according to the society pages of the *Times*. A middle-aged woman with three grown children, she is long and lanky, with long hair and a long, large face to match. Her big eyes are devouring: they swallow me up as I describe my book in progress. She is guarded, polite, intense. Then, abruptly, I am finished and Martha Hyder has started, her speech so steady and strong it lofts a single wave of words and words. Abhorring silence, she speeds up at the ends of sentences, or fills the gaps with slurred, swallowed ands and et ceteras. Agglomerated details and digressions create an initial impression of narrative disarray. Actually, Mrs. Hyder's narrative proves tenaciously purposeful—but the purposes reveal themselves gradually, on a grand scale. She moves fast but cannot be rushed. Nothing is skimped. And only the telephone can stop her.

"Music competitions are so easy to take potshots at. Because first of all there are too many of them. And I'm conscious of all the criticisms. I feel the same way. I mean, a lot of competitions seem to exist just to provide the excitement for wherever it is. You could say that about the Cliburn. It provides a lot of excitement. Every four years, everybody's mesmerized by all this marvelous music, et cetera, et cetera. And in a sense we could exist just as well without it. And the winner could go on his way. And basically in the beginning it started out like that. It started out as a wonderful event to honor Van and to find the great winner and give him ten thousand dollars and a Carnegie Hall debut and to set up a few concerts for him, and that was it. Because there was no concept of career management. I mean, who would have that concept here? Van was concertizing; it was in honor of him. The prize was given by the National Piano Teachers Guild, which was in Austin. The person who ran it, Grace Ward Lankford, was a wonderful music teacher, who was local and who had a lot of energy. She managed to put together a committee that was basically chamber of commerce, businessmen like Lorin Boswell, who owned the dairy, and a few others like me. And none of us knew anything about running a competition. It was set up the way a committee would be set up for the United Fund. And the reason it was so successful was that Sol Hurok, who was Van's manager, got completely behind it, and he gave us a good jury, people like Jorge Bolet, Lili Kraus, Leonard Pennario. So we had a wonderful jury from the beginning, and we just felt our way along. The only reason I got so involved is that I had three children who were taking piano from Grace Ward Lankford. Thirty minutes, thirty minutes, thirty minutes. And she said to me, 'Martha, you're going to be on my committee.' And I just said yes, not having the slightest idea what I was getting into or what was going on. I mean, I had my mother's bridge group here, working in the evening to put biographies together, because I realized that everybody who came to hear forty-two contestants would want to know where they came from. I was going to the printer at three o'clock in the morning. Things I'd never done before in my life. I also planned all the parties for the contestants and for the jury members. Forty-two contestants were coming, and I felt it was very important for them to have a chance to interact. You know, we've always had those snide remarks about the parties and entertainment. Well, I don't feel the least bit defensive about it. I think it's very important. You don't have to go to a party if you don't want to. But if you've been practicing for nine or ten hours, or maybe you're not crazy about the people you're staying with, then at least you have the opportunity to meet somebody. All this has to be organized. I wound up doing a lot of the housing, because I like the housing. Me, I'm a real flag-waver. So people who come here to Fort Worth for two weeks, I want them to have the warmest possible welcome, to live in the warmest family arrangement, and to have a good piano. The host families are told that this is the most important time in this young person's life. I mean, your entire two weeks must center around this person—whatever he wants to eat, he's totally spoiled, it's got to be quiet, et cetera, et cetera. And it's worked in most cases. Fort Worth has really risen to it. Because all the past winners have kept up with their host families here. That's a very important support to musicians who are moving about so much that they don't get a chance to make that many friendships. They need that support. We started the concept of tender, loving care for the contestants. The beginning was here in Fort Worth."

The Cliburn quickly acquired a reputation for handling its competitors with rare attentiveness and efficiency; the devoted host families really did become like surrogate parents and siblings. But it also acquired a reputation for producing winners without careers. Ralph Votapek, who took the first gold medal, in 1962, primarily became a teacher. Radu Lupu, the 1966 winner, made a big name, but only after finishing first at the Leeds Competition in 1969. Following his Cliburn victory, in fact, Lupu decided to return to his studies at the Moscow Conservatory—a move that, however well considered artistically, perplexed and enraged certain Cliburn backers, who afterward changed the printed regulations to stipulate: "Winners will be expected to fulfill all prize engagements." Though Cristina Ortiz, the 1969 gold medalist, fulfilled her engagements, her career, too, took off only when her Texas success was barely a memory. Vladimir Viardo, who won in 1973, was confined to the Soviet Union and Eastern Europe for thirteen years.

Viardo, a handsome, self-possessed twenty-three-year-old, seemed to some in Fort Worth the biggest talent the Cliburn had uncovered. His quick intellect—he delivered his presumptuous opinions with twinkling eyes and a knowing smile—informed a keyboard style itself suavely opinionated. He seemed a plausible enough candidate for professional celebrity. The Cliburn's failure to secure success for him pointed to necessary policy changes. Martha Hyder became the catalyst for these changes. She had been elected chairman of the Cliburn Foundation the year Viardo won. And the Hyders had been Viardo's host family for the 1973 competition; she had developed a close personal relationship to her charismatic Russian guest and believed in him as a pianist. More than anyone else in Fort Worth, she felt frustrated on his behalf. More than anyone else, she realized that not just the Soviets, with their travel restrictions, but the Cliburn itself was part of Viardo's problem: that of the twenty orchestras he was scheduled to appear with, in Arkansas, Delaware, Florida, Illinois, Indiana, Massachusetts, Michigan, New York, North Dakota, Ohio, Texas, Virginia, Washington, Saskatchewan, and El Salvador, only one—the Cincinnati Symphony—carried any prestige; that in general, the Cliburn administration, which had passed into the hands of Grace

Ward Lankford's daughter, was a provincial operation. Upon becoming chairman, Mrs. Hyder resolved to make Vladimir Viardo a "star" and to transform the Van Cliburn International Piano Competition into "the best and best-known in the world."

"We went to Ruth Johnson to be chairman, and it never occurred to us that Ruth Johnson wouldn't say yes. I mean, it was like finding out there was no Santa Claus. So we all looked at each other, and I tried to talk Nancy Lee Bass into it, but she said she had other things to do. So anyway I became chairman strictly by default. I never intended to be chairman of anything, because Elton and I were traveling all the time. He was the one who talked me into it. He assumed that I would do what everybody else had done. That I would hold four, five, six meetings a year, name an executive director, send out the brochures, and have the jury chairman set the repertory. But to our big surprise we had a Russian winner. And not only that, but our jury said this was a genius pianist that comes along once in ten years. And we were the host family, we were crazy about him, he had such a personality. But the Russians took him away almost immediately. Let's see, he played Saturday night and was told Sunday that he would win. And they took him away to New York on Monday, and then home two days later. Three weeks after that, we were informed by Madame Furtseva, the minister of culture, that she did not know that the Cliburn winner had a commitment to a list of concerts. And that she was very sorry, but Viardo couldn't come back here because he was graduating from the conservatory, et cetera, et cetera. So I was shocked. Here I was about to become the new chairman, and I didn't have the winner. Some people said to me if the Russians are going to act this way, forget it. And I said absolutely not, this is my genius pianist and we have to have him. So we sat down and worked three days and we drafted this wonderful letter to Madame Furtseva, saying you cannot do this because it takes away the credibility of competitions, it will give you a terrible name, we have our commitments to honor, et cetera. And I looked at the schedule and I kept six weeks in the fall and six weeks in the spring, making sure to include the Carnegie Hall recital and the Cincinnati Symphony, those two. And you know, she wrote us back almost immediately and said yes. So I had my genius first-prize winner coming back in the fall and spring. Now, if Christian Zacharias, who was German and who spoke perfect English, if Christian Zacharias had won instead of finishing second, I would have done nothing different than any of the other chairmen. I would have stayed in Fort Worth and held my meetings, I guarantee you. But I had a Russian who

I knew had to make a success—he told me, You know, if I get bad reviews they won't let me come back here. Somebody had to travel with him, because he didn't speak English and because it was very important that everything went well. So I ended up traveling with him, or one of my children did, or someone from the Hurok office. Somebody was always with him."

Mrs. Hyder's travels with Vladimir Viardo took them to New York City, where she arranged a meeting with RCA Victor and saw that Viardo had the finest concert attire for his American tour (previously, in Texas, she had kept Neiman Marcus open two hours past closing so that Viardo could shop privately); to Tennessee, where he gave his first American recital and met with the pianist Lili Kraus, a member of the 1973 Cliburn jury; to North Carolina, through which they drove in a rented car while conversing entirely in English so that Viardo could learn to speak it; and to Cleveland, where she chartered an airplane when a snowstorm delayed their scheduled flight. En route to East Lansing, Mrs. Hyder arranged a "retreat" at a Chicago hotel, inviting Radu Lupu, who was playing with the Chicago Symphony, Van Cliburn, who was also performing nearby, and, from Texas, John Giordano, the conductor of the Fort Worth Symphony and chairman of the Cliburn competition jury. As a result of this meeting, which lasted more than a day, Mrs. Hyder set off for Europe equipped with the names and addresses of influential concert managers, pianists, conductors, and pedagogues. In London, she met with Jasper Parrott of Harrison & Parrott, which agreed to present a London debut recital. In Moscow, she attended the Tchaikovsky competition and also (after spending three weeks trying to secure an appointment) met with Madame Furtseva, who promised that Viardo would play more often in Russia, make a solo recording there, and tour the United States in 1975 with the Moscow State Symphony. Eventually, Mrs. Hyder visited Geneva, Hamburg, Munich, Paris, Vienna, and West Berlin, among other musical capitals. Typically, she would bring along John Giordano, who would visit the local conservatories, hunting for potential jurors and contestants, while she tried cajoling local impresarios and orchestras into presenting the 1977 Cliburn winner. In the process, she not only learned the business side of music but discovered that she enjoyed it. Her personal wealth and international social connections opened doors and pocketbooks. And she reveled in her capacity for self-education. ("I'm a big question-asker. I'm a Sagittarius—it's part of my personality that I want to know everything before making a decision.")

The Soviets made good on their promise to Mrs. Hyder that Vladimir Viardo would tour America in 1975—but his visa was canceled the next year, and he was not allowed to return to the United States until 1988. Mrs. Hyder's ambitions for the Cliburn competition were more thoroughly realized. She did not act alone. On musical matters, she regularly consulted Van Cliburn. John Giordano's advisory role expanded. Robert Alexander, formerly manager of the Fort Worth and Dallas symphonies, became the competition's first executive director. Mary Lou Falcone, of New York City, was named its first professional press representative. John Pfeiffer, Van Cliburn's producer at RCA, was engaged to record all four rounds. Henry Grossman, a leading arts photographer, was made the official photographer. Cliburn and Giordano helped undertake major revisions of the repertoire: the addition of a second preliminary round (enabling the contestants to play twice before the first cut) and of a mandatory Mozart concerto. Though the cash prize of $10,000 for the gold medalist was retained, the tour itinerary was transformed from four dozen American dates over a single season to a two-year schedule including Europe and an impressive number of major orchestras. Tours were also initiated for the second- and third-prize winners. Mrs. Hyder and Giordano had personally prevailed on so many teachers and schools to send their best that the 1977 competition wound up with 192 applicants—more than it was prepared to process. A certain number were accepted or rejected by Mrs. Hyder's brain trust. The rest were referred to a hastily convened screening jury. Eventually, 104 applicants were accepted, of whom 76 competed. This group, representing twenty-five countries, comprised a piano cognoscenti's Who's Who in the under-thirty set.* Finally, Mrs. Hyder ensured national television exposure for the Van Cliburn competition. This was the centerpiece of her plan to make it the world's best-known. She started at the top, in New York, where WNET was interested in a PBS documentary partly modeled after commercial-television coverage of the Olympics. A budget of $1.3 million was drawn up. When the money was not forthcoming, Mrs. Hyder eventually succeeded locally—with a company called Fort Worth Productions,

---

* Among those who did not make the finals in 1977 were Gregory Allen, James Barbagallo, William Black, Boris Bloch, Michael Boriskin, Brigitte Engerer, Youri Egorov, Marian Hahn, Diana Kacso, André Laplante, Michael Lewin, Panayis Lyras, Alan Marks, Steven Mayer, Shigeo Neriki, Peter Orth, Pamela Paul, Cynthia Raim, Jean-Louis Steuerman, Nina Tichman, William Wolfram. The six finalists were Steven De Groote (first prize), Alexander Toradze (second), Jeffrey Swann (third), Christian Blackshaw and Michel Dalberto (tied for fourth), and Ian Hobson and Alexander Mndoyants (tied for fifth).

a $45,000 budget, and a last-minute grant from Charles Tandy. "Contest to Carnegie Hall," shown nationally over public television, legitimized the piano competition as home-screen high-culture entertainment; subsequent Cliburn competitions—and also piano competitions in Moscow and Salt Lake City—were shown on American public television as a matter of course.

Working hard for Vladimir Viardo, Martha Hyder worked hard to expand and enhance the Cliburn competition. Expanding the Cliburn competition, she took up the cause of young pianists struggling to break into the music business. Advocating the cause of young pianists in search of an audience, she became an advocate for disseminating high culture, for community uplift through art. In Fort Worth, the most impressive evidence of an elevating musical culture may not be the Cliburn competition but the Cliburn Concerts—an annual recital series undertaken by the Cliburn Foundation. While piano recitals languish elsewhere, Cliburn Concerts presents half a dozen and more ranking artists per season, plus chamber music. The series began in 1976 as lecture-performances to educate the city's growing piano audience. One instigator was Martha Hyder.

"Once I looked at the musical world, I realized it's an endangered species. It needs to be enlarged. I have so many friends that don't understand classical music. And I'm sure it's because they weren't educated that way. My mother saw that I went to every civic music program that came here. It's not that she went. But she dropped me off and she saw that I went. I just think that you have to build a love like they have in Europe, that it's terribly important here. That's one reason for the Cliburn Concerts. As for competitions, they get people excited who don't know much about music. They can help us capture a whole new audience—because of the personalities of the contestants, et cetera, et cetera. The audience gets involved like they do in the Olympics. Because if we don't become more populist about our music, we're not going to have any. Look at all the orchestras that are folding right now. We're losing our audience because of all the other things which catch people's imaginations. Barry Douglas on Johnny Carson—I think that's important. If classical music is to survive, it can't be so elitist and so snobbish that you can't have pianists on the Johnny Carson show." Mrs. Hyder believes that, in conjunction with the Kimbell Museum, the Cliburn Foundation has raised the civic identity of Fort Worth. "We have a big cultural life here. Fort Worth even got ahead of Dallas for a while. Everybody said so. Our Dallas friends used to come over a lot, before they got the new Dallas museum. And our ballet was better than their ballet. And the Cliburn was certainly much better than the Dealey music competition in Dallas. I mean, Fort Worth has done a lot."

Mrs. Hyder has plenty of detractors. In Fort Worth, she stands not at the center of the social set but somewhere to the side, as a popular or controversial iconoclast. With regard to music, she seems indiscriminately enamored of things Russian. Her obsession with Vladimir Viardo—whom she continued to visit in Moscow when he could no longer travel, and whose Moscow apartment she lavishly furnished—is said to have antagonized the Soviet bureaucrats she thought she could woo, and to have contributed to his thirteen-year exile from the United States. Even today, a Viardo recital or reception can rouse her to a state of determinedly frantic excitation. "Martha is a whirlwind," one longtime observer summarizes. "She's too busy and important for anyone. Probably, in her mind, she's the queen of this little empire, which she runs subliminally."

But Mrs. Hyder is bigger than any critique. She oversaw a revolutionary reconception of Irl Allison's mom-and-pop show. She ensured a permanent awareness of the Cliburn competition not only on New York's West Fifty-seventh Street, headquarters of the music business, but in Europe, where it had been ignored. In the process, she created career opportunities for the winners, and even the losers, where none had existed. Through a combination of bold instinct and shameless persistence, fortified by personal wealth and its prerogatives, she elevated Fort Worth's piano competition to a plateau of influence—or notoriety—no musician or music business-man could have envisioned. Of her signature parties, the best-remembered is one for Viardo, at the Kennedy Center. Its best-remembered momento is a photograph: of Viardo holding hands with First Lady Betty Ford, on his left Soviet Ambassador Anatoly Dobrynin and his wife, on his right Henry and Nancy Kissinger. Martha Hyder comments: "That's when Vladimir arrived as the star with the Moscow State Symphony. We had this great party not to raise funds, just to make friends. It was for our profile. We don't do that anymore. But at that time I was making a big statement."

Martha Hyder set out to make the Van Cliburn International Piano Competition "best" and "best-known." She achieved more than that. In transforming the scale of the competition, she transformed its meaning. Her "big statement" embraced an expanded role for concert music itself—in relation not just to high society but to society at large.

Where Piano Competitions Came From

THE HISTORY OF KEYBOARD COMPETITIONS SHEDS NECESSARY PERSPEC-
tive on the implications of Hyderization. This is a history, as old as
the keyboards themselves, documenting both continuity and
change: continuity, insofar as keyboard expertise has always pro-
voked an urge to compete; change, insofar as modes of combat have
shifted with the shifting place of music and its institutions.

Before pianists, there were organists, harpsichordists, and clav-
ichordists, the best of whom would test themselves against one
another. Typically, these tests were instigated by royal or aristo-
cratic patrons and took place in their palaces or homes. In fact, two
queens—Mary of Scotland and Elizabeth of England—were themselves among the first rival harpsichordists of note. Elizabeth sent
James Melville of her court to investigate Mary's instrumental competence. The latter inquired how well Elizabeth played her harpsichord and lute. "Reasonably for a queen, Your Majesty," Melville
is said to have replied. When he was later discovered eavesdropping
on Mary while she was at her harpsichord, he extricated himself
with the remark: "The beautiful melody which I heard ravished
and drew me within the chamber, I wist not how."

A 1708 musical duel between Handel and Domenico Scarlatti
was the highlight of a Venetian ball. Handel was judged the supe-

rior organist; as harpsichordists, they were declared equal. Nine years later, Johann Sebastian Bach and the French organist Louis Marchand tried outplaying one another. According to F. W. Marpurg's story, allegedly related to him by Bach himself:

> When . . . Marchand performed among other things a French ditty with many variations, and was much applauded for the art displayed in the variations as well as for his elegant and fiery playing, Bach, who was standing next to him, was urged to try the harpsichord. He accepted the invitation, played a brief preliminary improvisation (with masterly chords) and, before anyone realized what was happening, he repeated the ditty played by Marchand, and made a dozen variations on it, with new art and in ways that had not been heard before.
>
> Marchand, who had hitherto defied all organists, had to acknowledge the undoubted superiority of his antagonist on this occasion.

Mozart and Clementi, among the first virtuosos of the pianoforte, competed in 1781 at the invitation of Emperor Joseph II, who obliged them to vary a theme in alternation, each being accompanied by the other. Afterward, Clementi praised Mozart's "intelligence and charm," and Mozart denounced Clementi as a "mechanician" without "a penny's worth of feeling or taste." Joseph II judged the event a draw.

As the piano itself, in rapid evolution, grew more powerful, so did its celebrated exponents. In turn-of-the-century Vienna, the most famous pianist was the young Beethoven, whose fire and imagination held his listeners spellbound. Beethoven's temperamental extremes and reckless invention were epitomized by his improvisations; according to one contemporary report: "Now his playing tore along like a wildly foaming cataract, and the conjurer constrained his instrument to an utterance so forceful that the stoutest structure was scarcely able to withstand it; and anon he sank down, exhausted, exhaling gentle plaints, dissolving into melancholy." Such feats engendered rivalries so keen that devotees of the city's leading pianists organized contests between their heroes. One visiting contender was Daniel Steibelt, whose wife accompanied his "Bacchanales" on the tambourine and whose detractors considered him a charlatan. According to a story told by Beethoven's pupil and friend Ferdinand Ries, Steibelt in his first meeting with Beethoven "made a good deal of effect with his tremolos, which were then something entirely new." Beethoven could not be induced to play again. Eight days later, at a second meeting, Steibelt impressed with one of his quintets, after which he improvised on a theme used by Beethoven in his Op. 11 Trio.

This incensed the admirers of Beethoven and [Beethoven himself]; he had to go to the pianoforte and improvise. He went in his usual (I might say, ill-bred) manner to the instrument as if half-pushed, picked up the violoncello part of Steibelt's quintet in passing, placed it (intentionally?) upon the stand upside down and with one finger drummed a theme out of the first few measures. Insulted and angered, he improvised in such a manner that Steibelt left the room before he finished, would never again meet him, and, indeed, made it a condition that Beethoven should not be invited before accepting an offer.

In the Romantic age, the piano—newly reinforced by metal parts; newly responsive to every impulse of hand, foot, and brain—became music's central vehicle for heroic individualism. More than ever, its players were inherently competitive, and so, more than ever, was its literature, crammed with brave rhetoric and ingenious stunts. The consummation of these equations was Franz Liszt, whose playing was said to make the piano a self-sufficient "orchestra" and whose compositions culminated in righteous fusillades, healing visions, and other insignias of victory. It was Liszt who in effect created the solo recital format, dispensing with an orchestra, singers, or violinists to share the bill. He said: *"Le concert, c'est moi."* His larger-than-life presence and galvanizing musical imagination combined to create an overwhelming self-portrait of the pianist-composer himself. In 1836, at a joint concert with Liszt, Berlioz conducted the "March to the Scaffold" from his *Symphonie fantastique*. When the tremendous culminating fanfare subsided, Liszt performed his keyboard transcription of the same piece. According to Sir Charles Hallé, an important pianist and conductor of the day, Liszt's playing registered "with an effect even surpassing that of the full orchestra, creating an indescribable furore. The feat had been duly announced in the programme beforehand, a proof of his indomitable courage."

Liszt's most famous competition was with Sigismond Thalberg, whose fame rivaled his own. Thalberg was as perfectly poised as Liszt was demonically afire. He bowed with a polished reserve. He abjured superfluous movements of hands and arms. His trademark special effect was to swathe a melody, above and below, in swift, sweet arpeggios, as if three hands were playing. His arrival in Paris in 1835 split connoisseurs of the piano into two camps. The inevitable outcome was a competition—on March 1, 1837, in the salon of the Princess Belgiojoso. She charged forty francs a ticket and advertised in the *Gazette Musicale*: "The greatest interest . . . will be without question the simultaneous appearance of two talents whose rivalry at this time agitates the musical world and is like the indecisive balance between Rome and Carthage. Messrs Listz [*sic*] and

Thalberg will take turns at the piano." Thalberg played his *Moses Fantasy*, Liszt his Fantasy after *Niobe*. According to the critic Jules Janin: "It was an admirable joust. The most profound silence fell over that noble arena. And finally Liszt and Thalberg were both proclaimed victors by this glittering and intelligent assembly. It is clear that such a contest could only take place in the presence of such an Areopagus. Thus two victors and no vanquished . . ."

The Liszt-Thalberg duel encapsulates midcentury piano culture. The celebrity practitioners were distinguished by strikingly contrasted personalities and styles—not least because they usually played their own music, not someone else's. One of Liszt's historic piano "soliloquies," for instance, consisted of his own transcription of the *William Tell* Overture, his Fantasy on Themes from *I Puritani*, a set of original "Studies and Fragments," and an improvisation. Thalberg, Alexander Dreyschock, Louis Moreau Gottschalk, and Carl Tausig similarly produced études, transcriptions, and improvisations of their own. Even the enduring piano masterpieces of the period were composed by famous pianists: Liszt, Chopin, Mendelssohn. Schumann, too, was set on becoming a virtuoso until he damaged his right hand; his wife, Clara, was his inspired deputy at the keyboard.

Assessing the resonance of the Romantic hero with the contemporaneous piano and its audience, the piano historian Arthur Loesser has written:

> In Liszt, the human ideal of the age . . . was married to the musical instrument, newly perfected, that best mirrored the age's mechanical and commercial aspirations. In worshiping Liszt, his public also worshiped the piano, and in either case it really worshiped itself. Never before his time did the instrument soar to such blinding heights of social value, and never since. The time was about 1835 to 1848.

In decades after, as the piano receded from cultural centrality, the composer-pianists of Liszt's day gradually gave way to performance specialists. Competitions changed accordingly: toward the modern type in which fledgling virtuosos from several nations compete en masse, performing the composer-performers Bach, Beethoven, Chopin, Schumann, and Liszt. The first such event of note was the Anton Rubinstein International Competition, organized in 1886 by the Russian pianist many considered Liszt's truest successor. It was to be held every five years in a different city, administered by the head of the host country's state conservatory. Entrance was restricted to males twenty to twenty-six years old, without regard to class, religion, or nationality. Separate cash prizes, furnished by Rubinstein himself, were offered in performance and composition (Rubinstein was also a distinguished composer). The competition took place five times between 1890 and 1910—twice in St. Petersburg, otherwise in Berlin, Vienna, and Paris. Josef Lhévinne and Wilhelm Backhaus were two winners who made good. But Ferruccio Busoni, a player of Lisztian attainments, finished second in performance in 1890, behind Nikolai Dubasov of the host country. According to Busoni's biographer Edward Dent, Rubinstein felt at least one of the prizes should go to a Russian, and Busoni had already won the prize for composition. In 1910, Arthur Rubinstein (no relation to Anton) received an impromptu "special prize," first prize in piano having been awarded to Germany's Alfred Hoehn. In his memoirs, Arthur Rubinstein writes that Hoehn had brought a letter written on his behalf by the Grand Duke of Hesse to his sister, Empress Alexandra of Russia—a crucial advantage. When Rubinstein nonetheless proved the popular favorite, the conductor Serge Koussevitzky offered him a concert tour with a cash advance equal to Hoehn's winnings. Another distinguished loser that year was Edwin Fischer.

The Rubinstein competition did not survive World War I, after which two leading international piano competitions emerged: the Chopin, held in Warsaw, and the Queen Elisabeth of Brussels. The former was begun in 1927 by a Polish pianist, Jerzy Zurawlew, who was distressed by what he considered "gross misunderstanding" of his favorite composer. He later wrote: "Observing the sport craze of the young generation, I hit upon the obvious solution: competition. The advantages for young pianists were evident: financial awards and a good opening for a career. Not less evident was the subsequent popularization of Chopin's music." The first Chopin competition, under the patronage of the Polish president, was won by Lev Oborin of Russia. Alexander Uninsky—first of Russia, then of France—finished first in 1932, Russia's Yakov Zak in 1937. The Queen Elisabeth Foundation, named after Belgium's music-loving monarch, organized a Eugène Ysaÿe Competition for violinists in 1937; David Oistrakh won. The following year, the competition was opened to pianists, and Emil Gilels, Moura Lympany, and Yakov Fliere finished first, second, and third. Both the Chopin and the Queen Elisabeth competitions were interrupted by World War II, but two important American competitions were not. These were the Naumburg and the Leventritt, begun in 1925 and 1940. Walter W. Naumburg was a banker and an amateur cellist, concerned by the plight of young musicians without management or funds for a debut. The Naumburg Foundation's competition was the first in America focused on assisting nascent concert careers; it offered a debut recital at New York's Town Hall. Its notable piano winners have included Jorge Bolet (1937) and William Kapell (1941). Edgar M. Leventritt was a lawyer whose influential personal connections helped make the Leventritt competition, open to pianists and violinists, America's most important. Its first piano winners were Sidney Foster (1940) and Eugene Istomin (1943).

Once the war ended, piano competitions suddenly proliferated; the new ones included the Busoni (in Bolzano, 1949), the Munich (1952), the Maria Canals (Barcelona, 1955), the Vianna da Motta (Lisbon, 1957), and the Georges Enescu (Bucharest, 1958). In 1957, a Federation of International Music Competitions was formed, partly to coordinate dates. The Tchaikovsky, begun in Moscow in 1958, and the Leeds, begun in England in 1963, joined the Chopin and the Queen Elisabeth, both of which now resumed, as the most prominent of the postwar international piano competitions. In the United States, two comparably ambitious piano competitions were implemented and abandoned after a single run. These were the Rachmaninoff, whose prizes included engagements with the major American orchestras and whose jury included Vladimir Horowitz and Madame Rachmaninoff; and the Mitropoulos, whose jury included Arthur Rubinstein and Leopold Stokowski. The Rachmaninoff's sole winner, in 1948, was Seymour Lipkin. The Mitropoulos's, in 1961, was Agustin Anievas—whose sudden celebrity, like Lipkin's, was short-lived.

Though the Van Cliburn International Piano Competition, begun in 1962, endured, the most prominent American piano competition for three decades after World War II continued to be the Leventritt—and this notwithstanding its purposely low profile and relative confinement to American-born or -trained contestants. The Leventritt's prestige derived from its jury, which always included Serkin and Szell, and its victors, most of whom established careers of consequence; after Foster and Istomin, the piano winners included Alexis Weissenberg (1947), Gary Graffman (1949), Van Cliburn (1954), John Browning (1955), Anton Kuerti (1957), Malcolm Frager (1959), Michel Block (1962), and Joseph Kalichstein (1969).* For that matter, in the same postwar period, nearly all the winners of the four major European competitions showed staying

* See Appendix B.

power. The Queen Elisabeth competition, resumed in 1952, consecutively produced Leon Fleisher (1952), Vladimir Ashkenazy (1956), and Frager (1960). The Chopin's postwar winners were Bella Davidovich and Halina Czerny-Stefanska (1949), Adam Harasiewicz (1955), Maurizio Pollini (1960), Martha Argerich (1965), Garrick Ohlsson (1970), and Krystian Zimerman (1975). Leeds was won by Michael Roll (1963), Rafael Orozco (1966), Radu Lupu (1969), and Murray Perahia (1972). Cliburn (1958) and Ashkenazy and John Ogdon (1962) took gold medals at the first two Tchaikovsky competitions.

Cliburn's Moscow victory, as I have suggested, was the locus classicus: not only did it demonstrate the career efficacy of a first prize; it established new possibilities for personal glamour and popular acclaim. Warsaw and Brussels, too, were cities riveted by their visiting piano contestants. And as in Moscow, the glamour and acclaim were doubled by the cold war context. There was drama in the rumors of biased Soviet-bloc jurors, challenged by the wild popularity of certain Western competitors; in the state-sponsored preparation of Russians and East Europeans, versus the necessary self-sufficiency of the Americans. There were stirring opportunities both for patriotic display and for international concord. If Leon Fleisher's Queen Elisabeth victory, and Cliburn's gold medal six years later, marked the apogee of this exciting politicization, the excitement diminished not suddenly but gradually. At Warsaw in 1960, the six American contestants were closely tracked by the *New York Times*. Two months later, in Brussels, North American pianists took seven of the twelve top places—a showing juxtaposed by the *Times* with that of the Soviets, who, "having done well in the past, only placed fourth and eighth." Skeptical Russians, the *Times* commented, "ought to be convinced now [of American musical prowess]—and the rest of the world, too." When the Soviet Union, smarting from such disappointments, entered the already well-known Ashkenazy in the 1962 Tchaikovsky competition, Ross Parmenter of the *Times* suggested that America send Frager or, "even more exciting," John Browning, who was said to have finished "a sixteenth-note" behind Ashkenazy in Brussels. Misha Dichter's controversial second-place finish in the 1966 Tchaikovsky competition—the winner was sixteen-year-old Gregory Sokolov—was widely decried in the American press. He and other American winners were honored at a White House reception, with Van Cliburn as master of ceremonies. President Lyndon Johnson commented: "In the briefest time, in a foreign land with which we have great differences, you lifted the eyes of men beyond the things

which make us adversaries to the things which make us brothers."
Four years later, Garrick Ohlsson's Warsaw victory proved that the
novelty of an American winning behind the Iron Curtain could still
generate gales of publicity.

In moving from palaces and salons to the public arena, piano
competitions had retained their allure while vastly expanding their
audience.

But then their efficacy faded. Ohlsson's 1970 win, in retrospect,
came late in the day—it was partly through the services of an
aggressive publicity firm that he was belatedly feted in *Time* and
Newsweek; initially, the 1970 Chopin competition was relatively
ignored in the American press. Leon Fleisher, looking back to a
time of few international competitions, has observed: "If you won
in the thirties or forties, everyone noticed. The entire musical community was aware of it. And it opened doors." In fact—and this is
a fact worthy of italics—*not since Krystian Zimerman won the Chopin
competition in 1975 has a gold medal launched a major career*. Zimerman
feels he competed just in time: "The crush of the competitions came
somewhere around 1975. In this respect, I was lucky."

It is just possible that the post-1975 gold medalists are simply
inferior to their more celebrated predecessors: that as we lose touch
with the world in which the piano and its repertoire were born,
great talents are less drawn to the keyboard. A more obvious in-
ference is that diminishing political rivalries between East and West
diminished interest in cultural rivalries. Even more obvious is the
saturation point reached and surpassed by a deluge of new competitions. As early as 1948, the magazine *Etude* published a protest,
titled "Contest-itis," lamenting that "The multiplication of piano
contests, held everywhere, is [a] musical epidemic assuming major
proportions." Three decades later, this protest was as ubiquitous as
the competitions themselves. Even in paying tribute to Garrick
Ohlsson's Chopin victory, *Time* had occasion to complain that international competitions had become as numerous and indistin-
guishable as Vivaldi concertos. And increasing numbers of critics
labeled them destructive.

According to one tally, international piano competitions in Europe multiplied more than tenfold between 1950 and 1990. In
North America over the same period, the important new competitions included the Montreal (1964), the University of Maryland
(1971), the Three Rivers (Pittsburgh, 1975; since discontinued),
the Casadesus (Cleveland, 1975), and the Bachauer (Salt Lake City,

1976). Piano competitions now competed with one another for television, magazine, and newspaper coverage. They offered new and better prizes—more money, more guaranteed engagements—in competition for the best contestants. And the quest for a new Van Cliburn grew ever more elusive.

In part, the surfeit of piano competitions resulted from a surfeit of aspirant pianists. Essentially, however, the "more and bigger" syndrome was simply endemic to music as it had evolved since World War II. One catalyst was an audience of high-culture consumers grown more numerous and less tutored. In America, the "music appreciation" movement of the 1930s and '40s had consolidated a new audience for classical music with the help of the radio and the phonograph. After World War II came a "cultural explosion," assisted by television, capping and eclipsing the music appreciation era. According to the National Music Club in 1953, paid admissions for concert music throughout the United States surpassed what major league baseball took in at the gate. When ground was broken for New York City's Lincoln Center for the Performing Arts in 1961, the four new theaters were predicted to outdraw the New York Yankees two to one. These and similar cultural-explosion figures, analogizing concerts with spectator sports, paralleled the piano-competition surge. But in the eighties, when the New York Philharmonic began worrying about replenishing its aging subscribers, the Yankees proved to have more staying power. More than any baseball team, orchestras and opera companies resorted to promotional machinations—telephone marketing, computerized mailings, "radiothons"—to maintain tenuous audience loyalties and to convince fledgling fans that classical music was no antique. The climate for high culture grew more brash, more populist. Piano competitions absorbed both tendencies: diminishing interest, compensatory hype.

If the new, democratized audience counteracted an inbred smugness, the old audience was undeniably more learned—fortified with active listeners who made music at home. Rather than stressing specialized knowledge—how to play an instrument, how to recognize sonata form—music appreciation stressed Everyman's ability to understand Beethoven. Today's orchestras, with their fifty-two-week seasons, complete the cleavage between busy professionals and adoring spectators. Competitions trace the same tendencies toward a bifurcation of professional participants and passive laymen, with no gifted dilettantes in between.

That is to say: centuries before the famous keyboard jousts of Handel, Mozart, Beethoven, and Liszt, all music competitions were amateur events aimed at disseminating skills, not furthering careers. The ancient Greeks held such contests. Wagner's *Die Meistersinger* documents the singing tournaments of sixteenth-century Nuremberg, in which cobblers, clerks, and goldsmiths took part. In nineteenth-century England, towns and villages set their best singers against one another; as late as 1924, *Music and Letters* could report: "There is no large tract of country in England, Scotland, or Ireland without zealous workers in the cause of musical competitions. . . . Competitive festivals are now perhaps the most important force in our musical life." The place of the parlor piano in middle-class America around the turn of the twentieth century is suggested by such magazine articles for mothers and children as: "Octave Playing by the Grace of God" (1901), "Should Musicians Play Without Notes?" (1907), "Should the Untalented Study Piano Playing?" (1909), and "Housework and Piano Practice" (1910). Parents organized local piano contests, which in turn generated regional competitions. One, in Detroit in 1926, was publicized in the *Detroit Times* every day for seven weeks; it attracted 15,000 children from 177 area schools. The National Federation of Music Clubs, organized in 1898, began nationwide contests for singers and instrumentalists in 1921. Specifically for pianists was a national tournament begun in 1934 by the National Music Guild, itself spawned by the All-Southwestern Piano Playing Tournament of 1930. Irl Allison, who conceived both piano tournaments, aimed to "encourage each piano student to enlarge his repertoire . . . while at the same time [encouraging] perfection of performance." Though it admitted "all grade school, high school and college students of piano," the National Piano Playing Tournament expressly welcomed those students who were not "most talented and advanced." Participants were required to perform only "four selections, one polyphonic, one in sonata form, one romantic, and one modern." The awards consisted of five certificates: Fair Rating, Good Rating, Very Good Rating, Excellent Rating, and Superior Rating. "The great principle of this plan," Allison wrote in 1934, "is that everyone can win something. . . . It reaches out to all." He also wrote: "The position that the pupil would ultimately take in the cultural life of the community seemed as important to me as his personal attainments at the keyboard." Allison's competition eventually became known as the National Guild of Piano Teachers' National Piano Playing Tournament.

While the grass-roots efforts of the National Federation of Music Clubs and the National Guild of Piano Teachers continue to this day, they are far eclipsed by competitions, offspring of the Naumburg and Leventritt, for aspiring concert artists. This transformation, as I have suggested, parallels a related decline in domestic music-making. It also documents a paradoxical outcome of parlor-piano studies. The most gifted piano pupils of another era became private, public school, and college piano teachers. By the 1950s, they had fostered higher standards and expectations among their students, a growing percentage of whom sought performing careers. As music in the home diminished, conservatory enrollment shot up. Irl Allison's shifting tournament goals summarize these changes. In founding the Van Cliburn International Piano Competition in 1958, he retained the populist rhetoric of his All-Southwestern Piano Playing tournament; competitions, he maintained in 1978, disseminated "a feeling for music" like "nothing else in the world." At the same time, he had created an event superseding, as completely as possible, the modest amateurs to which his contests once catered.

Hyderization, then, completed a professionalization process begun by Irl Allison many years before.* It formalized and expanded the Cliburn competition's administrative bureaucracy. In competition with Europe, it maximized the Cliburn's scale and scope. And yet, because Texas is America, the populist underpinnings remained. In lieu of the government sponsorship of international competitions abroad, the Cliburn must rely on local volunteers to raise funds, house contestants, and keep the show running smoothly. Its backers continue to include the National Guild of Piano Teachers and the Fort Worth Piano Teachers Forum. As in Warsaw, Moscow, and Brussels, its contestants thrill an audience of piano enthusiasts. More than any European competition, it creates and sustains this audience. It boosts the communal pride of its thousands of listeners and participants. It thrives on the American genius for unembarrassed self-promotion. The first American piano competition to achieve the glamour and visibility of the Chopin, Tchaikovsky, and Queen Elisabeth, it eagerly popularizes high culture the American way.

---

* Driving home the "music equals sports" analogy invited by music competitions, the Olympic Games have been professionalized in much the same manner. See, for instance, "The Death of Amateur Sports," in Benjamin Rader's *In Its Own Image: How Television Has Transformed Sports* (1984), for an analysis of the professionalization of the Olympics and of college football. Television, a crucial validator for the Cliburn competition and others, likewise contributed to "the demise of the amateur model in youth sports." Rader also writes: "For more and more athletes, sports became a form of work rather than play; athletes 'played' for the external rewards rather than the satisfaction of the experience itself." Substitute "musicians" for "athletes" and "music" for "sports," and you are reading about today's fifty-two-week orchestral players. Also suggestive is Allen Guttmann's *Sports Spectators* (1986): e.g., "One facet of specialization was the separation of roles that put increasingly skillful players on the field and increasingly unpracticed spectators on the sidelines."

Elitists
Bite
the
Dust

THE DEMISE OF THE LEVENTRITT PIANO COMPETITION AND THE ASCENT
of the Cliburn were parts of the same popularization equation.

The Leventritt competition never courted popularity and even
shunned it. In its purest form—that is, before Van Cliburn's Moscow victory subverted its assumptions—the Leventritt invited no
audience. It announced its winner to the *New York Times* in a statement a few paragraphs long—about the same length as the announcement the *Times* printed. Its informality was such that there
was no budget and no scheduled frequency. Those years that it was
held, no prize was given if the judges found none of the finalists
ready for a major career—or there might be two prizes if two
finalists were found ready. No second or third prizes were offered.
Little or no money was awarded the winner, it being understood
that he or she would perform with certain leading American orchestras, including the Cleveland and the New York Philharmonic.

The privacy of the event reflected the instincts of the Leventritt
family, which began and administered it. Edgar Leventritt was a
prominent New York attorney of German-Jewish descent. He was
also a skilled pianist and violinist, whose friends included Adolf
Busch, Yehudi Menuhin, Rudolf Serkin, William Steinberg, and
George Szell. After his death, in 1939, a competition for pianists

and violinists was established in his name by his widow, Rosalie. The daughter of a Birmingham, Alabama, businessman, she retained a slight drawl that, in the opinion of Gary Graffman, "accented her impish humor and softened [her] sometimes needlesharp observations." Mrs. Leventritt's daughter, also named Rosalie, was a gifted amateur pianist (her teachers included Serkin; her potential suitors, Menuhin). Joining the family in 1938 was Rosalie's husband, T. Roland Berner. A nonmusician, eventually president and chairman of the Curtiss-Wright Corporation, he oversaw the finances of the Leventritt Foundation.

The spacious, book-lined sitting room of Mrs. Leventritt's Park Avenue apartment was New York's most prestigious private venue for chamber music. The room was also used regularly for practicing, for piano and violin lessons, and for rehearsals. Mrs. Leventritt sat in a corner with her needlework, taking it all in. She dispensed advice and encouragement to young artists. If they could not afford their lessons, she saw to that too. In fact, the family quietly subsidized the Marlboro festival begun by Busch and Serkin in Vermont, Pablo Casals' festival in Prades, France, and an organization called Young Audiences, which brings professional performers into grade school classrooms. Mrs. Leventritt's closest friends included Serkin and Szell—with both of whom she spoke constantly on the telephone, and of whom she would inquire: "Shall we have a competition this year?" They were the nucleus of the Leventritt piano juries, which were unpaid (not even transportation and lodging were reimbursed) and might include Steinberg or Mitropoulos or Bernstein. Characteristically, the Leventritt juries were of uncertain size, and their deliberations obeyed no rules. Contestants were asked to choose "important" solo works, plus three concertos, at least one of which would be by Mozart, Beethoven, or Brahms. Even the application process was vague: no tapes were requested; many (but by no means all) of the entrants were already well known to the judges. As Graffman has suggested, the competition "improvised" its rules to suit its opportunities. If, as in Van Cliburn's case in 1954, the most impressive candidate played Tchaikovsky and Rachmaninoff better than he did Beethoven, the jury made allowances. The goal was to identify talent.

The Leventritt was deeply, and rightfully, proud of its standards: its blue-ribbon jury and prominent winners (several of whom became Leventritt jurors) constituted an initiates' circle, including the close-knit Leventritt family. The Leventritt tone was serious, unabashedly elitist. Cliburn notwithstanding, the typical Leventritt winner was—like Serkin or Szell—more scholarly than flamboyant, "Germanic" rather than "Russian." And the winners were typically young, which welcomed a past or future mentor relationship with Leventritt elders. Graffman, a winner at twenty, later played for Serkin at Marlboro and appeared regularly in Cleveland under Szell, with whom he also recorded. Eugene Istomin, a winner at seventeen, had been a Serkin student; he later recorded with Busch. Malcolm Frager, a winner at twenty-four, was also regularly engaged in Cleveland. Generally, the career prospects of the Leventritt winners were well served by a compact network of influential conductors and impresarios. More than today, even a single appearance with the New York Philharmonic or the Cleveland Orchestra would attract substantial attention—toward hinterlands engagements, or a contract with Arthur Judson's Columbia Artists Management, or a recording for RCA Victor or Columbia. Spurning commercialism, anathematizing glamour, the Leventritt did not seek to maximize publicity or promotion—and did not have to.

As much as it was justly prized and admired, the Leventritt Olympus was envied and resented. Outsiders perceived the competition as a cliquish affair. And Mrs. Leventritt herself, for all her unquestioned generosity, was seen by many on the slopes as a daunting arts matron, more formidable than affectionate. Rudolf Serkin was especially controversial. Even Serkin's detractors conceded his musical stature and admired his ideals of sacrifice and self-abnegation. But Serkin appeared to some to relish the power he wielded on the Leventritt jury, or at Marlboro.

The eventual displacement of the Leventritt was not the result of animosities it may have engendered. Rather, the world of music outside Mrs. Leventritt's sitting room changed. Though members of the Leventritt/Berner family may deny it today, external events could impinge on their musical affairs, and nothing impinged more crucially than Van Cliburn's sudden fame and the possibilities for competition-induced mass appeal it disclosed. In an April 1958 press release, Columbia Artists hastened to remind America what few Americans ever knew: that Cliburn had previously won the Leventritt award, had consequently played with major American orchestras, and had thereafter toured the United States annually under Columbia's management. According to the press release: "The Russians' recognition of Cliburn's enormous talent . . . confirms the judgment of musical auspices and audiences in scores of . . . American cities." In fact, as even the Leventritt had to recognize, the Russian verdict created the American verdict. The following year, the Leventritt piano competition made a point of inviting foreign—and particularly Soviet—judges and contestants.

An appeal to the United States Information Agency for promotional assistance, cited in a Leventritt press release, argued in part:

> Although the Leventritt contest always has been conducted quietly and "out of the public eye," it is considered the most important international competition of its kind held in the United States, and that its standards always have been as high—and many musicians feel, higher —than any of its kind in the world. *In view of the international news attention accorded recently to contests held in other countries, it is felt that the existence of this 20-year-old, privately financed international competition held in the United States should be made known to a wider public around the world.*

Whereas the Leventritt finals had previously been witnessed by friends of the contestants and other initiates, in 1959 the general public was invited; Leventritt fliers advertised a "unique international event," and tickets were sold. Also, the final round consisted of concertos with orchestra, rather than, as previously, a mixture of solo and concerto repertoire, the latter accompanied by a second pianist. Media attention grew commensurately. One article in the *New York Times* carried the subhead: "Leventritt Contest Expands Its Scope and Aims for Big League Rating." The winner was Malcolm Frager. In 1960, the Leventritt finals were again publicized, and Mayor Robert Wagner proclaimed Leventritt International Competition Week—which backfired when the jury chose no winner, and the public objected. Letters to the *Times* called the competition a hoax and complained that the three finalists had been insulted. In 1961, there was no Leventritt competition; according to a *Times* article, the foundation was exploring ways to entice more foreign entrants. In 1962, the Leventritt reversed its course, moving from Carnegie Hall to a much smaller auditorium, whose doors were closed. The 1964 competition, for violinists, returned to Carnegie; it generated unprecedented publicity, thanks to a human interest story: the winner, Itzhak Perlman, lost his unguarded violin backstage. Through 1975, the Leventritt was either not held, or gave no award, with increasing frequency; Tong Il Han in 1965 and Joseph Kalichstein in 1969 were the only piano winners. The Soviets never did participate, nor did some important North Americans the Leventritt Foundation had courted: Richard Goode, Horacio Gutiérrez, Murray Perahia, André-Michel Schub. The Leventritt "standard," against which contestants competed, seemed increasingly elusive—as if the jurors, in other piano competitions pressured to pick a winner, were afraid to choose someone unworthy of the Leventritt imprimatur.

The watershed year was 1976. The Leventritt's earliest, essential strategies—the quiet solicitation of applications, the quiet competition, the quiet networking for the winner—seemed less effective than ever. The pressures to maximize media exposure and promotional opportunities had become irresistible. In an agonizing move, the foundation hired a professional arts publicist. According to Gary Graffman's wife, Naomi, who had worked for Columbia Artists before becoming an intimate counselor and helper to the Leventritts: "It was hair-pulling time. We began to see how it was possible to promote a classical artist so that he had unusual recognition and a better chance for a good career. Mrs. Leventritt, who had recently died, had abhorred the idea. But in order to do our best for the winner, we had to play the game." Gurtman & Murtha Associates, pioneers in using liquor ads and talk shows to help pianists and violinists, now drew up lists of Objectives and Needs, beginning: "To educate and inform the lay public, concertgoers, the press and the communications media what the cognoscenti in the musical world already know—that the Leventritt International Competition is the World's foremost prestigious competition of irreproachable character." The Immediate Needs list included: " 'Leventritt competition' to become household word." Gurtman & Murtha succeeded in committing CBS Television to produce a "Sixty Minutes" segment on the 1976 Leventritt. Concurrently, the Leventritt announced a cash award of $10,000. At the competition that May, the crush of cameras and reporters spread discomfort and confusion. Helen Epstein, covering the event for the *New York Times* Arts & Leisure section, felt she had invaded a fiefdom: "The way the Leventritt family reacted to me was just insane. They wanted to exercise complete control. They didn't know what they had gotten into." When the CBS crew, which had been promised complete access, began setting up lights in the jury room, Serkin disappeared. CBS left, but Epstein, who had been smuggled in, remained. She was "astonished by how mean and catty some of the jurors were"—yet less astonished, perhaps, than were the jurors themselves when they read about their deliberations in the *Times*. The verdict, which drew boos from a large Carnegie Hall audience, was No winner. Claude Frank, the jury chairman, felt that the additional money and publicity had made some judges circumspect about giving a prize "blown up so much as to practically guarantee instant fame." The reactions of the five finalists—Lydia Artymiw, Steven De Groote, Marian Hahn, Santiago Rodriguez, and Mitsuko Uchida—ranged from gratitude and relief to bitterness and rage. One later recalled: "After the final round, we were all herded into this room to await the result. And suddenly Serkin walked in. There he was with this big smile on his face—the one he wears when you know he's hiding something. And he said, 'To me, you're all winners!' And he patted us all and swept out of the room. It was about ten minutes later that we found out that none of us were winners. It was an ugly little scene."

In striving to obtain all it could for its winner, the Leventritt Foundation was impelled to promote itself. But instead of rescuing the competition, self-promotion killed it; the Leventritt proved inherently nonpromotable. After 1976, no Leventritt competitions were held. Instead, the foundation more than ever receded from view. It continued its policy of subsidizing concerts for past finalists—a generous consolation prize vital to several significant minor careers, even if some in the inner circle felt it diluted the Leventritt standard. After 1976, additional young artists were privately selected and patronized; one, the pianist Cecile Licad, was in 1981 given the Leventritt award—$10,000, a CBS Records contract, and major orchestral dates—without a competition. A nineteen-year-old Serkin protégée, she had been chosen, according to an article in the *Times*, by an "unpaid board of judges" including "many of America's most important musicians." But some former Leventritt jurors were annoyed that they had not been consulted. And some pianists who had competed in the Leventritt and lost perceived the Licad selection as biased. In subsequent years, the Leventritt Foundation lapsed into inactivity.

Even before the 1976 competition, Mrs. Leventritt and her daughter had soured on competitions—they decried a "new breed of contestants," mechanicians produced by the "circus atmosphere" of proliferating newer events. And with more and more applicants on the competition circuit, the sheer logistics of a low-cost, family-operated music contest became daunting. The deaths of George Szell in 1970, and of the two Rosalies in 1976 and 1983, were crippling blows. What essentially defeated the Leventritt competition, however, was Van Cliburn's victory. Pondering the future, if any, of the Leventritt Foundation, its president, Edgar Berner, remarked in 1989: "I'm not sure that there is a place for the Leventritt in today's world without destroying what my grandmother and mother created."

In a sense, the Leventritt competition is unfairly impugned by its own history. Until it lost its way in a new world of public relations, it never asked for attention, assistance, or approval. It had functioned admirably as a career springboard for two generations of American or American-trained pianists: the strong starts of such considerable artists as Eugene Istomin, Gary Graffman, Van Cliburn, John Browning, Malcolm Frager, and Joseph Kalichstein were Leventritt starts. In fact, the entire phenomenon of what Graffman has called the Outstanding Young American Pianists—the first crop of homegrown keyboard talent to achieve international prominence—was crucially supported by the Leventritt community. Naomi Graffman comments: "In going for a high profile, we risked getting egg on our face. The whole point of the Leventritt had been to be so independent it was nobody's business what we did. We weren't asking for help. We had our contestants, we had our judges, we had our conductors, who helped our winners. People who didn't like us didn't have to enter our competition." It was the unavoidable "high profile" gamble that made the Leventritt seem especially insular and aloof, and that underscored its suddenly reduced effectiveness.

To a striking degree, the world in which the Leventritt expired was a New World distinct from Old World Leventritt values and embodied by the Leventritt's upstart successor: the Van Cliburn International Piano Competition of Fort Worth, Texas. These two events, the one elitist, the other populist, are as different as Rudolf Serkin and Van Cliburn, as different as Serkin's wire-rim spectacles and Cliburn's occasional cowboy hat. They resonate with two distinct moments in America's high-cultural history, the first—of the forties and fifties—shadowed by Europe (its wars and refugees, its cultural colonization of the United States, its patina of worldly reflectiveness), the second—of today—bright with American optimism, gusto, and heedless naïveté.

Mrs. Leventritt kept company with refugee musicians, formerly friends, clients, and chamber music partners of her late husband. She admired these famous artists, but not from afar, as their audiences did. Rather, the pleasure she took in their presence, their conversation, and their music was that of a trusted peer. According to Naomi Graffman: "Mrs. Leventritt was a terrific personality, but not in the public eye; she didn't call attention to herself. I think her happiest moment at a concert would be if Rudolf Serkin was playing Schubert's B-flat major Sonata. That was the kind of thing she liked. She grew up in a gentler time. Her whole upbringing was genteel. She was not a socialite; she couldn't have cared less for bridge. And she wasn't one of these wealthy volunteers who get involved with the orchestra, the ballet, or the opera in order to have something to do." Martha Hyder's favorite pianists—Cliburn,

Vladimir Horowitz, Radu Lupu, Ivo Pogorelich, Alexander Toradze, Vladimir Viardo—are Russian by training or orientation.
They are her charismatic heroes. Her new enthusiasm for them
presses her toward telling anyone and everyone. She is a prosely-
tizer who wants Fort Worth's Van Cliburn competition to be the
biggest and best. (Cliburn himself said in 1977: "Tell 'em back East
what we're doing here. All they think about is the Leventritt. I love
it—I won it—but we have something bigger going on here.")

The Leventritt competition resembled a private event to which
the public was admitted. The Cliburn competition is committed to
pleasing the people. In most years, the Leventritt audience was not
even provided with a printed program. Referring to Mrs. Leventritt's daughter, whom she knew, Martha Hyder observes: "Rosalie
ran the Leventritt any way she wanted to, and she wasn't interested
in anybody's outside opinion." To the Cliburn, outside opinion
matters.

Edgar Berner says of the Cliburn competition: "It's a glitzy affair. It's not our style." The Cliburn style is an American style,
celebrating free enterprise and commercial sponsorship. Mobil and
Tandy underwrite the Cliburn's television expenses. General Dynamics donates flags. Fragrances are provided by Neiman Marcus
and Estée Lauder. The Cliburn is proud of its democratic largess
and self-reliance. It scorns European and Soviet arts subsidies, with
their restrictions and red tape. To assess the Hyderized Van
Cliburn piano competition, successor to the Leventritt as America's
most prominent, is to assess the trade-offs—the opportunities and
risks—of elite art in the throes of democratization. It is an assessment best made from the perspective of the competition's ostensible
prime beneficiaries: the pianists who have won and lost in Fort
Worth in 1977 and after.

II

SOME WINNERS
AND LOSERS

Steven
De
Groote

ONE FINE SUNDAY—SEPTEMBER 25, 1977—STEVEN DE GROOTE BECAME
a celebrated pianist with a major career. The day before, he had
been a finalist in the Fifth Van Cliburn International Piano Competition. A few weeks before that, he had been a fledgling twenty-
four-year-old playing obscure dates for low fees.

De Groote was surprised but not wholly unprepared. As a youngster, he had performed chamber music, and even half a dozen concertos, in his native South Africa. He had subsequently appeared
with the Belgian Radio Symphony and the Charleston Symphony.
Though he did not survive the first cut at the 1975 Leeds competition, he won the Young Concert Artists auditions in 1976 and was
a Leventritt finalist the same year. He had two or three recital programs ready to go, and three concertos with seven in reserve. Decades earlier, all this would have seemed sufficient for a young
pianist aspiring toward international prominence. But the Cliburn
gold medal conferred international prominence with aggressive suddenness. Mere musical preparation would not be enough.

De Groote was a tall young man with shaggy hair, guarded eyes,
and a pointed nose and chin. He was skinny, shy, and unworldly.
He had first glanced at the remarkable Grand Prize Tour the night
before the finals. He did not own concert tails. He shared a Phila-

delphia apartment in which the only piano was a red upright with four functioning keys. At the Cliburn, his awkwardness (he shrank when hugged) and odd attire (he turned up for his winner's recital wearing a blazer, dark pants, and a large black-and-white polka-dot bow tie) contrasted disconcertingly with Vladimir Viardo's aplomb four years before. And he was perceived as arrogant and withdrawn.

Two weeks after winning, De Groote was on the road, giving concerts. He was also propelled into an unfamiliar and exacting regime of socializing and publicity. While Fort Worth Productions edited its Cliburn competition television documentary for PBS (in which De Groote would be seen musing: "I wasn't expecting anything, really"), Cliburn publicists were contacting newspapers and radio stations along De Groote's route. In Wichita, Pasadena, Kansas City, and Baltimore, he was observed, feted, photographed, and interviewed. Of the early newspaper articles, the most important ran in the October 9 *New York Times* Arts & Leisure section under the headline: TRIUMPH AND TURMOIL AT THE CLIBURN COMPETITION. The writer was John Ardoin, music critic of the *Dallas Morning News*. The article read in part:

> It has been said that a competition is only as good as its most recent winner. By this standard, there are many who feel the Cliburn took a step backwards this year. . . . A detractor . . . would describe [Steven De Groote] as an example of the classic contest winner—a superb and fluent mechanism coupled with a common-denominator approach to music which is solid but not revelatory, and which gives offense to no one except those expecting an immense personality, one to match the prize. . . . It could well be that De Groote was a compromise among the jury which was, according to one of its members, split exactly in two over [second-prize winner Alexander] Toradze: "Half of them love him, half of them can't stand his playing."

In Ardoin's own opinion, Toradze had "almost literally played [De Groote] off the stage."

An interview with De Groote in the *Times* eleven days later was headlined: THE PRIZE IS HIS, AND DE GROOTE TAKES HIS DETRACTORS IN STRIDE. Ten days after that, the paper published letters from jury members disputing Ardoin's account of the voting, along with Ardoin's unrepentant reply. Meanwhile, De Groote was playing more than twice a week. He purchased concert clothes, rented an apartment of his own, and acquired a proper piano—exhausting the first $3,000 installment of his prize money in a matter of days. On December 12, he arrived at Carnegie Hall. He was greeted backstage by Toradze, by Lili Kraus and Rudolf Firkusny of the Cliburn jury, by the actress Arlene Dahl, by chairman Nancy Hanks of the National Endowment for the Arts. Harold Schonberg's *New York Times* review the next morning complained that De Groote had been "not fully up to" his program of Haydn, Prokofiev, Beethoven, and Chopin. The only thing Schonberg liked was an encore—Liszt's E-flat *Paganini* Étude.

> This was playing of strength, confidence and brilliance of sound. For the first time, Mr. De Groote really showed what he could do. A pianist with such natural virtuosity should stick to this element of the repertory. He can play it with fire and passion, whereas elsewhere he seems to play almost by rote.

The same month, *People* magazine named De Groote one of the twenty-five "most interesting people of 1977." Weeks later, Youri Egorov, in whose favor certain influential Cliburn patrons were ignoring De Groote, made his New York debut with their assistance.* Harold Schonberg wrote: "He has all the ingredients for success; there are not many young pianists in recent years who have so managed to involve an audience."

De Groote's Cliburn engagements lasted two seasons and took him to four continents. During one improbable stretch, he played successively in Sioux Falls, Taipei, Taiwan, Taichung, Hong Kong, and Kalamazoo. He lived in hotel rooms and returned home to pay his bills. In 1981, at the Sixth Cliburn Competition, he looked back and said: "The day I won this damned thing, one of the jurors came up to me and said, 'Watch it, you'll burn out. You'll see.' And there I was, I had this silver cup and this gold medal and this gold watch and this check and two years of concerts lined up and I thought, 'I can handle this, what's he talking about.' But he was right. . . . I'm four years older and I don't feel four years older at all. I haven't lived. I don't belong anywhere."

Times change. It is 1988, and Steven De Groote lives in Fort Worth, where he is director of piano studies at Texas Christian

---

* Though Egorov did not survive the second cut, it took a New York concert manager, Maxim Gershunoff, two days to raise $10,000—the equivalent of the first-prize cash award—from disappointed members of the audience. Gershunoff urged Martha Hyder to accept the money, toward a New York debut recital, on behalf of the Cliburn Foundation. When she hesitated, he told her that he would present Egorov's New York debut with or without the Cliburn's sanction. The concert was presented by Gershunoff "in cooperation with" the Cliburn competition. Egorov eventually established a major European career.

University. The furnishings of his studio, with its expensive Hispanic decor, were chosen and purchased by Martha Hyder. John Ardoin, in recent reviews in the *Dallas Morning News*, has called De Groote's playing "remarkable" and "sublime." With Van Cliburn and John Giordano, De Groote is a frequent artistic adviser to the Cliburn competition. And his noisily begun career has dwindled quietly.

At thirty-five, De Groote is no longer awkward or skinny. He is a large man with thick features, a weighty presence. He is not shy, but he makes no special show of friendliness. His eyes do not always participate in his smile. He feels that his clipped, precise speech creates a misimpression of arrogance.

"I think it's my accent, really. I've lived in the States now for eighteen years, and every time I get to know someone well, they say, 'I used to think you were aloof.' I have a new graduate student who's South African, and the first thing he said to me was 'Boy, they smile a lot in this country, don't they? And you never know if they mean it, because they do it all the time.' "

De Groote's musical upbringing discouraged anything like normal socialization. As the youngest in a family of musicians, he was touring South Africa, playing chamber music with his parents and brothers, by the age of ten. He left home at sixteen to study in Brussels, where his parents had met as violin students at the conservatory. Three years later, he moved on to the Curtis Institute, where his teachers were Rudolf Serkin, Seymour Lipkin, and Mieczyslaw Horszowski. His struggle for a career, he says, has not embittered him. But he recounts this struggle bluntly, ruefully, mercilessly.

"I have never felt any animosity toward the Cliburn competition at all. But the Cliburn people are pretending if they imagine they'll ever have a winner in the Van Cliburn superstar mold. I know it would have been impossible to turn me into a superstar. The whole package wasn't very presentable. I mean, that article by John Ardoin sealed my fate. And being South African, I could never have achieved the popularity of certain Russian emigrants and defectors. In fact, I maintain I'm not promotable. I'll give you an example. Before I played my Carnegie Hall debut in 1977, Bob Alexander, the executive director of the Cliburn, called me to say, 'I don't like your program.' I said, 'Well, what do you mean?' I had chosen precisely the kind of program I might play today. And I went ahead and played it. I began with an extremely rare Haydn sonata, which I think is a special piece. And then I played the Beethoven Op. 101 Sonata, and the Prokofiev Sonata No. 8, and the Chopin Scherzo

No. 4. I'm not going to play the Liszt opera paraphrases, and I'm not going to play the Chopin *Funeral March* Sonata. It's true I played a Liszt étude as an encore—which was the only thing well spoken of in the *New York Times* review. My second encore was the Sarabande from Bach's C minor Partita. Surely at Carnegie Hall, which is perhaps the most famous concert hall in the world, surely there you can play an intellectual program. But no, not if you're the Van Cliburn winner. You know, when you're a nobody, it's easy to be yourself. When you're a nobody, like I was before the Cliburn, you play whatever you like, and people listen. But if you're the Cliburn winner, people listen with certain hopes and expectations. 'Oh, he won the Cliburn; that means he'll probably sound something like this.' "

Harold Schonberg's hope, like Martha Hyder's, was that the Cliburn winner would sound something like Van Cliburn. In his review of De Groote's Carnegie Hall debut, Schonberg inferred that the artist had "crucified himself to try and play what he thinks should be played rather than the music with which he has a natural affinity." In fact, De Groote's natural affinity is not for Liszt's *Paganini* études but for Beethoven's Op. 101 Sonata (a subtler, more elusive work than the popular *Waldstein* or *Appassionata*), Prokofiev's Eighth Sonata (versus the Seventh, with its surefire, machine-gun finale), and Chopin's E major Scherzo (his least played and least heroic).

The pressure to please the crowd is great for any pianist. For young competition winners blessed with fabulous fingers, this pressure is insidious; onstage, the adrenaline rush attacks every conscious resolve to serve the music first. De Groote remembers feeling "the pressure to play differently" and remembers resisting it. He is the type of artist who could—a literalist whose unvarnished sound and undemonstrative technical command exude a truculent integrity.

De Groote's lucidity—his finely gauged balances and spare, precise pedaling—can verge on idiosyncrasy: in Schubert's F minor Impromptu, he barely shades the A-flat major theme in palpitating eighth notes, stripping away its usual Romantic veil. Some may find such playing "cold" or "stiff." But De Groote—who matter-of-factly says of his 1978 recording of Beethoven's *Eroica* Variations: "It's still the best"—seems not to care.

In January 1985, De Groote's life took a second sharp turn. Four years before, he had accepted a teaching job—a decision he ex-

plained to a *Washington Post* reporter at the 1981 Cliburn competition as follows: "I'm going to teach piano at Arizona State
University at Tempe, which, I am told, is the sixth-largest university in the country, and I'm damned pleased with myself. And if I
want to teach piano, I'll teach piano. I'm the one in control of my
life, not anybody else. . . . I'll have a library to go in and paths to
walk on and colleagues to whom I'll have something more interesting to say than 'Hey, I've got a plane to catch.' I'll have friends. Let
me tell you about friends. Friends are people who, even if you don't
see them for two years, are still your friends. I could count the
number of friends I have on the fingers of one mutilated hand. The
friends I used to have I lost. . . . And friends aren't the worst thing
you lose. I think I'm incapable of falling in love now."

At Tempe, De Groote rode motorcycles and flew airplanes. He
and his instructor were landing a single-engine plane one day when
it got caught in a wind shear and crashed in the Sonora Desert. A
man in a pickup truck happened to find them. The pickup truck
had a radio. A lonely ambulance, passing nearby, heard the radio
call. The ambulance called a helicopter. At the hospital in Phoenix,
De Groote was given a 2 percent chance to survive. His skull was
severely fractured; his aorta was severed. His hands were un-
harmed. A Dacron tube was inserted into his heart, a steel rod into
his leg; extensive plastic surgery left his face looking flatter and
fleshier. Eight weeks later, he was performing. Then his back was
found to be broken, and he spent almost a year in a body cast.

Two months after crashing in the desert, De Groote accepted a
teaching position at Fort Worth's Texas Christian University,
which offered him more money than he was getting at Tempe, and
also more authority. Memories of his 1977 triumph must have
influenced his decision; and the Cliburn Foundation extended a
friendly hand. He began playing regularly in Fort Worth. Then, on
March 6, 1987, he appeared with the Dallas Symphony in Beethoven's Piano Concerto No. 4. Eleven months later, he was heard in
Brahms's Second Concerto with the Fort Worth Symphony. These
were the performances that changed John Ardoin's mind, and no
wonder. Both were spacious interpretations, whose majestic steadi-
ness proved unifying: the many tempo changes commonly applied
to the first movements of both concertos, a result of their highly
contrasted materials, were minimized. Both performances, for that
matter, were singularly free of interpretive distractions: at thirty-
four, De Groote played as if all superfluous "expression" had already been burned away by experience. The Beethoven concerto's
many rapid scales and arpeggios, which easily reduce to filigree,

were made to speak. In the Brahms, a work so densely scored that pianists frequently smudge or simplify its textures, De Groote projected the insides of the massive chordal structures and maintained linear continuity where hastier players swallow the short notes. And he penetrated the depths of both concertos' slow movements without any affectations of profundity.

Ardoin, in the first of his reviews, pondered: "Perhaps it is too facile to link the expressiveness and depth of De Groote's Beethoven to his [airplane] accident, yet something has dramatically altered his playing." Eugenia Zukerman, in a "CBS Sunday Morning" television feature titled "The Man Who Fell to Earth," put the question to De Groote directly; he replied: "I think I'm more interested now in direct communication on every level—human and musical." Charles Kuralt, introducing Zukerman's report, called De Groote "a modern-day Icarus whose fiery fall from great heights brought him new understanding of the fragility and beauty of our human wings." De Groote is the type to wince at such language. In fact, he has characteristically refused to publicize his accident and recovery: "It never even occurred to me. I wouldn't have been able to live with myself. Suppose I did that and suddenly I had thirty more concerts a year than I had before."

As of 1988, thirty concerts a year is all De Groote has. His schedule had already dropped to that level before he fell from the sky. His best dates are in South Africa and Germany, where audiences, he feels, are more loyal, and the musical life is less commercialized, than in the United States. Though he plays almost no contemporary music (his repertoire stops with Bartók and Prokofiev) he has quickly acquired obscure concertos—by Dvořák, Reger, and Korngold—where they have been requested. He hopes some of his European broadcast performances will be issued as recordings.

De Groote is the first to point out that, if he is a better pianist today than when he won the Cliburn in 1977, he is also considerably older; his goal, he says, is "to be the best pianist I can be when I'm sixty." That his biggest career opportunity came too soon makes him philosophic; he does not feel singled out for punishment. The music business, he knows, increasingly promotes youth before experience—"the way Björn Borg was the only teenage-idol tennis player, and now there are six of them." He conjectures that Murray Perahia, born in 1947, is the only pianist of his generation "who may sustain a career into old age," and continues: "The fact is we're all becoming smaller and smaller because there are too many of us. We've reached a point of saturation. I remember how, way back in

'74, my teacher Mieczyslaw Horszowski told me that the golden age of virtuosos touring the world was over. The world is going to become a place where musicians establish themselves locally and function locally, he said. And I believe he was right. I can think of so many pianists who emerged since I won the Cliburn in 1977 and who are fading at about the same rate as I did. To me, what will never fade is the sense that I'm able to function as a successful musician without this compulsion to be famous. Or to play a hundred concerts a season, which is a desperate and greedy thing to do. Or to appear on the Johnny Carson show. The urge to be popular and the urge to exist with integrity are opposing forces. To me, success is something you can look back on and be proud of on your deathbed."

Like Ralph Votapek, who won the Cliburn in 1962, or Gregory Allen, who won Tel Aviv's Rubinstein competition in 1980, like numerous winners of the Bachauer and University of Maryland competitions, De Groote has become a hinterlands teacher, many of whose professional ties are local. And yet, even locally, he feels a stranger.

"I'm getting ready to leave Fort Worth, I think. I think as I get older I've started to hanker a little bit more for the country where I grew up. Because people there do not think I'm arrogant. Maybe my accident has contributed to the feeling that I'd like to be closer to what I was close to when I was younger. I don't know. I haven't decided. I'm still trying to make sense of it. I feel that despite the Cliburn competition I've kept a firm grip on my desire to evolve musically throughout my life. I know that you can have a glittery career and be doing absolutely nothing. For about two years after the Cliburn I wasn't playing well. And then I began playing fewer concerts and it got better. I'm a lot happier now. I don't want to go to Spearfish, and they don't want me there, either. It's a college town near Rapid City, with a really bad piano. An awful piano. There's no reason that piano needs to be played by someone in a suit. For people who pay five dollars a ticket and can't wait for it to be over.

"I'm asking myself now if the decision to come to TCU was a decision I made when someone should have told me I wasn't capable of making a rational decision. It was only two months after the accident. It would have been better to wait until my mind had cleared. I may have reached the same decision, but I probably wouldn't have. In many respects, this job is everything I wanted it to be. And it's also nice that I've gotten to play with the Dallas Symphony and been reengaged. And that I've played with the Fort

Worth Symphony. Here I can be the sort of local pianist that Mr. Horszowski was talking about. It's just that I think I'd like to be a local pianist in Johannesburg or Cape Town."

Steven De Groote looks up from his desk at the Mexican rugs on the walls of his studio, chosen by Martha Hyder.

Alexander
Toradze

OF THE THREE SOVIETS AT THE 1977 VAN CLIBURN COMPETITION, AL-
exander Toradze charmed the most intensely. Round-faced and
pudgy, sociable, demonstrative, he was a born performer. Earnestly searching for an errant English word, he would purse his
lips, knit his brow, and shut his eyes in a hard squint. In repose, his
features turned vulnerably soft. Pleasure crinkled his eyes, puffed
his cheeks, and stretched his mouth into a broad smile. He seemed
as forward as Steven De Groote seemed withdrawn.

At the piano, too, De Groote and Toradze were a study in
contrasts. De Groote was composed. From the moment he sat
down to play, Toradze was an adrenaline machine, arms fidgeting,
torso twisting, legs twitching, as he nervously glanced at the orchestra and the conductor. In action, eyes clamped, jaw clenched,
he crowded the keyboard like a pugilist, bowing his head, curling
his back, spreading his elbows. He beat time sharply with his left
foot. His powerful hands, with their surprisingly long fingers, stood
tall, tickling the keys or punishing them.

Interpretively, De Groote's performances ranged within the nor-
mal parameters. Everything Toradze touched sounded different.
His Bach—the Sinfonia from the C minor Partita—was Gothic.
His Haydn—the first movement of the G minor Sonata, Hob.

XVI:44—was relentlessly, formidably dour. He traversed a Scarlatti sonata in an eerie, mournful slow motion. Then, with boisterous abandon, he devoured chunks of Stravinsky—the Three
Movements from *Petrushka*—and Prokofiev—the Seventh Sonata
and Third Piano Concerto. In the Prokofiev concerto, Toradze's
vitality was assaultive. Prokofiev himself was a steely pianist, whose
caustically neutral interpretation of the Third Concerto was recorded in 1932. Toradze's version was aggressively human. In the
second movement, he costumed and choreographed the five variations as dance or fairy-tale vignettes. He slowed down Variation III
(marked *Allegro moderato*) to create a grotesque character piece, a
rhythmic tug-of-war between piano and orchestra whose writhing,
lunging cross-accents were both audible and visible. The smeared,
crystalline chords of the fourth variation (*Andante meditativo*), also
under tempo, conjured a glistening ice castle on a frozen lake.

If this in some ways qualified as "Romantic" playing, it was not
Romantic in the majestic Cliburn manner. Young Toradze was
always vehemently "on"; his intensity was unsettling, exhausting,
controversial. Lili Kraus, one of the jurors, commented afterward:
"The moment he enters the stage, there is a presence . . . because inside that man the creative power is at work, and this is
manifest. And besides all of this, he is lovable. . . . If they say that
he has a sound like the last judgment—yes, he has, thank God, he
has that. Yes, he's fanatical, as he should be. And he makes mistakes as he should because he's young. But he makes his *own* mistakes." Other jurors were less forgiving. Toradze's severest critics
considered him raw, gauche, a potentially embarrassing winner.
One juror, the composer Alberto Ginastera, reportedly argued during the deliberations that the two front-runners were as different as
Apollo and Dionysus, that no common criteria applied.

Martha Hyder has suggested that the 1977 first prize should have
been shared. But this is never a popular option. It complicates the
distribution of prize money, ruins the carefully planned itineraries,
upsets the presenters. It taints the imagery of victory.

Eleven years later, Toradze's English has vastly improved, but
he still squeezes his face shut when searching his vocabulary for a
missing word. His tiny New York apartment, near Lincoln Center,
is dominated by a grand piano and the photographs atop it: of
Toradze's mother and sister; of Toradze with Van Cliburn, with
Zubin Mehta, with the conductor Esa-Pekka Salonen posed alongside a smiling, life-size cutout of Ronald Reagan. The top third of

the bedroom door is a backboard for a miniature basketball net. In a closet, where it can sit privately, is a three-panel panorama of Tbilisi, the capital of Soviet Georgia, where Toradze was born. Toradze also retains ties to Fort Worth, which he occasionally visits. His memories of the Cliburn competition there are still vivid. In fact, all his memories are hot.

When I relate a recent conversation with a 1977 Cliburn juror who had found his playing "raw," Toradze steadies himself by grabbing his red suspenders: "I think he's right—and I hope I can stay that way all my life. I don't want to 'cook' this *raw* spontaneity by any recipe. 'Unpolished.' Big deal. I don't care. If it is interesting, inside. If it is moving. If it has been created on the spot and is unrepeatable. These are qualities which are much more rare than properness and polish." The juror in question had commented that compared to De Groote, Toradze had seemed the "bigger talent" but one best served by further years of study. De Groote himself—as I inform Toradze—once remarked that Toradze was fortunate to have avoided the gold-medal itinerary. Toradze is now chain-chewing nicotine gum. Words rush to his mouth faster than his thick English can spew them out. "I would never say this in criticism of Steven, because he is my friend. But I am *delighted* to play as many performances as I can. At any time. At that time, especially. Because for any Soviet pianist to come here and win a competition and tour the United States for two years—it's a *major* life undertaking. You could *dream* about that. It was a total desire of mine. That was the whole purpose I was preparing for the competition. You don't think I was preparing to get the second prize?"

The difference between gold and silver mattered most to the three Soviet contestants. Since Lev Oborin won in Warsaw in 1927, many Russians have taken first prizes in the major international competitions. In the Soviet Union, these prizes have automatically meant more dates, higher fees, and—the crucial reward—foreign tours. Second- and third-prize winners are expendable. In a sense, the entire system is organized to groom and manage successful contestants. Whereas elsewhere young talent may wither unnoticed, the Soviets scout their kindergartens and summer camps. Fledgling virtuosos are directed to the central music schools at the age of seven—before bad habits can form. At the conservatory level, teaching is an honored profession; at the Moscow Conservatory, apex of the system, the master teachers are the master musicians: a Khachaturian, an Oistrakh, a Rostropovich, a Heinrich Neuhaus.

Toradze was born in 1952 to a musical family: his father, David, was a leading Georgian composer. He entered the central music school at Tbilisi at six and first played with orchestra at nine. He won the Trans-Caucasian Competition at sixteen and was third in the Soviet Union Competition a year later. He entered the Moscow Conservatory in 1971 to become a student of Yakov Zak—then one of the great names of Russian pianism, after Richter and Gilels. The story of his subsequent conservatory regime, as he tells it, is an epic, a tale of loyalties and betrayals, of crisis and rebirth. A tumble of personalities and events, the long, convoluted paragraphs are sustained only by the high energy with which they begin, and which binds the many breathless hesitations and novelistic digressions. Toradze starts by rubbing his hands and looking out a window. Then he raises both his arms from the elbow and leans back.

"Now, how I was prepared for the Van Cliburn competition is at the same time very simple and very complicated—as everything is. To begin with, by 1974, after being so promising, I was not able to compete anywhere, because Zak wouldn't approve. Zak, who could be very constructive and helpful for his other pupils, was not a supportive teacher for me. He was an intelligent and powerful figure, but nervous and fearful. He had passed through Stalin's era, and maybe because of that he was a frightened man, especially in his later years. He disbelieved in me so much that finally when the time came for him to listen to a program I was preparing, he didn't allow me to play for himself only. He asked me to bring my father. He wanted my father to see how disabled I am, and that it was not Zak's fault. Well, oddly enough, I played brilliantly, as Zak said himself. He said he didn't recognize me. But I knew while I was playing that I would never go to Zak again. Because of his mistrust for me. So in the middle of the year I told Zak that I was leaving him. This was a very risky step, which made him and all those connected with him enormously furious. It was maybe the first time a quite promising student had left a great-name teacher during the final year. Zak tried to stop me. He said, 'I hope you are not thinking of going to the "housekeeper," ' meaning Zemliansky. I didn't give an answer, because at that time I didn't know who would risk helping me and, by that, risk jeopardizing relations with Zak. But Zemliansky welcomed me. I bless that day: October 22, 1974. I'm sorry I have this feeling toward Zak, but I cannot get over it. I realize he is already in his grave. But he hurt *very much* Zemliansky, and me, and my father too. I will always remember that, as long as I am alive. Do you understand what I mean, or not?"

Boris Zemliansky, who as Lev Oborin's assistant had been Vladimir Ashkenazy's principal teacher, became Toradze's teacher when Toradze left Zak. Remembering Zemliansky, Toradze gently presses his palms to his chest.

"He was the greatest human being I have ever known. With Zemliansky I became a different person. And a different musician. What did he do? Nothing. He was just calm, human, quiet—all the things which I am not, talking to you now. The way he taught was unique. First and foremost, time was not limited with him. You had all the time you needed. You needed five hours, you got five hours. You needed the whole day, you got the whole day. Somehow, he managed in this way. And that was the case not only for one or two favorite students—every student was a favorite. Secondly, every lesson was like a performance. He sensed that I needed that. Even if it would be the Liszt Sonata, he would let me play the whole thing, not once interrupting. Studying with Zemliansky, I received my conservatory diploma in 1975. I received five-plus, which is A-plus. Zak, who was on the jury for the diploma recital, Zak personally came up to me, being extremely nervous and uptight and almost yelling: 'Don't think I want to sign your A-plus. It is not my opinion that you are A-plus. It is *their* opinion!' "

When in 1975 Toradze, as a postgraduate student, decided to enter the Van Cliburn competition, Zemliansky set about preparing him for the elaborate internal competitions that would determine the Soviet contestants. Months afterward, in 1976, one of Yakov Zak's best students, Youri Egorov, defected, leading to Zak's intense interrogation and disgrace. Later that year, Zak died. In February 1977, Toradze won the All-Soviet Competition, assuring his selection for the Cliburn. Nikolai Petrov—whom Zak considered his chief protégé, almost his son—had been named to the 1977 Cliburn jury and therefore also judged the February competition.

"The best musicians of Russia were all gathered there. And Zemliansky was there, my teacher. And Petrov said: 'Yes, I acknowledge Toradze as the winner. But I have to protest the bad teaching of Zemliansky in the Prokofiev Third Piano Concerto. Because it's absolutely antimusical.' And people—you know how people are. People love to hear how you put me down. So nobody stopped this attack. Zemliansky couldn't say anything, because he was in a way a helpless person. Very quiet, a beaten-by-life type of personality. He had even spent time in prison during the KGB's 'cleansing of society' campaign, for a supposed homosexual affair twenty years before. After Petrov's remark, he ran out of the room, and nobody could find him for several days. We didn't know where he was. Later, we discovered he had been walking, walking around the city. My selection to the Van Cliburn competition was his last pedagogical victory. In May, he committed suicide. He was fifty-two years old."

Toradze now had to prepare for the Cliburn without Zemliansky. But he managed to obtain the tutelage of Lev Naumov, the esteemed teacher of Vladimir Viardo and Andrei Gavrilov, and formerly a principal assistant to Heinrich Neuhaus. Naumov and Toradze removed themselves to a dacha, where Toradze performed his Cliburn repertoire day after day. He also got to perform both his concertos with orchestra four times. These arrangements typify the thoroughness of the Soviet system. Equally typical was that Soviet musical politics dictated that Toradze take steps to smooth his relationship with Petrov. "I was never even thinking about this when Zemliansky was alive, but the closer we got, we realized it was probably essential that I play for Petrov and listen to his ideas about music. It took five, six people to *push* me to do it. It took Naumov. Naumov only supported this step to help me."

Martha Hyder and others in Fort Worth had picked Nikolai Petrov for their jury because he had won the silver medal at the first Cliburn competition, in 1962. They had prevailed on Youri Egorov to enter, because Radu Lupu and others had predicted great things for him. And they had welcomed the participation, as well, of Vladimir Viardo's friend Alexander Toradze. The resulting Russian contingent was more than wary of itself. In Petrov's opinion, Egorov's defection had contributed to Yakov Zak's death. In the opinion of Toradze, Petrov was predisposed to penalize both him and Egorov for disloyalty to Zak. Egorov (who died of AIDS at thirty-three in 1988, by which time he had established a significant career in Europe) blamed Petrov for his surprising failure to survive the final cut. Petrov insists (and others confirm) that he was one of Toradze's loyal supporters on the 1977 Cliburn jury, and counters unprovable allegations regarding his behavior toward Egorov with plausible stories of his own. Whatever actually happened, these inflamed personal relations illustrate a common circumstance at international music competitions: jurors and contestants know one another, and harbor strong opinions, before a note is played.

Toradze returned to Moscow frustrated and exhilarated. As the Cliburn silver medalist, he toured the United States four times in 1977, 1978, and 1979. Then the Soviet invasion of Afghanistan caused a hiatus in cultural exchange with America. Toradze festered. He was earning the equivalent of $80 to $120 per concert. He felt discriminated against as a Georgian. He was galled by the constant company of KGB "interpreters." At a Paris airport in 1977, he ran into Mstislav Rostropovich, a family friend, and walked away from his escort; Rostropovich told him: "When you go back, kiss the ground of our country. But when are you going to do something?" In 1982, he refused to take part in a gala Prague concert honoring "Soviet-Czech friendship"—which he did not believe existed. In August 1983 he was sent on a tour of Spain with the Moscow Radio and Television Orchestra—only to discover that, as the Spanish had not been told he was coming (an intentional oversight, he believed), he would not be able to perform. He asked to return early to Moscow but was denied permission. On August 25, he entered the American embassy and requested refugee status. Two days later, the Moscow orchestra's concertmaster hung himself in a hotel bathroom. On August 28, the Spanish police granted Toradze asylum. He was not able to communicate with his parents until October 31, when he succeeded in telephoning them from Fort Worth. On November 4, his father was interviewed by the KGB. He died of a heart attack three days later. Toradze—who had been scheduled to give the Moscow premiere of his father's new piano concerto that same month—learned of his death the night before he began a nine-city tour with the Los Angeles Philharmonic: his first American concerts in more than four years.

According to a much-rehearsed stereotype, today's Russian pianists are assembly-line products, machine-tooled to bang accurately and hard. The Soviet conservatory system, in this view, serves politics first, while treating music and musicians as accessories in a game of cultural propaganda and prestige. Toradze himself says he would have preferred Western freedoms to Russian regimentation. Like other Moscow Conservatory pianists of his generation, he was permitted to compete only in selected international competitions. Even once he was chosen to represent Russia abroad, there was no guarantee he could get out; in 1971, his participation in the Montreal competition was canceled—apparently as a result of a bystander's assault on Soviet Prime Minister Alexei Kosygin during a Canadian visit.* And the training regime for competitions, Toradze maintains, is crudely specialized: "If you are well prepared, as I was, you are training toward a peak that will last a week, ten days at most. The goal is to hit 110 percent the moment of the final round."

*The same year, twenty-three-year-old Boris Belkin was already at the Moscow airport, preparing to leave for the Paganini International Violin Competition in Genoa, when he was told he would not be permitted to go. His fingers went numb, and he dropped his violin case. Shortly afterward, he had himself admitted to a Moscow psychiatric clinic.

Yet the thoroughness of Russian training remains enviable. John Browning, who won the Leventritt competition in 1955 and finished second in Brussels a year later, follows conventional wisdom when he observes: "If the Russians don't come, the general standards are not nearly as good. . . . You know, they're ready to give concerts at the age of fifteen—they're truly ready." Toradze had performed with orchestra on more than a hundred occasions by the time he arrived in Fort Worth at the age of twenty-five. His intense, intimate relationships with Zemliansky and Naumov make Juilliard look like the factory. At the Moscow Conservatory, a continuity of tradition, lost in the West, remains precariously intact. If one can no longer speak of a flourishing English, French, or Viennese school, the Russian school is still apparent. It is Romantic/heroic, and traces its lineage to the eruptive Anton Rubinstein (1829–1894). It correlates with Russian music, which underwent no Baroque or Classical phase; with huge spaces and personalities; with unfettered emotion versus ratiocination. Its famous exponents included Sergei Rachmaninoff and Vladimir Horowitz. Theodor Leschetizky, once Vienna's leading piano pedagogue, summarized the Russian piano attributes a century ago: "passion, dramatic power, elemental force, and extraordinary vitality."

If Russian schooling fabricates competition winners, it also produces a high percentage of individualists. Viardo (who places himself within a Russian "Dionysian tradition of spontaneous initiative") is one. Valery Afanassiev, Stanislav Bunin, and Andrei Nikolsky are also prominent subjectivists. So are Radu Lupu and Ivo Pogorelich, both Russian-trained. Toradze personifies this individualism and its source in nineteenth-century heroism—personifies, that is, a subjectivism predating the modern emphasis on self-effacing "textual fidelity" and "authenticity." Obviously, with no "objective" textual evidence to validate their liberties, pianists like Toradze can seem self-indulgent or sincere, according to taste; they engender impressions as personal as their playing. My own impression is that Toradze is not a frivolous artist; that the agonized yet urgent forward motion of his performances—so similar to his style of speech—serves the music and the artistic response it compels.

The composer Francis Poulenc, who knew Prokofiev's piano playing well, once likened it to "the steady unwinding of a precision clockwork motor spring." According to Poulenc, Prokofiev performed his own music "quite straightforwardly. . . . Rubato made his flesh creep." Toradze's performance of the first movement of Prokofiev's Piano Concerto No. 2 is slower, moodier, more shockingly tortured than any performance the composer might have given. It is a reading whose darting swells and stabbing staccatos and syncopations amass a welter of sharp detail. The movement's centerpiece is a five-minute cadenza, the most punishing in the standard concerto literature, marked triple-*forte* and *colossale* and culminating with a chordal barrage climbing toward the tonic—the arrival of which coincides with the orchestra's pounding reentry and with hammered arpeggios up and down the keyboard. The traumatic intensity with which Toradze lands on this crucial downbeat ("It's not that I'm getting goose bumps; my *goose bumps* are getting goose bumps") is reinforced by a sudden, preliminary pause—a gasp for breath not found in Prokofiev's score. Also unnotated is the suddenly thundering timpani crescendo Toradze asks for at this point. It is a moment both uninhibited and plotted, as true emotionally as it is false to the score. Toradze comments:

"I have the dearest feelings for this concerto, because I can identify very easily with young Prokofiev. The concerto is dedicated to Maksimilian Shmitgoff, who was his close friend. We're talking about Prokofiev and Shmitgoff being twenty-two, when Shmitgoff committed suicide. I can identify with Prokofiev's personal loss because I experienced the loss of a close friend even at an earlier age. So Prokofiev wrote this concerto, dedicated to his friend, and the concerto is his friend's life and funeral, the devastation Prokofiev experienced and his desire to turn the clock back. The *misterioso* beginning, pizzicato, is like a heartbeat—that's why I take it so slowly. At the start of the piano part Prokofiev writes 'narrante'—he begins his talk to you, he starts his story telling you about his beloved friend who died. He asks you to share his pain. The second theme, in A minor, shows the youngster's playfulness; he remembers funny stories associated with him and elaborates on that. Then all of a sudden this stops, and he's back to his sorrow. The cadenza is unique in all Prokofiev's music; you will never find in the other concertos, or in any of the sonatas, such *intense* devastation. Without Shmitgoff's death, this would not have been possible. The climax of the cadenza is the entrance of the orchestra, which is itself an unusual thing. This is very democratic, if you follow the thought process. It says that you cannot grieve all by yourself—without sharing your sorrow, your pain, with other people. The orchestra's theme here is the theme of the heartbeat from the beginning. But now it's not only Prokofiev's heartbeat—it is *everybody's* heartbeat. In Russia, and also in Georgia, death is a huge public event. *Everyone* comes to the funeral. So that Prokofiev's heartbeat becomes something bigger. A processional. A heart *bleed-*

ing. It sounds so trivial to say these words, but this is such an *honest* description. I'm sure if you were to talk to Prokofiev, he never would be able to talk to you as sensitively as he speaks in his music here."

What most makes Toradze's performance matter is neither its remarkable physical excitement nor the debatable accuracy of his scenario; rather, he has the capacity to probe himself: to extract subjective truths resonant with young Prokofiev's violent world of feeling. In other concertos—the Beethoven *Emperor*, which he scans with a moment-to-moment intensity at odds with its grandeur; or the Ravel G major, to which he brings a combination of insouciance and motoric drive so heady it makes the score sound small—the resonance is skewed, and yet exerts a fatal fascination. "Lexo playing Beethoven!" I once heard a Toradze detractor exclaim. "I wouldn't miss that for the world."

Toradze's volatility is chronic. Even his weight fluctuates by thirty pounds and more. His career, too, seems forever in flux. He began one recent season with fewer than twenty dates, yet wound up with twice as many, including an eight-city tour with Rostropovich and the National Symphony. Ernest Fleischmann, the savvy manager of the Los Angeles Philharmonic, has frequently engaged him, as have John Giordano, Zdenek Macal, Gerard Schwarz, and the New York Philharmonic. Elsewhere, he is regarded as difficult, or musically anathema.

The night of his London debut, Toradze slipped in a hotel lobby and injured his right arm; he arrived late at the Royal Festival Hall, but performed. He missed his plane back to New York because he dreaded returning to the United States. He canceled concerts with the Dallas Symphony when a scheduled recording with that orchestra fell through and he was not told. He once canceled at the Hollywood Bowl because he decided the Rachmaninoff Third Concerto, a new work for him, was not ready. His cautiousness about acquiring new repertoire discourages record companies and orchestra managers.

One seminal event since his defection was the four-month visit of his mother in June 1988—made possible by his rehabilitation in Georgia, where he had become a nonperson prior to *glasnost*. With Van Cliburn's help, their airport reunion was documented in *People* magazine. Toradze decided to hire a publicist to place similar "personality" stories elsewhere. This is a service most solo performers, even the most august, consider vital, but it costs about $1,000 per month.* Toradze wonders whether to look for a teaching position to supplement his income. He is thinking of marrying and raising a family. He still "plays for" the eyes and ears of his parents and others he left behind in Tbilisi and Moscow—and yet he adores American freedoms, gadgets, and amenities.

Part of Toradze thrives on the drama of his instability. And the loneliness of exile, he believes, fosters personal and artistic growth. "Why are teachers so important for youngsters?" he asks. "Because of their life experience, their knowledge. That is the difference between children and adults. And unfortunately, people who have passed through deeper, more dangerous, more painful processes become more interesting. Because they experience something which others have not. This may be one reason why certain circles of American intellectual and musical life are attracted to Russians and what they are bringing here. Because the Russians, and everybody associated with them, Georgians included, and Jews, and Armenians, and others—they suffered more than Americans. So many of the major events of the twentieth century have included Russians as their main subject: whether it was war, or revolution, or Stalin's purges, everything seems to include them.

"I think that suffering is part of the Russian experience. It is part of my experience as a musician. I can't just look at a score and think: Gosh, what a beautiful concerto; I'm going to make it just delicious. That doesn't interest me. Composers, if they are expressing something, they do it because they cannot express it in other ways, because there is something they need to get out of their system. You don't need to get out of your system pure happiness and joy. No, because it's comfortable. So you need an element of discomfort, of irritation, certain spiritual urges that make you create this or that. That's where our real differences are—in pain. Tolstoy, at the beginning of *Anna Karenina*, says: 'All happy families resemble one another; each unhappy family is unhappy in its own way.' So I have to find this element. I have to find two or three pages of pain. Then I use that, because I can associate with that, and elaborate. I can use my own experience. And fortunately, my own experience with pain is quite considerable. It has been enough."

---

*Though pianists of Toradze's stature earn $5,000 to $10,000 per engagement, hotel and travel expenses are not included, and management takes 20 percent of all fees. Pianists in top demand earn $15,000 to $30,000 per recital and somewhat more for a pair of orchestral dates. "Superstar" singers like te Kanawa, Pavarotti, and Domingo command at least twice as much.

André-
Michel
Schub

WHAT KIND OF PLAYING SUCCEEDS IN COMPETITIONS? UNSURPRISINGLY,
pianists who win say honest playing succeeds—not the kind that is
tailored to please or impress. Typical is Barry Douglas's remark
about finishing first at the 1986 Tchaikovsky competition: "I went
with no expectations, and just played." Or Malcolm Frager's explanation of how he won the 1959 Leventritt after failing twice
before: "I had been afraid—too much aware of the jury. My new
attitude was to forget I was competing." But Vladimir Viardo, a
dense stylist, felt the need to rein in his interpretations at the 1973
Cliburn. "I didn't want to play Bach and Mozart too Romantically.
And in the Liszt [*Funerailles*], I was preoccupied with certain technical aspects—I wanted the jury to hear my octaves." Viardo advises his students at the Moscow Conservatory to "narrow their
range of personal expression" in competitions, because "new personalities usually disturb people. I tell them: 'You have to try to
play *one* head above the others, not two heads.' "

André-Michel Schub, the 1981 Cliburn winner, did not consciously alter his interpretations. But he did calculate a precise
musical strategy. For one thing, he chose repertoire to highlight
what he played least controversially. To this end, he eliminated all
Schubert, Schumann, and late Beethoven, because he felt the con-

sensus on correct interpretation was too vague. For the finals, he chose the flamboyant Tchaikovsky First over either of the Brahms concertos, which, he anticipated, needed more rehearsal and a better orchestra than the competition would provide. He readied his pieces not toward spontaneous, inspirational performances but toward performances that would leave nothing to chance, even under abnormal pressure. His only goal was to win.

Schub's entry surprised many. At twenty-eight, he was not part of the competition circuit and already had a big enough name to have played with the Boston and Chicago symphonies, the Cleveland Orchestra, and the New York Philharmonic. Most of his dates, however, were with the Chamber Music Society of Lincoln Center, and he craved a prominent solo career. In interview after interview, explaining why he had come to Fort Worth, his answers were variations on the same theme: you only live once. He was impatient to maximize his chances for major exposure. He felt the Cliburn, which accepted pianists up to the age of twenty-nine, was an opportunity he could not afford to miss.

That it was also a risk was a point driven home in a series of ten articles filed by Harold Schonberg of the *New York Times*, who covered the entire fourteen-day event. Schonberg's first story, on May 18, identified Schub as the heavy favorite and added: "He must know that it will be a blow to his career if he does not win top prize." In later articles, Schonberg respectfully, but unenthusiastically, classified Schub as a "cool," "analytical," "Apollonian" player. Schub read Schonberg's articles, which convinced him that he had gambled his future on the verdict of twelve colleagues of whom half had never attained performing careers as prominent as his own. Meanwhile, Mitchell Johnson of Fort Worth Productions had been engaged to produce a live, ninety-minute Cliburn competition special, which would be televised nationally over PBS the evening of the finals. The 1981 winner was certain to be the most publicized Cliburn medalist since the competition began nineteen years before.

Unlike Steven De Groote in 1977, Schub was a seasoned professional; he knew the pressures the winner's itinerary would inflict, and was ready. Like De Groote, however, he cut an awkward public figure; with his furrowed brow and hunched shoulders, his eyeglasses and anxious eyes, his clean, tensed features growing soft around the jaw, he looked wrong posing for photographers in a cowboy hat. Onstage, his bows were stiff and self-conscious, and his smile frayed at the corners. At the keyboard, he radiated concentration, not pleasure. The Fort Worth audience responded accordingly. On the sidelines, De Groote commented to a journalist:

"I'm hearing so much more acutely people saying the sort of things I heard last time. . . . 'That guy, you know, he plays well, but when he comes offstage, he's got this strange manner about him, and I don't know if it's going to work.' These are the lines I've been getting from the top echelons of this organization. I think it's shameful." Schub was the favored pianist, but not the favorite.

Outwardly, Schub maintained his cadet-like discipline. Inwardly, he was experiencing what he later described as "a war—it was the Battle of Gettysburg, and by the end the wounds and sickness were everywhere. It's the most awful period of your life, but you learn how tough you are." The war inside exaggerated the tightness of his playing. Brahms's Variations on a Theme by Handel, the centerpiece of his semifinal recital, turned hard and precariously brisk. But being a superb musical athlete, Schub was able to keep up without stumbling. If his performance, like De Groote's of the same piece four years earlier, was not notably warm or colorful, his intentions were always lucid, and lucidly realized: he left nothing in doubt. Schub faced the finals nervously contemplating the hardships of preparing for the 1981 Leeds if he failed to win—yet he dispatched both his concertos commandingly. Stamina is a perennial issue in piano competitions. Schub's stamina seemed limitless, and so did the power and security of his whipsaw Tchaikovsky. The final, machine-gun blaze of octaves drove the audience to its feet. Schub's gold medal conferred $12,000 and some three hundred concert dates, including a Carnegie Hall recital, recital debuts in Hamburg, Amsterdam, and London, and appearances with the Chicago Symphony, the Philadelphia Orchestra, and some four dozen other orchestras.

The immediate ordeal seemed over, yet was not. During PBS's live television coverage of the competition's final hour, all the stresses Schub had held in check—the distorting self-consciousness produced by his strategizing, by his social discomfort, by his frontrunner status—converged in a rush. Billed as a "magical distillation of the fourteen-day Van Cliburn competition into ninety exciting minutes of television entertainment," Mitchell Johnson's telecast ritualistically surveyed the parties and "photo opportunities," rehearsals and backstage hugs; music was relegated to a background role. But Johnson's portraits of the leading contestants were sensitively handled. And in televising the awards ceremony live, Johnson presented not only fifteen minutes of uninterrupted speeches and announcements by Cliburn, John Giordano, Chairman Phyllis Tilley, and Texas First Lady Rita Clements, but fourteen minutes of uninterrupted music: an impromptu minirecital by the gold medalist. Home viewers saw Giordano, as jury chairman, name Daming Zhu, Christopher O'Riley, and Jeffrey Kahane as the sixth-, fifth-, and fourth-prize winners; name Panayis Lyras and Santiago Rodriguez as co-winners of the second prize; and—to cheers and rising applause—present the gold medal to André-Michel Schub, who shook Giordano's hand, endured a bear hug from Van Cliburn, and proceeded to wander away, only to be sent back toward the many smiling, open-armed dignitaries. Finally, clutching his silver trophy with both his strong hands as if he were afraid he might drop it, Schub was escorted backstage and into the arms of the pianist André Watts, who was hosting the concert for television. "You gonna play?" Watts inquired. *"Really???"* Schub tremulously quipped, and disappeared from the screen. Cliburn now remarked to Watts: "You know, that is a terribly nerve-racking thing—to sit there not knowing whether you're going to have to play, having to be concentrating on something to play, just in case, and then to know you have to." Watts, filling time, looked at the camera and asked: "Where is Mr. Schub? We want Mr. Schub! . . . Someone has just relieved him of his wonderful trophy. So his hands are free and we can get him over here." Cliburn and Watts now debated whether to talk to Schub before he played. Schub returned and asked Watts: "Why don't *you* play?" Then, suddenly, he was onstage, performing Debussy's *Reflets dans l'eau*. While the cameras scrutinized his face, which was shut in a grimace, a microphone fastened to the piano, inches from the strings, turned Debussy's tonal washes into cactus needles. Schub plunged ahead with Liszt's second *Paganini* Étude, a thundering showcase for alternating octaves—if one is missed, the others fly off course. Schub began losing control of these octave cascades. Bending low over the keys, redoubling his concentration, he never gave up, but the dazzle of the piece, the breathtaking continuity of its ingenious obstacles, was grimly denied. Even the closing arpeggiated chords were dirty. The very last note split. A shadow of pain crossed Schub's perspiring features just before he smiled, rose, and bowed. Backstage, he was waylaid again. Watts, prodded by the impatient camera, now remarked: "So you've won this competition and already it starts: you see, you've just finished playing, and people are grabbing you on television. . . . Do you feel good?" Schub erased his smile, shut his eyes, and glanced at his feet before answering: "I'd just like to play well from now on." When Watts asked if he had acquired all six *Paganini* Études, he replied: "I have. They're just extremely hard in a situation like this." His face glistened with sweat. His arms dangled uselessly.

*   *   *

Schub's reputation as an impersonal musician is belied by his personality. His thin, trembling tenor simmers with temperament. His speech is articulate but halting. When he discusses his career and profession, his manner is courteous, even deferent, yet pained.

His childhood was insular and specialized. He was born in Paris to a French mother and an American father, both students at the Sorbonne. The family moved to Brooklyn before he was one. He began studying the piano, with his mother, at the age of four. While in high school, he studied privately with Jascha Zayde. He attended Princeton for a year, unsure whether to pursue music. A successful audition for Rudolf Serkin sealed his fate: four years of study, mainly with Serkin, at the Curtis Institute.

"At Curtis I worked all day. All day equals eight hours, ten, twelve, seven days a week. I went to the record store to buy a record, that would almost be a day off. Meals: I ate Franco-American spaghetti out of the can, unheated. I'm not kidding. Cereal for breakfast. You do have to see people: there was a hamburger joint, and I might hang out there for an hour. But as much energy as I had I applied at the piano. Because I realized I had quit everything else to do this, and I wanted to get as much control of the piano as I possibly could. It was also the time to learn the basic concerto repertoire. Which I did. I mean, I can count on one hand the standard pieces which I didn't work on then. It was a tough regime."

The Curtis Institute of Music, located in four turn-of-the-century mansions near Philadelphia's Rittenhouse Square, may be the closest American equivalent to the Moscow Conservatory of Viardo, Egorov, and Toradze. Rather like the Leventritt competition, to which it seemed affiliated, Curtis is small, selective, and rarefied. Mary Louise Curtis Bok, whose father began the Curtis Publishing Company, founded the Institute of Music in 1924. With an endowment of $12.5 million, it provides free tuition to all its approximately 180 students. Its graduates include Samuel Barber, Leonard Bernstein, Jorge Bolet, Lukas Foss, Eugene Istomin, Gary Graffman (the present director), Gian Carlo Menotti, Leonard Rose, Peter Serkin, and Benita Valente. Unlike Moscow's conservatory, Curtis cannot claim to transmit a nation's cultural inheritance, nor is it integrated into a national system of education and performance. Though preteenagers—some as young as seven—may enroll, the average age of entry is seventeen or eighteen, and there is no postgraduate curriculum for instrumentalists. The faculty has included Emanuel Feuermann, Josef Hofmann, Wanda Landowska, Gregor

Piatigorsky, William Primrose, Fritz Reiner, and Elisabeth Schumann. When Steven De Groote and André-Michel Schub were students at Curtis, the central luminary was Rudolf Serkin, who served as artistic director from 1968 to 1976.

From Serkin the teacher, Schub absorbed the trademarks of Serkin the pianist: absolute intensity of commitment and selfless dedication to the composer's text. "There was a lot of pressure with lessons. Lessons were almost every week, normally for an hour. They would sometimes go over, but rarely. Because, basically, I would play the piece I had prepared, and I would either get raked over the coals or not. I think they were mainly lessons of inspiration. Not even musical inspiration. They made you work harder. I also had some lessons with Horszowski, who was just the opposite of Serkin. He was angelically inspired without any of the tyranny. But I, for one, thrived on the tyranny. I needed that. It's how I am on myself, so I was getting an even heavier dose of it, and at a very young, impressionable age."

Through Serkin, Schub spent three summers at the Marlboro Festival—an invitation denied to De Groote. Unlike De Groote, he chose not to enter the Leventritt competition: at the age of twenty, having completed Curtis's undergraduate curriculum, he felt he had had enough of the Serkin milieu and was restless to move on. At twenty-one, he entered the 1974 Naumburg competition. A memory lapse in the first round left him pondering medical school—but he won anyway. The prize included two New York recitals. He was also able to acquire management and to audition for some important orchestras. He played with the Boston Symphony and the Cleveland Orchestra, and waited. Nothing much came his way. In 1977, he was named winner of the Avery Fisher Award, for which there is no competition. A flurry of Lincoln Center engagements followed, then an invitation to become the resident pianist of the Lincoln Center Chamber Music Society. After six lonely years on his own, the attraction of stable employment with reputable colleagues was great. But Schub did not want to be labeled a "chamber music pianist." He agonized before accepting the offer. I interviewed him for the *New York Times* several months later, and reported:

In the coming season, [Mr. Schub] will appear with the New York Philharmonic, in recital at Alice Tully Hall, and with the Chamber Music Society of Lincoln Center. . . .

Such concentrated exposure in a world music capital is the dream of many a young artist. In a recent conversation, however, Mr. Schub, an earnest man with worried eyes, seemed unimpressed. In fact, following a series of polite evasions, he quietly confessed that he feels fairly frustrated about the progress of his career so far.

"If five years ago someone had suggested that at this point I would have played with some of the orchestras I've played with, I guess I'd be happy. On the other hand, one ingredient of success is to have the highest aspirations. And when you have the highest aspirations, you don't see yourself the way the outside world does; you just see day-in and day-out. So some positive things happen, and also a lot of frustrating things. And at the age of 26 I'm quite impatient, and quite impetuous, too. I think it's part of my playing. It's certainly part of my personality."

Schub also said:

"When you go around the country and play with mediocre orchestras, the rehearsal circumstances are such that it's usually professionalism that carries the day, rather than optimum circumstances. It can be very painful. When you're playing a concerto, for instance, you actually have to avoid listening to the orchestra; you have to sort of protect yourself in order to play. Very often the conductor doesn't agree with you; he might have different tempos, or a different pacing for a piece. In very few cases do you have orchestra players actually listening. When they do, it's a great treat, but usually they don't.

"I remember doing the 'Emperor' Concerto once with an orchestra in a smaller community. There's a spot in the last movement where, just before the piano comes in, there are two measures of triplets for oboe and bassoon. And no one played. Just silence. That experience taught me that you have to hear an ideal orchestra in your mind. . . . Basically, you go out with a certain commitment, and you won't let anything rattle you. . . ."

Balancing intellectual rigor with increased interpretive liberties, and a bolder application of color, has been an overriding objective for Mr. Schub in recent years, and he sees himself improving. About the direction and destination of his career, he is less certain.

"The only thing you can do is work on the music you play, and have that go in a positive direction," he said. "Everything else is circumstantial; I'm not in control of it."

For a moment, Mr. Schub seemed disquieted by his own words. Then he retraced his thoughts, and spoke again: "But I guess deep down I believe you do make your own way, and that if you persevere long enough, everything comes out right in the end. You have to believe in that."

Schub had calculated he could use the Chamber Music Society position as a steppingstone. It quickly began to feel like a rut. Less than a year after joining the Society, he entered and won the Cliburn competition. Whereas De Groote, at twenty-four, had been a bewildered victor, Schub at twenty-eight knew what he wanted. But the Cliburn Foundation also wanted certain things from him. During the competition, he was already perceived as a "difficult" case, resistant to being interviewed or photographed. When the Cliburn produced a live recording of Schub's semifinal recital, for distribution by Columbia Records, Schub objected: he found his competition-style Brahms *Handel* Variations too fast. When the Cliburn persisted, Schub killed the plan by recording the same repertoire for another label, forcing Columbia to withdraw. Also, rather than entrusting his concert itinerary to the Cliburn administration, he stuck with his New York management, which was able to book certain important engagements at much higher fees than the $1,000 Cliburn dates. To the people in Fort Worth, Schub seemed selfish and unreliable. To Schub, the Fort Worth people seemed exploitative. "I felt there were some musical decisions that should have been mine to make. You know, I wasn't twenty-one. I think their philosophy was: the more concerts, the better. Sure, some of the Cliburn engagements were really great. But it was equally important to them, even if it meant killing yourself, to fly three thousand miles to Eugene, Oregon, when you could have had a four-day Thanksgiving break instead. One thing that made me really furious was the party they threw after my Carnegie Hall recital. I could invite my date and my parents, and that was it. I thought the party was in my honor. And I had some friends who had come from very far away. But that was it. All this kind of built up."

After two years of Cliburn dates, after playing at the White House and being recognized in restaurants, Schub saw his itinerary drop in half. He likens the Cliburn tour to having been "a farmer with a big piece of land and a lot of seeds, some of which took root and some of which didn't. I had no machinery, no assistance—just all this land and a whole bunch of seeds. I really had no time to think about it. I had no time to do anything except go out and play."

Schub acknowledges that he owes his post-1981 career to the Van Cliburn competition. But he has never shed the image of a competition athlete, an interchangeable winner—an image once summarized by a prominent New York critic with the savage quip: "André-Michel Schub? Why, I knew him when he was Steven De Groote."

*   *   *

Schub and De Groote do share certain musical affinities with Rudolf Serkin. Jorge Bolet, a juror at the 1974 Naumburg, told Schub afterward that from the "first two notes" he had known he was listening to a onetime Serkin student. The remark rankled because Schub understood it. For a time, he took lessons with Bolet himself, who cultivates a suave touch and is no literalist. And he pursued a catholic repertoire, rather than concentrating on the Germanic composers Serkin favors. But Schub's approach is too high-strung for him to have discovered a model either in Bolet or in warm-toned (and technically fallible) Germanic subjectivists like Edwin Fischer or Wilhelm Kempff—alternatives to Serkin too little known in the United States. Rather, he is seduced by Sviatoslav Richter and Maurizio Pollini: players who combine something like Serkin's intensity with awesome, potentially depersonalizing polish and control. A perfectionist, he has acquired a technical command that is the envy of many a more flamboyant player. His octaves are heroic. He takes skips fearlessly. With his finger strength and chiseled articulation, he is the rare player who can make a simple scale—such as the one in streaking tenths at the close of Chopin's G minor Ballade—a gripping event. But the same piece's rhapsodic episodes disarm him. In fact, the "gracefulness" and "poetry" of Schub's playing—the teasing hesitations and tapered phrase endings—can sound superimposed. To some listeners, he is like a cook who seasons the dish only after it is out of the white-hot oven.

The Cliburn competition showcased Schub's stiffness, his forceful but unglamorous Liszt and Tchaikovsky. But his Serkin-style Mendelssohn—a fleet, febrile version of the Fantasy in F-sharp minor—struck sparks. A work that shows Schub off to even better advantage, but that he did not perform in Fort Worth, is Schumann's *Symphonic Études*. Here, Schub does not look for charm or grandiloquence or variety of color and mood; more than any other pianist of my experience, he relishes the challenge of treating Schumann's études as an étude set, pure and simple. Honoring such markings as *sempre brillante, con energia sempre, sempre marcatissimo, con gran bravura*, and *presto possibile*, he penetrates the dense patterns at full speed, scorching them clean, binding them tight.

Splashier pianists make quicker careers. If Schub is to attain something like Serkin's depth of agitation, or the Romantic elegance some find in Bolet's playing, or the Olympian probity of Richter, it will take time. His recent second marriage, he feels, has shifted his priorities in healthy ways. He still sees himself as a "loner" and his profession as essentially "solitary." His principal recreation—on tour or at home in Manhattan—is a daily twelve-mile run. But he says he no longer works as compulsively to "play 100 percent of the notes the way you planned to play them." He performs about seventy times a year, mainly concertos and chamber music. A number of conductors—Mstislav Rostropovich in Washington, Zdenek Macal in Milwaukee, Jerzy Semkow in Rochester, Joseph Silverstein (who considers him the finest American pianist of his generation) in Utah—reengage him regularly. He speaks of the music business as "almost a crapshoot" and feels it is becoming harder and harder to launch a piano career. "I think that were I to be ten years younger and to enter the 1989 Cliburn, winning it would have nowhere near the same impact that it had for me in 1981." But fundamentally, he seems less anguished about his professional future. "Whoever you are, there's always more you would like. But the seasons roll around, and I do work. It pays the rent, comfortably. I am doing what I love to do. I've had a taste of absolute celebrity—TV hype, and all that—and I know that I don't want that. That's not me. So it's happening. I'm one of the very few who do work regularly. I really have to put that in perspective."

There is nothing craven about Schub's career drive. He acutely understands that professional opportunities—the conductors, orchestras, and audiences with which he interacts—will help determine his ultimate artistic potential. He is of a generation that is dangerously remote from Mozart, Beethoven, and Brahms to begin with. Serkin, born in 1903, knew the Berlin of which Bruno Walter wrote: "The common denominator, the characteristic sign of those days, was an unparalleled mental alertness. And the alertness of the giving corresponded to the alertness of the receiving. A passionate general concentration upon cultural life prevailed, eloquently expressed by the large space devoted to art by the daily newspapers in spite of the political excitement of the times." Walter, Erich Kleiber, and Otto Klemperer headed separate opera houses. Wilhelm Furtwängler conducted the Philharmonic. Arnold Schoenberg taught composition; one of his pupils, in a class of only six or seven, was Serkin himself. The city's other younger pianists included Claudio Arrau, Wilhelm Backhaus, Edwin Fischer, Artur Schnabel. The violinists included Adolf Busch, with whom Serkin performed regularly, and whose daughter he married.

This legacy is both a treasure and a burden to those who would inherit it. Schub ponders Serkin's long shadow and says: "I don't think it's particularly healthy to distance yourself. You can't talk about the Brahms D minor, or the *Emperor* Concerto, or the Beethoven Fourth, if you're talking about whose playing has made an impact, without mentioning Serkin. And when you play it, you can't go out of your way, because you don't want to imitate, to play it differently. I mean, a lot of it is right. A lot of it is great. And he was an incredibly strong presence. Stronger, I think, than almost anyone else I've come in contact with."

Jeffrey Kahane

PANAYIS LYRAS AND SANTIAGO RODRIGUEZ, WHO SHARED SECOND prize at the Cliburn the year André-Michel Schub won, are both graduates of the Juilliard School, where they studied with the same teacher: Adele Marcus. Lyras, born in Greece, was a veteran of the competition circuit, with major prizes at the Bachauer, Rubinstein, Three Rivers, and University of Maryland competitions. In an interview with the *Washington Post* halfway through the 1981 Cliburn, he commented: "Who knows what they're looking for? Once you get down to the finalists, there's not that much difference between them. It's a very subjective thing. Sometimes you wonder what it takes to make it in this business, whether it really comes down to being good-looking, to having an exotic name or staring a lot at the ceiling while you play. And if you're someone who is very honest about his music, who is sincere about what he is doing and loves it, it hurts that those things might be a factor; yes, it hurts. But time is a great equalizer—if you live that long." Lyras left Fort Worth feeling he had deserved the gold medal; he declined to be interviewed for this book. Rodriguez, born in Cuba, is a thin, dark, intense man, gauntly handsome, a ravaged matador. We have already encountered him as one of the five finalists (with Steven De Groote) in the 1976 Leventritt competition. A year before, he took first prize at the Maryland competition. As was the case with Lyras, the 1981 Cliburn competition was Rodriguez's second and, necessarily, his last. He prepared, he recalls, like a "lunatic," practicing ten and twelve hours a day. Going into the final round, he was widely considered Schub's closest rival. But the Rachmaninoff Third Piano Concerto found him "burned out" and ill; a severe ulcer, stemming from his junk-food diet as a closeted piano student, was acting up. The 1981 Cliburn left Rodriguez "catatonically depressed." He also developed a crippling hand ailment, which took three years to cure. Though he credits the Cliburn silver medal with boosting his career, his fifty concerts a season are seldom major dates, and his only post-Cliburn recordings are on a label begun by his devoted Russian wife (whom he met at the 1978 Tchaïkovsky competition). Since 1988, he has taught at the University of Maryland. Surveying his prospects in the shadow of encroaching middle age, he ponders: "I've never had such a bout with the piano as I had this past summer. I just didn't feel like practicing. Until about two years ago, I practiced eight to nine hours a day; I can't remember a day I went without practicing. Now I'm aiming for a middle ground—a coexistence with the piano, instead of letting it dominate me." And: "I just thank God I'm still kicking. So many other pianists my age have no concerts at all. I'm still in this holding pattern." And: "All of a sudden you have somebody who comes from another part of the world and makes a big splash. All of a sudden he's playing dates with orchestras that supposedly book three years ahead of time. Or you have a person who says, 'I want this kid to play with X.' These are things that can happen. They happen all the time. It's so difficult to make it without a powerful helper, just doing it on your own, not owing anything to anybody." And: "I know I'll get there sooner or later. I don't think I could get up and practice if I didn't think things were going to change. But really, it makes you humble."

In fact, the healthiest career among the 1981 Cliburn finalists probably belongs not to Schub or Lyras or Rodriguez but to Jeffrey Kahane, who finished fourth (third place being voided by the twin silver medals). More than the others, Kahane is a pianist of pronouncedly personal gifts; but he is not a pianist for all seasons. His diminutive size—even his hands are small—discourages Romantic power and sweep. Rather, he is a player of delicacy and crispness, balanced by a febrile, Mendelssohnian vigor. In Fort Worth, he made a memorable impression in Dvořák's Piano Quintet, which he undertook not only as an experienced chamber musician but as a friend and colleague of Peter Oundjian, then the new first violinist of the Tokyo String Quartet. Kahane's crystalline passagework and fragrant, minutely inflected *pianissimos* aerated the legato textures of the Tokyo strings—an ideal complementarity resulting in a performance both vibrant and warm. Of his solo performances, the most notable was of Chopin's rarely heard *Variations brillantes*, Op. 12—a gossamer reading of microscopic virtuosity. In Schumann's big C major Fantasy, which anchored his semifinal recital, Kahane's cleverness and clarity seemed not enough. But his downfall was Brahms's Piano Concerto No. 1—a work seemingly chosen to showcase his deficiencies. In other Romantic concertos—by Chopin, or Mendelssohn, or Saint-Saëns—a taut, crystalline approach might have created the necessary intensity. In the Brahms, amplitude of phrase and depth of tone are normally considered prerequisites. And—more damagingly—Kahane's performance suggested that he lacked the high temperament to dominate the concerto's emotional landscape of rage and grief.

Later, Kahane asked himself if he had chosen the wrong piece. But he had already made his strongest impression in contradistinction to the competition's Goliaths. Among those who liked him best was Edna Landau, partner in a tiny New York management firm called Hamlen/Landau Management. After hearing Kahane's solo and chamber music rounds, she told him she was interested in representing him even if he failed to make the finals. Upon finishing fourth, Kahane decided to sign with Hamlen/Landau rather than hold out for a big-name manager. It is a decision he has never regretted.

Kahane's career reverses the De Groote scenario of celebrity turned local pianist: he is a local pianist who gradually, even tentatively, acquired a national solo career. He was born in Los Angeles in 1956. His first teacher, for ten years, encouraged him to improvise and compose. In fact, until he was fifteen he was mainly interested in popular music, writing songs and playing guitar and keyboards in rock bands. He applied unsuccessfully to the Curtis Institute in 1972, his biggest piece being a Chopin polonaise. He attended the San Francisco Conservatory instead, graduating in 1977. Two years later, he married. By then, he had been playing chamber music around town for years. In the summers, when Robert Shaw led a San Francisco choral festival, he had been the rehearsal pianist. He had also handled various keyboard assignments for the San Francisco Symphony—and this at a time when Edo de Waart, as music director, Michael Steinberg, as artistic adviser, and John Adams, as composer in residence, were impressively committed to fostering an audience for new music with the help of local musicians. Looking back, Kahane feels grateful to have been spared a more prestigious, more high-powered musical education.

"People think of the West Coast as representing the self-involved and narcissistic side of American culture. But I found a sense of musical community in the San Francisco Bay Area unlike anything I've seen on the East Coast. The San Francisco Conservatory had something they called a community service program. From my first year there, when I was sixteen, I was playing with chamber groups in convalescent homes, doing prison concerts, that type of thing. And there was nothing like the high-pressure competition you get in the more traditional Eastern schools. The conservatory was small—about 275 students altogether; at Juilliard, there were two hundred pianists alone. The students were basically friends; there were no young hotshots. Part of the reason was that there were opportunities enough to go around. Even the orchestras took an interest in local talent. My first really important solo opportunity was with the San Francisco Symphony, playing the piano part in Messiaen's *Trois petites liturgies*. It's not a piano concerto by any means, but it has a highly exposed piano part. And shortly after that, the Oakland Symphony engaged me to play Bernstein's *Age of Anxiety*. And then Edo de Waart engaged me on John Adams's New and Unusual Music series to play the Berg Chamber Concerto. There was really a lot of wonderful stuff going on."

In recent years, the wear and tear of a busy concert schedule has softened and frayed Kahane's ruddy, firm-featured face. But he retains the quiet speech and sane manner he must have acquired growing up in California; in an emotional profession crowded with intense personalities, he seems precariously mild. He predictably disliked the "jealousy" and "competitiveness" of Juilliard when he transferred there in 1975; even members of the piano faculty seemed to him "destructive," "malicious," and "warped." Discovering himself to be "basically a Westerner," he returned to San Francisco. When in 1977 he finished second in Switzerland's Clara Haskil competition, his success surprised him. Three years later, he ventured to Warsaw for the Chopin competition, and did not advance past the second round.

"I came back from Poland very shaken up. I felt that I could never make it in an international competition. That I wasn't cut out for it. That competitions were inherently bad. I remember feeling I couldn't find how to be involved in the competition without compromising myself. And I felt dehumanized by the way the contestants were treated. There must have been 170 of us in the first round—the Chopin is a real cattle call—and each one played a Chopin étude, a Chopin scherzo, and so on. When I returned home, I found myself thinking about a career conducting or composing. So when I found out I had been accepted for the 1981 Van Cliburn competition, I was astonished. I had had a horrible time with the videotape audition. But Anthony Phillips, the executive director, was very encouraging, and everyone else in Fort Worth seemed very fair, very humane. After Warsaw, where we were housed in a functional high-rise hotel, the hospitality of the Cliburn actually came as a shock; no effort was spared to make everyone as comfortable and happy as possible. Still, I thought to myself: This is ridiculous. What am I doing here? And I was incredibly nervous during the first round. I remember completely screwing up the coda to the second movement of the Schumann Fantasy. And then I had to play the finale of Mozart's K. 570 Sonata without repeats, which was so bizarre that at one point I just froze; it really rattled me. So I was sure I would be knocked out—which I wasn't. Anticipating the second round was absolutely thrilling—I could go out and simply play a recital, and also could play chamber music, with which I was very comfortable. But then, the day of my recital, I happened to hear Schub on the radio. And again I began thinking: Oh, this is ridiculous, and I got very depressed. What saved me was finding a way of saying to myself: I just want to go out and make music. I went onstage thinking: I actually am going to make it to the finals."

Kahane did make it to the finals. But the final-round concertos— he played Mozart's K. 271 as well as the Brahms First—undid him. The trouble began the night the finalists were announced: the jury did not reach a decision until around midnight, after which the six finalists were kept up posing in cowboy hats for photographers. And Kahane had to rehearse and perform both his concertos the next day. In retrospect, he feels that the Brahms was unready in any case.

Kahane's fourth-place finish entitled him to $4,000. Though fourth prize carried no concerts, his Cliburn exposure resulted in a contract with Hamlen/Landau Management, a television cameo in Mitchell Johnson's documentary, and scores of good reviews, including favorable notice from Harold Schonberg in his series for the *Times*. Two years later, Kahane consolidated his reputation as an important newcomer by winning the Rubinstein competition in Tel Aviv. The event itself was unpleasant. Contestants were housed two to a room in a motel on the outskirts of the city. The required repertoire included Prokofiev's *Suggestion diabolique*, which Kahane "hated" learning. As winner, he received "not a single engagement from the day I left Israel; I never heard from them again." And yet, in the musical community, his strong Van Cliburn showing seemed validated. "It was like a pedigree. I mean, I was able to get a date with the Philadelphia Orchestra—which is so absurd."

Kahane now decided that if he was serious about tackling a major career, it was time to move East. Manhattan seemed untenable. And so in early 1984 the family relocated to the Boston area. In addition to using his new home as a strategic Northeast base, Kahane was determined to become part of the local scene, as he had in San Francisco. His first Boston recital attracted an audience of twenty. Eventually, he found a job at the New England Conservatory and got to know the composer Leon Kirchner, a goad and an inspiration to Yo-Yo Ma and scores of others who took part in his Harvard classes and Sanders Theatre concerts. Kahane performed the Berg Chamber Concerto under Kirchner's baton, gave the first performance of Kirchner's Five Pieces for Piano, and played Kirchner's First Piano Concerto. Meanwhile, Charles Hamlen and Edna Landau were booking him at the rate of sixty to seventy performances a season, including dates with the Baltimore Symphony, the Chicago Symphony, the Los Angeles Philharmonic, the New York Philharmonic, the Pittsburgh Symphony, and the San Francisco Symphony.

Kahane's decision to pursue a solo career had come remarkably slowly and fitfully. "I was on a psychological seesaw about it. I think it was because I started so late—I didn't get serious about studying the piano until, I would say, the age of fourteen, by which time many of my colleagues were already playing all the Chopin études. I alternated for years between feeling this was something I wanted to do and was capable of doing, and feeling that I could never be the kind of pianist that I wanted to be." Even now he sounds self-conscious saying: "I'd *love* to be able to play in Berlin, and Vienna, and Paris, and with the Cleveland Orchestra. I guess the crudest way of putting it is that I'd like to have what's considered a Big Career."

Kahane is glad he did not win the Van Cliburn competition. He would have been completely unprepared for the sheer volume of activity André-Michel Schub undertook. Also, the Cliburn scenario makes no allowances for family responsibilities—and Kahane became a father six weeks after the 1981 competition ended. For that matter, any Cliburn medal would have disrupted the continuity of his fledgling career, with its late start, local roots, and gradual pace. And these are all factors he has turned to his advantage. For a classical musician, his early socialization—he was playing at school dances from the age of eleven—was surprisingly normal. His interest in jazz, rock, and composition broadened his musical purview. His chamber music experience fostered relatively harmonious collegial relations as well as vital career networking. He is not known to sulk, fume, or procrastinate. He interacts smoothly with conductors and presenters.

Kahane's is also the rare piano career that has tangibly benefited from good management. Lazy or ineffectual professional representation is a chronic complaint among concert artists. Too many managers wait for the telephone to ring. They lack even a pretext of musical training. They become more important than their clients, whom they derogate behind their backs. When Schub won the Cliburn, his manager did not even show up in Fort Worth. Both Charles Hamlen and Edna Landau are modest, musically literate, and predisposed to close personal relations with their clients.

In a sense, Kahane, Hamlen, and Landau grew up together. Hamlen and Landau were working out of a basement in 1981 when they decided Kahane was the pianist they had been looking for. The office moved aboveground, expanded and refinanced, as IMG Artists in 1984. Itzhak Perlman and André Watts were two clients who came over from bigger, more glamourous managements. As television and recordings, jet planes and fifty-two-week seasons, have accelerated and expanded the music business, the prepotency of individual music brokers has diminished; no one controls the American destinies of the important conductors and instrumentalists to the degree Arthur Judson's Columbia Artists once did, or tours whole ballet and opera companies with the personal aplomb of a Sol Hurok. In signing with Hamlen and Landau, Kahane became an early beneficiary of a new management style, tailored to new needs.

If IMG contributes a sort of professional-family security, Kahane is finally rooted by his actual family: unlike most pianists of his generation, he has a wife and children. At the same time, these roots are now being powerfully jarred by Kahane's brisk career ascent—and so, ironically, are the "local musician" roots that have nourished his artistic identity. In 1988, Kahane decided he could no longer sustain his multiple life as husband, father, teacher, chamber artist, and touring soloist. He accepted a full-time teaching job at the Eastman School of Music in Rochester—much more lucrative employment than his part-time appointment at the New England Conservatory.

"Moving to Rochester, and giving up my artistic life in Boston, was in some ways crazy. I see it as a kind of gamble. The last several years have been a constant struggle to figure out how I can be a better musician and still be a better husband and parent. If it's true that I seem 'whole,' my family has a tremendous amount to do with it. And that nourishes my artistic side. But it also complicates it. I'm always having to justify not spending an afternoon with my wife and children in order to learn a new piece by Leon Kirchner. Or having to justify *not* learning all the Chopin études, which I've always wanted to do. One of the painful things that happen is that I spend less and less time working, and get by on my facility. You know, if I have a month when I'm only playing Beethoven Fourths and Mozart C minors, I don't have to sit at the piano for hours a day. And sometimes I'll be going along like that and suddenly I'll say to my wife, not necessarily in a very gentlemanly way, 'I have the feeling that if I just went on doing this you wouldn't notice.' Which isn't really true. But suddenly I'll feel intensely deprived, wishing that I could spend unlimited time each day not just practicing but thinking about music, learning.

"So I may have a healthy career, but I have made it by running myself ragged—by being willing to acquire an enormous amount of repertoire in a relatively short period. And at times my playing has suffered because of that. I wasn't able to be more selective and not take every single concert that came my way. That was the logic of going to Rochester. So that when Charlie or Edna calls up to announce, 'We have a date for you with the X Symphony for Y dollars,' I'll be able to say, 'No, I don't think so.' Which I've never been able to do. That possibility is like a precious dream. That means that for the week I would have been playing in city X, I'll be at home or teaching. I don't really like to travel."

Kahane says his first year at Eastman took a "terrible toll"; he now teaches half time there and feels ready to pursue his career more constructively. Having emerged from the Cliburn competition admired as a miniaturist, having been "traumatized and confused" by his Brahms debacle there, he first made his name in chamber music and in the pre-Romantic literature from Bach to Schubert. Then, not without resistance even from Hamlen and Landau, he ventured gradually into heavier repertoire. He now feels he has proved to himself that he can succeed with Brahms, Prokofiev, and Rachmaninoff.

Kahane's current wish list reflects continued breadth of interest.

He feels ready to return to the Brahms First Concerto and is looking for a conductor and orchestra to play it with. He is eager to find
further opportunities to perform the Kirchner First and to acquire
some solo pieces by Roger Sessions. He would like to record with
orchestra—which he has never done. He wants to establish himself
in Europe. And he intends to maintain his commitment to chamber
music, including a duo with the violinist Joseph Swensen, whose
repertoire includes improvisations on American popular songs.

His mildness and modesty, while career assets, may prove artistic liabilities as he ascends toward bigger repertoire. And he may
never regain all the equanimity he knew before his professional life
turned hectic. But Kahane has cast his net wide. Even if he cannot
realize the Big Career he seeks, he will have explored an array of
possible compensations.

José
Feghali

IN RUDOLF SERKIN'S BERLIN, PIANISTS WERE NOT INTERVIEWED IN THE
daily press (even today Serkin does not grant interviews). When
Van Cliburn won the Tchaikovsky competition thirty years later,
he was interviewed and photographed for newspapers and magazines of every description; on television, he appeared on a game
show and a variety show. Today, classical musicians regularly participate in television "talk shows," delivering rehearsed anecdotes as
deftly as their morsels of Chopin and Kreisler.

Compared to such talk show types as Itzhak Perlman and Luciano
Pavarotti, Steven De Groote and André-Michel Schub had been
throwbacks to another, media-innocent era. But José Feghali, the
twenty-four-year-old Brazilian who won the 1985 Van Cliburn competition, was television-ready: comfortable, confident, instantly likable. His creamy, light-brown complexion, his black hair, dark eyes,
and full lips, were sensuously Latin. His smile was engagingly boyish. His baritone, which rose an octave to italicize a stressed syllable
or word, was eager and smooth. In Bill Fertik's TV documentary of
the 1985 competition, talking about the importance of "love" in
reaching an audience, Feghali was ardently direct yet exuded the
coolness that television itself propagates and craves. And when the
time came for him to accept his gold medal—at an awards ceremony

hosted by F. Murray Abraham, who himself had won an Academy Award for *Amadeus*—he instinctively understood how to brandish his trophy proudly yet modestly, a victory gesture evoking the Academy Awards or the Olympics as surely as Schub's televised awkwardness had contradicted the Cliburn competition's mediation between popular and high culture.

The memorable musical feat of Fertik's documentary was his ability to intercut different performances of the same piece. Viewers watched four pianists give a single continuous performance of Chopin's C major Étude, Op. 10, No. 1. Five pianists were seen in Bach's *Chromatic* Fantasy and Fugue, three in the *Scherzo* from Schumann's Piano Quintet. The telecast's virtuosic high point was Fertik's split-second splicing of the seventeen final measures of the *Scherzo* from Brahms's Piano Quintet, divided between seven contestants.

José Feghali did not take part in any of these group renditions. Instead, he was seen playing eighty seconds of Haydn and eight minutes of Tchaikovsky (the close of the first movement of the First Piano Concerto). Feghali proved as pleasurable to watch in performance as in conversation. He sat erect, chin up, and smiled easily. During rapid passages he sometimes mimed each note, his lips pursed, his eyes dancing to the sight of his fingers.

Would it have occurred to Bill Fertik to fracture human speech by leaving sentences unfinished, or by completing them by having each in a series of speakers utter a single word? Fracturing Bach, Haydn, Chopin, Schumann, and Tchaikovsky, he ensured that the competition's visual content would silence its musical impact. Notwithstanding ninety seconds of intriguing inwardness—a portion of the *Chromatic* Fantasy played by the Taiwanese-American pianist Hung-Kuan Chen—the televised pieces and performances blended indistinguishably into one another. The musical message was blandly efficient, as if this competition—despite such undeniably personable contestants as Feghali or Philippe Bianconi and Barry Douglas, who placed second and third—had produced no commanding talents and no clear winner.

And this message was reinforced in the press. The pianist Ivan Davis, a Texas native who himself had won Europe's Casella, Busoni, and Liszt competitions in 1958 and 1960, covered the 1985 Cliburn competition for the *Dallas Morning News* (John Ardoin was on tour with the Dallas Symphony). Davis wrote in part:

> This year's Cliburn was particularly arid. Only four pianists from the preliminaries seemed worthy of international consideration.

One, David Buechner, was inexplicably eliminated, causing a veritable hue and cry from the not unperceptive public.*

Of the remaining three, the ultimate silver medalist, 25-year-old Philippe Bianconi of France, proved to be the most professional. . . .

José Feghali . . . is a major talent whose personality easily vaults the footlights, winning the affections of the audience. His performance of the Dvořák Quintet . . . was wreathed in tender smiles and glittering elegance. His solo recital revealed both his current strengths and weaknesses—truly personal ideas undermined by a lack of finesse and experience. The bronze medalist, Barry Douglas, 25, of Northern Ireland, gave a fascinating account of Mussorgsky's *Pictures at an Exhibition* and more sober-sided views of everything else.

The nine other semi-finalists were all disappointing in various ways, although blandness usually prevailed. The one contestant with a real musical personality, Hung-Kuan Chen, . . . astounded many with an incandescent Scriabin Fifth Sonata but offended more with a truly perverse Liszt sonata. . . .

[In the concerto finals,] Mr. Bianconi proved to be the only [contestant] who might possibly cope with the demands of the ordeals facing the gold medal winner. . . .

Young artists, no matter how talented, need time to learn about themselves and the music world. They need time to experiment, to question, to say yes, to say no, to taste triumph, even to fail. A recital in Carnegie Hall or on stage with the Chicago Symphony is not the place to learn.

The value of the first prize at the Cliburn is estimated to be in excess of $200,000. Now that is a potent lure, but if no new Horowitz or Hess is discovered—as it has been in the past and probably will be in the future—one hopes that the Cliburn competition will have the courage to declare no gold medal.

The world is already too full of competent, conscientious assembly-line prizewinners—who could lull us all into thinking that music might actually be dull.

Feghali did receive some excellent reviews in the course of his gold-medal tour. But his crucial Carnegie Hall debut was crushed by the critics. To Bernard Holland of the *New York Times*, Feghali seemed "a skilled orator without a topic, a novitiate who has memorized his Bible but cannot preach it. . . . At the moment he is neither intellectually nor spiritually equipped for the spotlight into which he has been cast." To Peter G. Davis in *New York* magazine, "everything sounded tasteful and correct. And dull—colorless, im-

---

* Davis, who did not attend the preliminary rounds, based parts of his coverage on what others had reported.

personal, mechanical, and without an expressive point of view or even a clue as to why Feghali ever wanted to become a musician in the first place." Like Ivan Davis, both writers were especially harsh on the competition itself. Holland thought Feghali's recital exemplified "the great damage that the Van Cliburn and competitions like it perpetrate. They convey the instant stamp of mastery to those who are not yet masters." Peter G. Davis wrote:

> the reasons for [Feghali's] triumph in Fort Worth continue to be obscure, although I have a theory. Some contests have become so big, costly, and image-conscious that the judges are encouraged to award top prizes to bland, safe, conventional musicians rather than risk the competition's prestige and good name by gambling on a more controversial, exciting, original talent. Consciously or not, this seems to have been the Van Cliburn's policy from the very beginning, and after anointing so many mediocrities since 1962, the competition has by now completely lost its credibility.

It is June 3, 1988. José Feghali has arrived in New York from Stara Zagora, Bulgaria. Last night, after going twenty-five hours without sleep, he participated in a Carnegie Hall gala concert honoring Steinway & Sons. He next plays in London. He says he feels "full of beans."

In person, Feghali is as fresh-faced as on television. His enthusiasm is tempered by thoughtfulness. His conversation is flexible and sincere.

He was born in Rio de Janeiro in 1961. At age fifteen he moved to London, where he eventually studied at the Royal Academy of Music. He won two competitions in Britain and took part in a number of others before preparing in earnest for the international circuit in 1984. At Leeds that year, he made it only to the quarterfinals. He won the Cliburn nine months later. At the time, he was playing twenty-five to thirty concerts a season, of which about one third were chamber music. He had given recitals at London's Queen Elizabeth and Wigmore halls. The most important of his orchestral dates—about fifteen in all—had been with the City of Birmingham Orchestra. He knew about a dozen concertos, of which six were by Mozart (learned in a single year when he "just fell in love with Mozart"). His first Cliburn season, he played ninety-two times.

Notwithstanding his relative inexperience, Feghali was in some respects better suited to the Cliburn itinerary than De Groote or

Schub had been. He seemed neither a novice nor a young man in a hurry. To Andrew Raeburn, the Cliburn executive director, who monitored Feghali's progress from Fort Worth, he was "amazingly resilient. He never wilted. Even bad reviews didn't faze him." Feghali himself remarks, his voice itself smiling: "There are very few times onstage that I wish that I weren't there. It is of immense importance to me—the day that I don't enjoy playing the piano I will cease playing the piano and do something else. I mean, every performance is special in certain ways. At one point, I performed the Tchaikovsky concerto ten times in a row. And you know, people are always telling you that if you repeat something too often it's going to go stale. Well, I suddenly realized that during one performance, when I found myself wandering off, almost on automatic pilot. But I pulled myself together for the second movement—and actually began discovering things that I *had never noticed*. So I came out of that experience with a very important lesson learned, which is that you can always make a piece fresh and spontaneous, especially if you do not subscribe to rituals of preparing in a certain, specific way, mentally."

Feghali at twenty-seven seems both very young and very poised. His inner life remains hidden. Outwardly, he appears to have quickly understood and accepted his new situation, with its particular opportunities and constraints.

"The hardest part of this business is not the music but the other 95 percent. For every two hours you spend onstage, you spend countless more traveling, living in hotels, dining in restaurants. Some pianists are satisfied with a piano, a room, and a meal. In my case, I like people. I like talking. And these became luxuries I could no longer afford. At the time of the Cliburn competition, for example, I had been thinking of getting married. I was not quite engaged. The competition was not the only factor, but that relationship ended a year ago, and my new schedule played a very important part. There was a complete change of priorities. A complete change of everything, basically. Now, sometimes that's just not what a person wants. Some people like a life fixed in one place. If that's what you want, then a concert pianist is not the life for you. I do hope to marry and have a family, but I can't say that that's something I spend any time thinking about. Frankly, I believe it would be irresponsible right now to consider marrying. At one point I was depressed about it—but only because I was looking at what I had left. When your life takes such an abrupt turn, you have to adapt your expectations. I try to focus on the people I've met and the personal experiences I've gained that I otherwise wouldn't have.

So I've gotten some things I've always wanted, and other things I've lost. And the bottom line is I have no regrets. No, better: I have no *resentments* because my life has been changed.

"I have a very simple ambition at the moment. My ambition is to be a musician and to carry on enjoying music, hoping that five years from now I'll look back and come to the conclusion that I'm a better musician than I was five years before. That's basically what I'm trying to achieve. I'm not trying to play with the Berlin Philharmonic. I've played with them. The Amsterdam Concertgebouw, I've played with them. Of course, I'd like to play with them again, but that's not the goal. The goal, as far as I'm concerned, has nothing to do with fame. The most important aspiration is to improve. To learn as much as you can. I mean, I have so much to learn just in terms of repertoire. The year of the Cliburn, I learned one new concerto, and that was about it. Now I'm learning the Beethoven First and I want to learn the Beethoven Fourth. I want to look at one of the Prokofiev concertos very soon. I'm relearning some of the concertos I've played, such as the Rachmaninoff Third. And I'm consolidating my recital repertoire in some areas where I'd like to make it stronger, like the late Beethoven sonatas. I'd like to have some more Bach. I'd like to play more twentieth-century music: Berg, Schoenberg, Webern. I've never wanted to specialize. So there are odd spots in almost every area of repertoire that need attention."

Currently, Feghali plays sixty-five to seventy times a year. Some of his best dates have been in Europe. He especially remembers a Beethoven Third Concerto with Kurt Masur and the Leipzig Gewandhaus Orchestra as "very special. I felt on top of the world. And I had the eerie feeling that the audience knew every note of that piece." He has been asked back to Leipzig, and to Baltimore, Dallas, Fort Worth, Honolulu, Milwaukee, New Haven, and Omaha. But he has given no New York recitals since his Carnegie Hall debut, nor has he performed with orchestra in Boston, Chicago, Cleveland, Los Angeles, Philadelphia, or San Francisco. And he has made no major recordings.

Feghali knows that on New York's Fifty-seventh Street he is often spoken of in the past tense. He feels New York's critics are needlessly abrasive and that the New York ambience is unhelpfully competitive. "People look at me and wonder: What happened to you? Well, why do you have to have sixteen recordings in every shop and be on the front page of the *New York Times* Arts & Leisure section? Some of the best pianists in the world started slowly. Look at Richter, or Bolet, or Arrau. Or look at Malcolm Frager: he's a *superb* musician. And when did you last see his picture in the *New York Times?*"

Feghali maintains his home in London. He has also, like Steven De Groote, purchased a house in Fort Worth. He performs on the Van Cliburn Foundation's recital series, and with the Fort Worth Symphony. His girlfriend works for the Cliburn Foundation. "Fort Worth is a lovely place, with lovely people," he says. "In New York, people say, 'Why *Fort Worth?*' as if it were a cowboy town. Well, it's not like that at all."

José Feghali's intelligence and spunk inspire people to like him. Like Jeffrey Kahane, he is considered a pleasure to work with. When he disappoints musically, no one will begrudge him the benefit of the doubt.

It may be worth considering that Feghali's most insecure playing at the Cliburn competition came in the spotlighted concerto round. Having pulled a back muscle rehearsing with the Tokyo Quartet, he had taken a muscle relaxant, to which he reacted with dizziness, fainting spells, and a skin rash. Though he recovered the day before the finals, he had interrupted his practicing, and now overpracticed. Performing the Mozart C minor Concerto and Tchaikovsky's B-flat minor, he experienced tightness in his right hand and also some lingering sluggishness. In the Tchaikovsky, particularly, his labored playing suggested the effects of slowed reflexes.

If at Carnegie Hall, some four months after the competition, Feghali seemed dwarfed by the 2,800-seat space, this is what happens to most of the pianists who risk giving recitals there. The conductor Wilhelm Furtwängler, when he first led the New York Philharmonic in 1925, found Carnegie "too large" for *orchestral* concerts; then, as now, Europe's leading orchestras played in substantially smaller auditoriums. Vienna's Bösendorfer Hall, where Liszt, Clara Schumann, Brahms, and Anton Rubinstein once gave recitals, had four hundred seats. For a solo artist to project into an area seven times this size demands special force of personality, even specialized interpretive skills. Lofting a Haydn sonata (itself a questionable choice) from Carnegie's vast stage, Feghali employed nuances that might have charmed an intimate audience equally appreciative of his expressive face and hands.

The ordeal left Andrew Raeburn feeling that the Cliburn Foundation should have waited fifteen to eighteen months after the competition before presenting its winner in Carnegie Hall, that future gold medalists should only play "between two dozen and fifty con-

certs the first year, with a concentration on less prestigious auspices." But eighteen months after his victory, Feghali was still only
twenty-five years old. With his eclectic enthusiasms (he has no
favorite repertoire and lists Gilels, Horowitz, Kempff, Michelangeli, and Richter as the pianists who have most impressed him in
live performance), he has not fully focused his artistic identity or
glimpsed his full potential.

Ivan Davis, in the *Dallas Morning News*, discerned in Feghali's
playing more promise than fulfillment; he considered him unready
for the Cliburn gold medal "at this stage in his career." In the jury
room, too, there was substantial sentiment against awarding first
prize to any of the 1985 finalists. Technically, the rules permitted
such a verdict; Andrew Raeburn had even prepared an appropriate
"contingency plan." But failure to award the gold medal would
have vexed the audience and the contestants. It would have
complicated the television documentary, tangled the itineraries,
disappointed the presenters, annoyed the sponsors. The jury understood these pressures.

One juror, Jorge Bolet, declared afterward that he would never
again judge a piano competition. He commented: "These kids are
turned overnight from promising talents into international super-
stars. I'd like to see a completely different kind of prize. Instead of
lots of money and 10,000 engagements, I would give a monthly
stipend for five years to take care of living expenses, plus twenty-
five guaranteed performances a year in colleges and with small
community orchestras. The winner would have three or four
months off in the summer for study. It would be a five-year ap-
prenticeship to develop and mature into a major career."

When Steven De Groote won the 1977 Van Cliburn competition, his victory was described and disputed in John Ardoin's
lengthy *New York Times* account, with its two-column photographs
of De Groote and Alexander Toradze. The 1981 competition was
the subject of ten Harold Schonberg articles; André-Michel Schub's
gold medal was worth a clarion headline, plus a follow-up interview
two weeks later. The *Times* announced José Feghali's victory with
a nondescript Associated Press story, eight sentences long.

In retrospect, Feghali's lower visibility may have helped him to
acquire a protective anonymity De Groote and Schub never enjoyed. He himself has elected not to hire a publicist, not to buy a
Manhattan apartment, not to covet fame.

His wholesome charm should win him allies. And he is fortunate to be managed in America by Charles Hamlen of IMG, who considered him the only 1985 Cliburn contestant "who seemed to enjoy what he was doing there."

Between 1985 and 1988, Feghali played with the orchestras of Atlanta, Baltimore, Cincinnati, Dallas, Detroit, Houston, Indianapolis, Milwaukee, Pittsburgh, and St. Louis, and with Washington's National Symphony—Cliburn engagements at a minimal fee. The inevitable public perception of Feghali's failure to return to most of these cities—that he is not wanted back—is naive: rebookings would cost up to twice what was paid initially. As of early 1989, Baltimore, Dallas, and Milwaukee have reengaged Feghali, and Hamlen is feeling optimistic about Washington. About New York, where Feghali has not performed a recital or concerto since 1985, Hamlen feels discouraged. Renting a major hall is expensive (at least $10,000) and risky (what if nobody comes?). Preferably, recitalists are presented by the halls themselves, on popular subscription series like Lincoln Center's Great Performers or the 92nd Street Y's Distinguished Artists. But Feghali's dim New York reputation precludes these opportunities, and as a Cliburn winner, he is *too* reputable to appear among the youngsters on Lincoln Center's "Next Generation" series or as a Y "bonus" recitalist. The New York Philharmonic is unlikely to book him. One of Carnegie Hall's visiting orchestras is a better bet but tricky, because IMG does not tour orchestras. And then there is the problem of interesting a major record company in Feghali—a prospect about which Feghali's own attitude seems typically patient or circumspect: "I'd like to make a recording at some time. I'm really not prepared to do one next month. If I do a record I want it to be something special. A first record is very important. And once you do it, that's it, it's permanent."

Building Feghali's career, according to Hamlen, is no longer a process of capitalizing on his Cliburn success. "It's like redeveloping his career on its own terms."

William
Wolfram

JOSEPH KALICHSTEIN, WHO WON THE LEVENTRITT IN 1969, COMMENTS about piano competitions: "The biggest mistakes are made in the early rounds. It's the time pressure—the judges simply don't know the contestants yet. Sometimes in the first round you'll get half a movement of a Beethoven sonata. And usually there are études, which to me are a waste of time. So you're left with question marks about everyone." Kalichstein was chairman of the jury for the 1988 Oslo competition, in which the player he found "the most riveting" did not survive the first cut.

Charles Rosen, a pianist who enjoys a singular reputation for intellectual achievement, also faults the judging process. "For instance, I was on the jury of the 1975 Leeds competition. One of the most distinguished pianists in that competition was Steven De Groote, who was knocked out after the first round. The trouble with De Groote was that he was controversial—people either liked his playing very much or found it cold and didn't like it at all. This becomes fatal when the jury votes on who will advance. Let's say there are twenty places. If pianist A, who is nobody's favorite, is disliked by two members of the jury and considered all right by ten others, he'll get in. If pianist B is disliked by six members of the jury, and the other six think he's exceptional, he won't make it."

All observers of this skewed elimination process have their favorite stories. At the 1988 Gina Bachauer competition, in Salt Lake
City, a twenty-seven-year-old Japanese pianist named Shinnosuke
Tashiro seemed to me the most individual, most arresting contestant. Tashiro's version of the *Appassionata* Sonata eschewed every
"traditional" rubato and ritard; he projected the three movements in
a single, concentrated arc culminating in the furious F minor downbeat of the final measure. In Toru Takemitsu's *Uninterrupted Rests*,
Tashiro's karate attacks and floating watercolor sonorities sustained
an exercise in pure concentration and sound. When he failed to
make the semifinals, I asked several jurors why. One told me that
in the *Appassionata*, Tashiro should have slowed down (as nearly all
pianists do) for the second subject of the first movement. Another
felt his playing lacked "freedom." These same opinions were delivered to Tashiro in person at a breakfast for the eliminated contestants. Their effect may be to push an unusual pianist, whose
strength transcends ego, toward mainstream mores.

Every piano enthusiast knows the story of Ivo Pogorelich, who
became the most famous contestant in the 1980 Chopin competition
after failing to reach the final round. At the Van Cliburn competition, Youri Egorov has been the most celebrated loser. The 1985
Cliburn competition produced its share of similar controversies.
Many agreed with Ivan Davis, in the *Dallas Morning News*, that
David Buechner's early elimination was inexplicable. Another
prominent early casualty was Dickram Atamian, a controversial
player who won the 1975 Naumburg competition and performed at
Carnegie Hall and with the Cleveland Orchestra before his career
unraveled. A third unlucky candidate was William Wolfram, whom
many in Fort Worth had picked to do well. A leading New York
manager had contacted him months before the competition began.
And when the Sunday magazine of the *Dallas Morning News* decided
to track a single 1985 Cliburn competitor, Dusty Rhodes of *Dallas
Life* chose Wolfram as a possible winner.

Like Buechner and Atamian, Wolfram was cut the fifth day, after
the two preliminary rounds. But Dusty Rhodes wrote her piece
anyway. Wolfram, she reported, was a big man (even taller than
Van Cliburn, a photograph showed), twenty-nine years old, with
a gruff voice and an incongruously high-pitched laugh. He smoked
cigars, liked Motown music, considered *Cosmopolitan* magazine
great comic literature, and relaxed by playing tennis and watching
basketball and hockey on television. He said he had participated in
so many piano competitions that "it's ridiculous—I literally couldn't
even possibly count them all." He felt competitions inculcated a

"sterile approach" to music and that winning them "involves a lot of luck. It's not like a sporting event, where, for the most part, the better team wins. . . . If you hit a home run, then it's a home run. Here, it's a judge's *perception* of a home run." He thought he had played well at the Cliburn competition, but accepted his loss with surprising equanimity. "This is a colossal disappointment, there's no doubt about it, but I felt very good. . . . I know it's a little irrational, but somehow I do feel guilty. I feel that somehow, the situation—and I'm the agent of that—has let people down. . . . I almost feel like, at this point, avoiding my friends, because I'm going to have to go through the whole story. That bothers me. Nobody knows what really happened down here; there's no way to describe it. I think that I'll end up telling very little. It would all sound like sour grapes."

Among those disappointed by Wolfram's showing was Andrew Raeburn, who later commented: "I can't make up my mind what happened. There's no question that the jury asked him to play a selection of pieces that wasn't really fair. He wound up playing fugues in both preliminary rounds. He wasn't able to show off his best playing." Raeburn helped arrange for Wolfram to perform with the Fort Worth Chamber Orchestra and on the Cliburn Foundation's recital series.

The "ridiculous" list of major competitions William Wolfram has entered includes the Bachauer, the Bartók, the Chopin (twice), the Cliburn (twice), the Kapell, the Leeds (twice), the Naumburg (twice), the Queen Elisabeth, and the Tchaikovsky. His only first prize came in the defunct Three Rivers competition, in Pittsburgh. But some of his losses were impressive. In Moscow in 1986, he finished eighth in a diverse international field and was accorded a "winner's recital"—which some who placed higher were not. At Warsaw in 1980, the students of the Chopin Academy voted Wolfram a "special prize" when the jury decided not to advance him to the finals—after which Pagart, the Polish Concert Agency, sent him on a two-week tour and arranged for three recordings.* At the 1987 Naumburg, Wolfram's third-place finish appalled the jurors Jacob Lateiner and Jens Nygaard. Lateiner, a pianist and peda-

---

* According to Jeffrey Kahane, who competed against Wolfram in Warsaw and who also knew him at the Juilliard School: "The people in Poland just went berserk over Bill." Kahane considers Wolfram "unquestionably a great pianist" and finds his lack of greater success "baffling."

gogue with a reputation for kindness, sat with his face in his hands when the verdict was announced; he later called Wolfram's performance of Liszt's *Dante* Sonata "one of the most poetic Liszt performances I have ever heard." Nygaard, a locally prominent New York City conductor not known to mince words, afterward remarked: "The decision in that competition violated every musical tenet I believe in. I was mortified. When it was over someone came up to me and said—as if I had *injured* myself—'You'll be OK. You'll get over it.' But the more I get to hear Bill, the more I believe in him." Nygaard speculated that some jury members voted against Wolfram out of "unconscious envy."

But Wolfram's strangest and most controversial loss was at the 1987 Kapell competition at the University of Maryland. The competition itself was in transition. Eugene Istomin, having become artistic director the year before, had renamed it after his late friend and colleague William Kapell, had added a Philadelphia Orchestra engagement and a New York recital to the list of prizes, and had transformed the jury into a Leventritt-like panel of prominent concert artists. In order to obtain the services of such jurors as Emanuel Ax, Paul Badura-Skoda, and Ivan Moravec, however, he required their attendance for only a single day: the final-round concertos. A separate jury was established to hear the earlier solo rounds. At the 1987 competition, the piano professionals who patronize the University of Maryland Piano Festival, of which the competition is a part, were agog at Wolfram's performance of Rachmaninoff's Piano Sonata No. 2 in his semifinal recital. Of the judges for that round, Joseph Kalichstein found Wolfram's performance "tremendous." The American pianist James Tocco, also on the first jury, thought Wolfram "was absolutely robbed" of first place, and said of his performance of the Rachmaninoff sonata and of Scriabin's Fourth: "I have never heard either piece played as well—certainly not better, but not even as well." George Moquin, the festival's executive director since 1982, considered Wolfram the strongest contestant the competition had fielded in five years and was confident his victory would enhance the Kapell's own reputation. But Wolfram's subsequent performance of Prokofiev's Third Piano Concerto revealed a fraction of his talent. The piece itself is relatively impersonal; worse, much of the piano writing is buried by the large, noisy orchestra. On this occasion, Istomin, himself a member of the second jury, was especially intent on imposing a high standard: he felt the previous year's first prize had been undeserved. At his insistence, an initial vote was taken whether to give a first prize. The vote was close, but no. And so Wolfram was awarded second prize. Many in the audience who booed and hissed this decision had heard substantially more of Wolfram's playing than the jurors had. Moquin and others now decided Wolfram nevertheless deserved the first prize New York recital, at Alice Tully Hall. In a flier for that event, prepared by the Kapell competition, Wolfram was lauded for "taking top honors," and the judges' decision was termed "controversial." The flier continued: "Few can name many first prize winners, even in major league competition. But many runners-up have achieved lasting public applause and critical acclaim. How many would recall the name of the first prize winner of the first Van Cliburn competition? Yet the fourth-place prize that year went to French pianist Cécile Ousset, who currently enjoys an international career and a major recording contract." Wolfram's Tully Hall recital received notably better reviews from Bernard Holland and Peter G. Davis than either had given José Feghali two seasons before.*

In fact, Wolfram's reading of the Rachmaninoff sonata is of a caliber rarely encountered in any competition—good enough to bear comparison with the remarkable concert recordings of the work by Van Cliburn and Vladimir Horowitz. His technique handsomely encompasses Rachmaninoff's extremes of power and lilting nuance. He knows how to dangle and tease the melodic thread, testing its elasticity; how to calibrate the surge and fall of the elusive larger structures. His instinct for the long line, his undemonstrative virtuosity and singing tone, actually suggest something like the young Van Cliburn.

Wolfram also shows an unusual affinity for Liszt. His pianistic finesse enables him to project a poised image of this maligned composer. And he gorgeously realizes the Lisztian upholstery of plush, dark-hued satins and velvets. Few pianists in my experience so instantly conjure up the starry void of *Harmonies du soir*, the cosmic solitude of *Vallée d'Obermann*.

In other music, Wolfram remains a polished Romantic. This is one reason he stumbles in contests that stress purported versatility in varied repertoire: many find his Haydn too aromatic, his Beethoven too suave.† Some competitions favor relatively young,

---

* The Kapell competition now includes recitals as well as concertos in its final round.

† James Tocco remarked of certain jury colleagues who expressed reservations about Wolfram's Beethoven in Maryland: "It really disturbed me to hear people trying to make him into something he's not. It's a distressing aspect of piano competitions in general—the policy 'Let's hear a little bit of Bach, and a little bit of Beethoven, and a smattering of twentieth-century music.' What's wrong with playing Romantic music well and nothing else? What's wrong with playing Bach well and nothing else?" And Tocco added: "Every person on a jury

malleable winners, whom certain of the judges or sponsors will enjoy guiding as mentors; to the degree that he is no stylistic chameleon, but a stylist, Wolfram sounds—in the words of one former teacher—"not teachable." Also, his rejection of surface intensity in search of the long line can make him appear a diffident player. This is an impression reinforced by his easy technique and by details of demeanor: that he walks to the piano in stiff, straight-legged strides; that he does not smile when bowing; that his head wanders while he plays.

Some who know Wolfram's playing find him and it diffuse. Perhaps in time his musical personality will acquire a sharper focus, will more completely span the Romantic extremes of demonic and religious possession. Already, however, he has more to say than many a touted young virtuoso in whom an all-purpose intensity makes do for understanding and conviction.

Some pianists consider themselves experts in jury behavior. They will research the recordings and repertoire of the judges. They will choose pieces that sound equally well on a variety of pianos: instruments of different makes with different potentialities. They will even enroll in master classes with X of West Germany, or Switzerland's Y, because—and only because—X and Y are frequent international jurors and allegedly favor who favors them.

William Wolfram volunteers no such subtleties of explanation to account for his twelve-year record of competition defeats. "It's very hard to say what happened," he begins. "Quite honestly, when I was younger I used to logically come up with what repertoire would be good for me in a competition, and what would be bad. But after a while I stopped doing that. . . . I have sometimes believed that I didn't succeed in competitions because of doing things my own way. For one thing, I have a propensity for doubling octaves and breaking the hands—I do those things constantly. This turns a lot of people off. It's like a crusade: a lot of pianists—the zealots, the Pat Buchanans of the piano—are outraged. At the same time, I have to say that I think I'm a late developer, that I am playing the piano better now."

At thirty-three, Wolfram is at last too old to enter any more major international piano competitions—a fact he receives as casu-

---

has a vested interest in propagating his own attitudes toward the music that he plays, and if somebody comes along with different attitudes and obviously feels perfectly comfortable about it, I suppose it can be threatening."

ally as he does my visit to his Manhattan apartment, itself casually strewn with books, records, and papers. His six feet four inches slouch across a venerable sofa. His gaze, under dark, curly hair, is mild and meandering. His voice is soft, his tone impassive or quizzical as he recounts a musical odyssey worlds remote from the concentrated tutelage of a Vladimir Viardo or an Alexander Toradze. Born and raised in an affluent New York City suburb, he could not integrate his piano education with his social environment.

"I did not have the classic happy childhood. My parents sent me to parochial school first, which was strict. Then I went to a progressive school. Finally, I wound up going to public school—I think it was in the seventh grade; I'm not sure. Which was a tremendous help. I needed to exist in the world and not in a shell.

"When I was younger I had been discouraged from taking part in sports, but I always found sports very alluring. I'd play games in the backyard, invented by myself. Then, in high school, I developed an absolute mania for ice hockey. I was not on the White Plains High School team; I was on a team that was better. I also played a lot of tennis. In fact, if some of those people who knew me in high school could see me now, they wouldn't believe it.

"Meanwhile, completely independent from school, I had been pursuing music, from the age of about five. It was something I had to do before going to school, and which I didn't like. I really did not like doing it at all. Music was an impediment to a normal life. Every Saturday, my mother would drive me into Manhattan and I would attend classes from ten to five in Juilliard's Pre-College Division. I remember how on Fridays I would have one of my two weekly hockey practices. I would get back at about two in the morning. Of course, that was much more important to me than music, so I would always be exhausted Saturdays at Juilliard. Those years were completely sacrificed—I couldn't have cared less about solfège, piano, composition. I think if I had had a different avenue— if there had been something else to get into deeply—I would have dropped music. Because I was finally growing into a more normal kid. Before that, I had been socially maladjusted, extremely shy. And as I got over this, being normal became so important to me, I enjoyed it so much, and it was so necessary, that I really had no interest in music. I never really thought about stopping music; I just put it on a back burner, where it continued to sit even in college."

"College," for Wolfram, mainly meant Juilliard, where he obtained a bachelor's degree and where his main teacher was Irwin Freundlich.

"Everyone I know—absolutely *everyone* I know—has a hatred of that place and of that building. I never had that. There were a lot of unpleasant things at Juilliard—the cutthroat students, the teachers who encouraged the run-of-the-mill—and I avoided them like the plague. I went for the things I enjoyed, and I had a wonderful time there. Like Harvey Shapiro, an incredible cello teacher; he was such a thrilling musician that I accompanied his class for a couple of years. And Freundlich was truly a great teacher. I was very close to him and admired him extremely—he was the closest thing to a Renaissance man I've ever seen. He had been a psychology major at Columbia, he played third base on their baseball team, he was a sergeant in the army. He often brought his sergeant's training into the classroom: he could be a very rough, [Vince] Lombardi-esque teacher. Which always worked with me. He was a tremendous motivator. When he died, in 1977, I reached my lowest point—I so loved him, and so much of my motivation was tied to him. Which made sense at that time, because I had—and I still have—such a weird tie to music. The lowest point was also a function of my own growth, or lack of it, as a person. I wanted to have fun. Having worked quite hard when I was fairly young, I was goofing off and having a great time. I was losing interest in music so much that it's kind of amazing that I ever got back into it."*

Wolfram mainly undertook the international competition circuit after Freundlich's death. The opportunity to play for excited audiences in major cities, sometimes with orchestra, was heady. He

---

* Among pianists of my acquaintance, Jeffrey Swann most provocatively analyzes the pathology of social dislocation endemic to his profession. As he now plays more extensively in Europe than in the United States, he is a master of cross-cultural comparisons. He says: "Compared to other musicians, pianists start earlier, practice more—because of the number of notes and the amount of repertoire—and are by themselves more. In Western Europe, they nonetheless seem to be able to begin their lives more or less normally—they're not considered odd. In the Soviet Union, they're isolated, put in an incubation tank to pursue their specialized training. In the United States, they experience a different kind of isolation and incubation, often overseen by older ladies; they then go to Juilliard, which means going from one weird neurotic environment to another, even weirder, more neurotic environment. When I was a kid in Texas, all my friends were male pianists. I never went out on a date. All we ever did together was listen to music. Texas is like the rest of the U.S., only more so. I mean, when you come from such a huntin', fishin', and whorin' society, if you want to play the piano you find yourself in a world dominated by older women, many of whom have unfulfilled relationships with their huntin' and fishin' husbands. They seem to encourage an undirected sexuality. This may be one reason for something that isn't written about but which everyone in music knows: that—compared to, say, violinists—there are an awful lot of homosexual pianists. In Texas, when I was growing up, pianists were *expected* to be gay. Flirting with them was acceptable and fun because it was *safe*." A better illustration of America's ambivalence toward Art—of the dual impulse to revere and control, glorify and castrate—would be hard to find.

especially recalls the 1980 Chopin competition for its "overflow crowds and incredible World Cup atmosphere." He has seen many colleagues on the circuit turn bitter. Americans who compete in Poland and Russia, for instance, insist that contestants from those countries benefit from partisan Soviet-bloc jurors, extra rehearsal time, and other concealed advantages. Wolfram himself believes that his 1980 Warsaw showing was impaired when he drew an early-morning slot—he plays better later in the day—and that a Russian contestant had initially drawn that time but was permitted to reschedule. The memory that grates most is of an American competition in which he had, as he afterward learned, tied for first place—at which point one of the jurors agreed to change his vote. That taught him, he says, to "just play, get the results, and go have a drink." Santiago Rodriguez, reflecting on the rigors of the Leventritt and Cliburn competitions particularly, says: "You *bleed* too much, if you're sensitive. You just *die* a little bit every time you compete. You get so tough your musicality is blocked. Meaning you've got scars and scabs where the blood was; you lose the freedom to take risks. Your frame of mind is self-protection: let me get through this thing without breaking down." But Wolfram seems to have known how to prevent competition wounds—or perhaps how to anesthetize them.

Today, he plays about fifty times a year—a schedule he feels is right for him. He says his "luck turned" in the early 1980s, around the time he acquired small-time management. One catalyst was years of playing with orchestra—with ample rehearsal and multiple performances—for ballet companies in Pittsburgh, Boston, and Miami, an opportunity that arose when the ballet conductor Ottavio De Rosa heard him at the 1980 Three Rivers competition. Another valuable springboard was Affiliate Artists, whose Xerox Pianists Program provides two-week "residencies" with American orchestras; following a successful 1985 Affiliate Artists audition, Wolfram appeared with the symphonies of Canton, Fort Worth, Indianapolis, Richardson (Texas), Syracuse, and Tucson, and with Tampa's Florida Orchestra. At one time he spent twelve hours a week accompanying Suzuki violin classes; he now supports himself completely as a performer. He does not play with the major American orchestras but is a visible presence on the New York piano scene. He also occasionally appears with the violinist Oscar Shumsky, whom he considers "one of the greatest musicians I've ever encountered." Abroad, he has been heard in Holland, Italy, Peru, Spain, and Thailand. And the Poles have asked him back to perform and record in 1990. He partly credits his progress to "feeling more relaxed as a person: I get along very well at these after-concert things now. That produces reengagements." He married in 1985; his wife, an ex-singer, attends law school. The Wolframs look forward to having children in several years. "My career," he says, "has actually proceeded in a stepwise, logical fashion. When I didn't care that much about it, for whatever reasons, I didn't have anything really going. As I got more serious—and now I'm completely serious—things progressed slowly but surely. As a matter of fact, I'm more nervous now than ever before. There's so much more opening up."

Every time I have asked William Wolfram to summarize his feelings about piano competitions, he has volunteered a different answer. He blames them for "standardizing interpretation" but feels he "would be nowhere without them." He says they forced him to narrow his repertoire—and yet they motivated him, in the wake of Freundlich's death, to work hard. He detests the " 'say cheese' situations" endemic to them, yet thinks that "as a learning experience, competitions, for me, would almost be worth five concerts. I respond best when there's fear and pressure." Even his defeats, he believes, disseminated and validated his name. To a farcical degree, he was helped by Bill Fertik's Tchaikovsky and Van Cliburn documentaries, in which he was seen saying things like: "I would like to play like the Edmonton Oilers now, but I wouldn't want the same results, because they were kicked out [of the Stanley Cup] this year. But they did win the cup twice, and they played with great abandon, flair, and style. But usually the competitions like a little bit more of the Philadelphia Flyers organizing tactics." After which one New York music critic wrote: "If Wolfram . . . can make it as a pianist, he should be in demand for talk shows."*

Wolfram's one certain conviction about competitions suits his ironic observational style. His 1980 Polish tour, the most intense and thrilling of his career, was at the same time "fracturing"—it gave him a taste of doing too much too soon. "To tell you the truth, when I didn't get to play with the Philadelphia Orchestra as a result

---

* Some other Wolfram comments from Fertik's television documentaries: "All my friends are leaving—they're dropping like flies." "Uppermost in my mind is whether the Red Sox are still in first place." And: "I always thought that a good test would be having a pianist play under grave physical duress—like three people trying to beat him up at the same time." Wolfram comments: "Quite often I gave a lot of sports analogies, because I found it easier than to think. And when they got hold of that, they used it, went with it. Very often they would ask a question that would lead me into the ballpark, because that had become my identity."

of not winning first prize at the Maryland competition, it didn't bother me that much. Of course, I would love to play with the Philadelphia Orchestra. But if I could be guaranteed that my career, instead, would continue at the rate it's going now, building only a couple of rungs every year—gradually, slowly—I'd be the happiest person in the world. If I play with the Philadelphia Orchestra someday, that's all I want. For now, I think I need more time and experience. Because—and this always drives me nuts—I feel very strongly that every year, and even sometimes at six-month intervals, I know more and play tangibly better. I'm still honing my style. It's almost like getting control of your shots in tennis."

Looking back at the 1985 Van Cliburn competition, in which he was lapped by José Feghali, Philippe Bianconi, Barry Douglas, and dozens of others, Wolfram says: "I realize now I wouldn't have been quite ready for the gold medal. If I had won third or fourth, it might have helped a lot. But in general, I think that if I had done better in competitions, it would have gotten in the way."

For every aspirant thirty-year-old pianist with a name—for every Steven De Groote, Alexander Toradze, André-Michel Schub, Jeffrey Kahane, José Feghali, or William Wolfram—there are nameless hundreds who have had to abandon their concert hopes and teach, or who have changed professions altogether. (One winner of the University of Maryland competition, also a medalist at the Bachauer competition, became a computer programmer.) Onstage, the artist-in-tails embodies glamour; offstage, he may be beset by actual poverty. (Many a struggling concert artist with one foot in the door on Fifty-seventh Street can barely afford a small studio apartment on Manhattan's Upper West Side, yet cannot risk leaving New York.) His public face exudes poise; privately, he may feel enraged and mutilated. (One New York pianist, once a frequent also-ran on the competition circuit, calls jurors of his acquaintance "frauds" and summarizes: "Competitions did me a lot of harm. You cannot help but be aware of who is winning and advancing; you can't help but prostitute your integrity to fit into their kind of approach.")

As even our relatively privileged group of six Cliburn participants makes clear, playing the piano in concert can be an onerous profession. The regime of daily, solitary practice turns pianists into social misfits early in life. On tour, pianists must suffer the vagaries of bad instruments, halls, and audiences, the coldness of strange restaurants and hotels. Career opportunities are hard to come by and getting harder. And the biggest talent does not ensure the biggest reward.

The experiences of our six pianists also suggest—as the first of four interim conclusions about pianists and piano competitions—that in any competition *the best pianist does not necessarily finish in the running*. Illness and stress, envy and bias, unsuitable repertoire, insufficient playing time—all these can become factors in the verdict. The very notion of "best" is not only subjective but inappropriate: how choose between a De Groote and a Toradze? It is enough to observe the vehemence with which "experts" of the jury can disagree with one another.

Second: *as talent showcases, competitions unquestionably help pianists, but not necessarily the ones who win*. In Fort Worth since 1977, the prime beneficiaries have been Toradze, Kahane, and Egorov, none a gold medalist. Over the past decade, the most spectacular competition-sprung keyboard career is that of Ivo Pogorelich—a result of his controversial elimination in Warsaw in 1980. The fates of Dang Thai Son, Tatyana Shebanova, Arutiun Papazian, Akiko Ebi, Ewa Poblocka, Eric Berchot, and Irina Petrova—the Chopin competition's top winners that year—are (at least in the West) obscure. Considered as a group, De Groote, Schub, and Feghali have not thrived on their Van Cliburn victories. And yet . . .

These Cliburn gold medalists are better than the musical public believes: the prevalent stigmas of "sameness" and "blandness" are unjust. As we have seen, *no* international competition has produced a winner with staying power since Krystian Zimerman won the Chopin competition in 1975. The years are long past when Van Cliburn or Leon Fleisher could automatically achieve fame by winning in Moscow or Brussels. Gone forever, as well, are the opportunities for intricate networking the Leventritt seized in quietly securing nascent careers: the premier conductors are globe-trotting; the big and powerful managers are not as big and powerful; it now takes more than a few major orchestra dates for a young talent to attract notice. It is worth asking what might have happened to the likes of Eugene Istomin or Gary Graffman had they won the Hyderized Cliburn as young men rather than the Leventritt three decades earlier. Would they have been media-ready? Could they have handled the instant celebrity? the nearly one hundred engagements per season? For that matter: De Groote and Schub, both Curtis products, would have made perfectly plausible Leventritt winners forty years ago, with plausible expectations of healthy careers. But the career expectations attached to Cliburn winners are crippling: their ballyhooed debuts are bound to disappoint. In fact . . .

The Cliburn competition's trademark itineraries are booby-trapped.
More than opportunities, they ensure overexposure and fatigue.
For some gold medalists, the London and Carnegie Hall recitals are
premature. For others, the concerts in Fishkill and Greenville are
superfluous. The crowded itineraries preempt opportunities for
learning and living. They dictate a future decline in engagements,
and attendant perceptions of failure. They are less the result of
planning than of circumstance: Martha Hyder's determination to
expand a prize deemed insufficient for Vladimir Viardo. They
anchored her impressive success at enticing the best media coverage
and contestants. But they were arrived at with no true understanding of the artistic consequences. No wonder Jeffrey Kahane and
William Wolfram are glad they did not win.

III

THE EIGHTH VAN CLIBURN INTERNATIONAL PIANO COMPETITION

Preparations

"MY OWN EXPERIENCE OF THE JOB WAS THAT IT WAS RATHER MORE than half dealing with the power elite of Fort Worth," recalls Anthony Phillips, executive director of the Cliburn Foundation for the 1981 competition. "The whole thing simply does not get off the ground without the initiative and support of movers and shakers of various kinds, and their wishes always have to be accommodated to the abstract demands of one's vision of the ideal." A gentlemanly Englishman new to America, Phillips ran afoul of local music interests when he presented the Saint Paul Chamber Orchestra—a group superior to Fort Worth's chamber orchestra—on the Cliburn Concerts series, and again when he proposed presenting the Dallas Symphony. Ironically, he had been hired partly to make the Cliburn more cosmopolitan and to improve its image abroad. He did succeed in expanding Cliburn Concerts into a regionally significant chamber music and recital series. But his sophistication contradicted certain provincial agendas. Some "movers and shakers" mistrusted his loyalty to Fort Worth, hoping and expecting that he would move on to someplace bigger. After presiding over a single competition, he resigned to become general manager of London's Royal Festival Hall. He is currently one of London's major artists' managers.

Phillips's successor, Andrew Raeburn, remembers his three and a half years with the Cliburn Foundation with a philosophic ambivalence. As a newcomer to Fort Worth (where he continues to live), he was startled and touched by the local hospitality. He feels the Cliburn looks after its winners more painstakingly than any other competition. He equally remembers that part of his work required him to "scream bloody murder whenever I saw extramusical factors intrude on the musical purposes—things like an irate board member entering the jury room to complain that only one juror had attended a dinner party the previous evening." Raeburn resigned after the 1985 competition, feeling "still of two minds" about music competitions. "One was enough. It was worthwhile, but I'd never do it again."

For the third time in a row, the foundation had to find an executive director for its next competition. A search committee formulated a job description listing an unlikely diversity of responsibilities—a mirror of the competition's unlikely diversity of objectives. The new director would administer an office of nine with an average annual budget of more than $1 million. He would be a fundraiser and promoter. He would know music and the piano, and enjoy good rapport with musicians. As artists' manager, he would oversee the winners' new careers. As impresario, he would supervise the Cliburn Concerts series. And ideally, he would be a prominent and persuasive civic figure—if possible, with powerful and glamorous international friends.

Inevitably, the search invited reevaluation. Especially in its Hyderized form, the Cliburn competition's crowning aspiration has been to anoint a keyboard gladiator to tour the world's music capitals with Roman pomp and splendor. As everyone knew, nothing like that had happened in 1977, 1981, or 1985. And why had Youri Egorov, potentially the most plausible champion the competition had fielded in those years, failed even to make the final round? With all the money, hard work, and goodwill the foundation commanded, was it doing the best it could? Interviewing applicants for Andrew Raeburn's job, some members of the search committee found themselves pondering strategies proposed by John de Lancie, formerly director of the Curtis Institute and the chief revisionist on the final list of candidates. Echoing Jorge Bolet's advice following the 1985 competition, and supported by Steven De Groote, whom he knew from Curtis, de Lancie advocated a different type of Cliburn prize, weighted toward further education and more gradual career development. In effect, he advised the Cliburn Foundation to distinguish Fort Worth 1989 from Moscow 1958—to understand that the Cliburn competition would not find another Van Cliburn to win its gold medal and seize an instant major career fortified by fame, publicity, and one-hundred plus dates a season.

The candidate the foundation settled on, and who became its new director as of July 1986, was Richard Rodzinski. Born in New York in 1945 and raised in Italy, he is the son of Artur Rodzinski, the late Polish-born conductor of the Los Angeles Philharmonic, the Cleveland Orchestra, the New York Philharmonic, and, briefly, the Chicago Symphony. His maternal grandfather was the violinist Henryk Wieniawski. He studied musicology at Oberlin College and Columbia University and had thoughts of becoming a recording producer; instead, he served as artistic assistant to Kurt Herbert Adler, general director of the San Francisco Opera, from 1969 to 1975. For the next four years, he was the Metropolitan Opera's artistic administrator (where, as in San Francisco, he assembled and served on juries for opera auditions—his only prior experience with music competitions).

Rodzinski is a tall, mercurial man with curly gray hair and a bushy black mustache. His intense face, dominated by a large, dilated nose and penetrating eyes, makes him look older than his forty-four years. Temperamentally, he is poles apart from Andrew Raeburn, whose very British demeanor—urbane, low-keyed, amused—belies a surprising bluntness of opinion. Rodzinski's playful or combative bluntness is not surprising. At the same time, his dimpled, toothy smile projects a reassuring warmth. In laid-back Fort Worth, he is a driven Yankee conspicuous for his rapidity, volubility, and gesticulatory gusto.

Rodzinski's musical affinities equally set him apart from Andrew Raeburn. Before heading the Cliburn, Raeburn had served as musical assistant to Erich Leinsdorf at the Boston Symphony and as artistic administrator of the Detroit Symphony under Antal Dorati—Central European conductors of a sober, literalist bent. In his 1985 charge to the jury, he emphasized the importance of respecting the composer's text. He expresses some impatience with Fort Worth's hunger for a glamorous winner. "I don't think you can expect a great star to emerge from any competition except once in a while," he says. "And I'm tired of reading reviewers who think someone is an interesting 'personality' because he brings a new interpretation to a piece of music." When Richard Rodzinski talks about future Cliburn winners, he stresses not fidelity but "communication" and "charisma." He grew up in a family closely linked to that of Arthur Rubinstein, whose trademark was panache. His list of the "great young pianists" includes names that make Raeburn blanch.

Also, unlike Raeburn or Anthony Phillips—or Grant Johannesen, chairman of Cleveland's Casadesus Piano competition, or Seymour Lipkin, artistic director of the University of Maryland's William Kapell competition, or Paul Pollei, founder and director of Salt Lake City's Gina Bachauer International Piano competition— Rodzinski comes across as a true believer in piano competitions. He exudes certain faith that in any well-run music contest, the best man will win, or at least finish in the money. He says: "I don't think you can work in the arts unless you have a sense of mission. It certainly is the case for me. And I happen to believe that competitions do some good. Not just for those kids who happen to win but for the entire musical scene. Because a competition serves a tremendous function as a screening agency for musical directors and presenters, to identify those young musicians who are the most talented. I believe that. If I didn't, I would quit right away. Especially with the present proliferation of musicians, it becomes all the more important to find a way to select a few, because everybody's not going to make a career. I remember when there was an opening for second horn in the Fort Worth Symphony. Eighty candidates came down. Wow. That's a lot of people. From all over the country. So they have orchestral screenings. We have screenings for solo instrumentalists who play the piano. Same thing."

Rodzinski tenaciously pursues this argument and its naive implications. In a panel discussion at the 1987 Kapell competition, his remarks underlined his confidence in the jury system for music. The Cliburn's "screening process," he said, identified "the best available talent ready for an international career. . . . In other words, it's a safe bet." And he characterized competitions as inherently "educational" for the pianists themselves—they "learn" and "grow" by finding out from the judges how good they are. Some time later, when the *Dallas Morning News* ran an article claiming that the Cliburn competition "transforms the art of classical piano playing into something like a blood sport," Rodzinski scribbled a furious rebuttal that, had the *Morning News* printed it, would have astonished many a purported beneficiary of juror wisdom:

> the most socially and humanly significant aspect of a music competition goes by unnoticed, receives no press, perhaps because it is not glamorous, and there is little negative one can say about it. Namely, com-

petitions are an invaluable forum for young musicians to learn how they measure against their fellow musicians. . . . The competition allows a young pianist early on to assess his potential for a performing career.

In the year preceding the 1989 competition, it became apparent that Rodzinski's zeal would help secure more widespread recognition for the Cliburn than even Martha Hyder had achieved. As the foundation had never enjoyed full validation abroad, Rodzinski's assets as a candidate had included strong European ties, via his family and his operatic experience. And he had stressed the need to find international funding sources to compensate for diminishing Texas oil wealth—a factor tangibly affecting the Cliburn's local gifts and subsidies. Concomitantly, he had maintained that a more aggressive marketing effort was necessary to combat chauvinistic resistance to the Cliburn and Fort Worth in countries like France and Italy. As executive director, he quickly followed his own counsel, undertaking an international mailing of eight thousand applications and ten thousand brochures ("First held in 1962, the Competition serves as a living testament to the tremendous impetus that winning a major competition has on launching an international career," etc.). He also redirected certain promotional strategies. Abandoning Bill Fertik's formulaic treatment of the Cliburn as a horse race with music, and characteristically embracing the validity of the jury system, he charged Peter Rosen to produce a ninety-minute television documentary explaining "the moment of discovery of great music-making"—the reasons why the 1989 gold medalist "would rise above the others—his or her charisma, desire to communicate, to persuade, to make music." For radio, he arranged for an unprecedented thirteen-week series of national broadcasts, including live coverage of the awards ceremony, plus recorded excerpts from the competition.

Thanks to Rodzinski's vigor and idealism, and also to *glasnost*, the 1989 Cliburn has attracted a record number of potential contestants: 214 pianists from 37 countries filed applications by the November 1988 deadline. And this total does not include applicants from the Soviet Union, which has agreed to send pianists for the first time since 1973, or China, which sent pianists to Fort Worth only once before. Rodzinski's agreement with the Soviets, moreover, includes these novel provisions: Goskoncert, the official Soviet artists' agency, will organize tours of the Soviet Union for the Cliburn winners; should a Soviet pianist win the gold medal, he will be allowed to tour ten months for each of two seasons; and the Cliburn Foundation will help organize American tours for the winner of Moscow's 1990 Tchaikovsky competition.

As of the beginning of 1989, with the Eighth International Van Cliburn Piano Competition five months away, the proverbial high expectations seem plausible. Not only are the Russians coming, but a number of the American and European applicants are endorsed by eminent teachers and conductors as "certain" winners. Richard Rodzinski, a popular activist, predicts the success of the coming contest as an article of faith. Mindful of past disappointments, he projects a contagious confidence that the Cliburn can do better.

In any music competition, the jury is crucial and problematic. The problems begin with the necessary subjectivity of evaluation and the necessary vagueness of standards and criteria. And the better the contestants are, the more subjective and vague the evaluation becomes.

Roughly, music juries are of two types. The first, recalling the methods of the Leventritt competition, deliberates informally and includes friends and associates of the organizers, who may themselves preside in the jury room. Juries for the Naumburg piano competition, for example, tend to include friends and associates of Lucy Mann, the executive director, and of her husband, Robert Mann, first violinist of the Juilliard Quartet; and the Naumburg jury "talks out" its verdicts with the sanctioned participation of both the Manns. Susan Wadsworth enjoys similar prerogatives during her Young Concert Artists auditions. One possible result is the perception—and actuality—of bias. But the bias may be informed and constructive.

In the big international competitions, directors like Richard Rodzinski are expected to relinquish control of the outcome. As a member of the Geneva-based World Federation of International Music Competitions, the Cliburn must see that at least half its jurors are not from the "host country" (i.e., the United States). Theoretically, bias and the perception of bias are minimized.

And yet the international juries typically invite cynicism and ridicule. One senior American pianist expresses the opinion of many intimate observers: "You see the same jurors at many of the major competitions. They are mostly piano teachers who don't play concerts and from whose studios you never encounter major talents—unless major talents go to them because they judge competitions. And they're invited because they come from all these different countries and it's nice in an international competition to get representatives from many different countries. And in their hometowns each of them is one of several or many piano teachers and doesn't get terribly much attention otherwise. As itinerant jurors, however, they're wined and dined, they stay in hotels they normally couldn't afford to stay in, they get their three meals paid for, they're treated as being very, very important, they live in a way that they're not accustomed to—or that they become accustomed to, because they hope to be invited to continue this existence. There's this hierarchy of who gets invited to, say, Moscow, where the level is higher. And they make their jury colleagues feel it. 'Will I see you in Tokyo next month? And after that will you be in Salt Lake City? Oh, they've even asked you to Moscow!' That kind of thing."

Everyone on the competition circuit can cite instances of jurors who were senile, or hard of hearing, or mentally impaired, or (as quite commonly happens) biased in favor of students or countrymen. In fact, jurors are often chosen for extramusical reasons. Those who administer competitions of their own are especially popular with one another. Jurors from out-of-the-way countries—China, for instance—are counted on to promote at home the competitions they visit abroad. In pre-Gorbachev times, Soviet jurors—chosen by the Soviets themselves, rather than by the competitions they judged—were typically expected to know the Soviet contestants, and how to help them.

One class of jurors is notoriously hard to obtain. In bygone years, the judges in Brussels, Warsaw, and Moscow included Casadesus, Annie Fischer, Gilels, Michelangeli, Richter, Rubinstein. Today, such distinguished concert pianists rarely turn up on "distinguished juries." For one thing, there are many more juror slots to fill. For another, distinguished performers tend to be busier than before, jetting from country to country twelve months a year. And many of them simply do not believe in piano competitions.

The Leventritt juries were unsurpassed for their inclusion of ranking performing musicians. As we have seen, Mrs. Leventritt commanded the loyalty of certain instrumentalists and conductors, and she would hold the competition only if these and other key artist-jurors were available. Nowadays, the closest approximation to a Leventritt-style jury is at the Kapell competition, whose present artistic director, Seymour Lipkin, was himself a member of the Leventritt "family"—as was his predecessor, Eugene Istomin. A respected pianist and teacher of long experience, Lipkin enjoys social and professional ties that enable him to prevail on reluctant colleagues. His 1989 jury notably includes Jorge Bolet, who previously announced his disgruntled retirement from jury duty following the 1985 Cliburn.* The other members of the 1989 Kapell jury are Rudolf Firkusny, Peter Frankl, Charles Rosen, Tamás Vásáry, Vladimir Viardo, and Ventzislav Yankoff—all but Yankoff, who is among the best-known French pedagogues, pianists with active international solo careers. But Lipkin must rely on two special enticements to obtain such busy professionals: Kapell jurors are offered full-fee recitals at the University of Maryland during their stay; and (as we have seen) they are required to adjudicate only the final round, lasting one or two days, a separate jury having been impaneled for the preliminary and semifinal rounds.

The typical piano jury, however, is not remotely of the caliber of Lipkin's *secondary* jury. Even at the Bachauer competition, in some respects bigger than the Kapell, the jury never includes famous performers. Unlike the Kapell or Bachauer, the Cliburn competition offers jurors a substantial stipend—$10,000. But then the competition is a long one—sixteen days. And scores of pianists can earn more than $10,000 for a single performance. In past years, the Cliburn has managed to secure a few big-name jurors, including Bolet (1962 and 1985), Leon Fleisher (1969 and 1977), Firkusny (1977), and Alicia de Larrocha (1966). Rodzinski has had less luck in 1989. Of his fourteen jurors, those with the most visible international careers are probably John Lill of Great Britain, who shared first prize at the 1970 Tchaikovsky competition and is prominent in Europe, and the Brazilian-born Cristina Ortiz, who won the 1969 Cliburn competition and is perhaps best known in London, where she lives. As Rodzinski is quick to stress, "some people who are wonderful pianists are simply awful on a jury. We were looking for jurors who could recognize a communicative artist without necessarily agreeing with the way that artist expresses himself. Sometimes a teacher is better able to do that than a performer, because a teacher is trained to accept fifty different interpretations of a work. But it's impossible to generalize. I mean, there are certain great performers who are totally convinced of the way they play and cannot accept another view. And others are great because they are broad-minded."

Rodzinski has also sought to include "people from different walks of musical life—not just pianists. We discussed quite a few singers, for instance. This was very much Van Cliburn's idea. We actually

---

* Bolet had to withdraw owing to ill health. He was replaced by Grant Johannesen.

spoke to a few." Though none of the singers worked out, Rodzinski did engage a composer: John Corigliano. When Corigliano decided to withdraw, he was replaced with a conductor: Maxim Shostakovich, the son of the composer, and now music director of the New Orleans Symphony. A second conductor on the 1989 Cliburn jury is Lawrence Leighton Smith, music director of the Louisville Orchestra. As George Szell and William Steinberg once helped promote the careers of the Leventritt winners, Shostakovich and Smith will potentially engage the pianists they like best in Fort Worth. Rodzinski's most unorthodox selection is that of John Pfeiffer, the veteran RCA recording producer who has worked closely with Van Cliburn, among many other artists.

The remaining 1989 Cliburn jurors are all pianists and piano pedagogues. The Russians are sending Sergei Dorensky, chairman of the piano faculty of the Moscow Conservatory and a well-traveled pianist and juror. Poland's Jan Ekier heads the piano division at Warsaw's Chopin Academy; he was president of the Chopin competition in 1985. Li Mingqiang, vice president of the Shanghai Conservatory, is, like Ekier, a former prize winner in the Chopin competition; he served on the Cliburn jury in 1985. Takahiro Sonoda is one of Japan's prominent pianists. The Spanish pianist Joaquin Soriano teaches at the Madrid Conservatory. The French pianist Nicole Henriot-Schweitzer, who teaches at the Royal Conservatory in Brussels, is serving on the Cliburn jury for the fourth time. Ralph Votapek, the Cliburn's first gold medalist and now artist in residence at Michigan State University, is one of two American-born pianists on the jury. The other is the venerable and much-recorded Abbey Simon. The Hungarian-born György Sándor, now an American citizen, is best known as an exponent of Bartók, with whom he studied and whose entire keyboard output he has recorded.

Taken as a group, the 1989 Cliburn jurors are neither famous nor obscure. Their considerable prior experience in Moscow, Warsaw, Brussels, and Leeds suggests the presence of several "professional judges." Some of the older members are fading performers certain to envy the new gold medalist's itinerary. One juror, Sándor, happens to be an outspoken critic of piano competitions; he calls them

> very unwholesome; a contagious disease which now covers the whole globe. . . . They can do tremendous damage to young artists. But they are good for the committees who participate, for the jury members and for building teachers' names. I myself very often judge international competitions. It's like playing God . . . but I try to play God the way

I think God should play. I always look for that talent which has a quality of originality, instead of the uniformity which has become the status quo.

If Sándor, at seventy-six, is no Arrau or Serkin, he projects an easy personal authority, which cannot be said of all Rodzinski's choices. Taken as a whole, the 1989 Cliburn jury is notably heterogeneous: its teachers, pianists, conductors, and recording executive, representing nine countries and four continents, include reputed pedants and free spirits, literalists and Romantics, specialists in Bartók, Beethoven, Chopin, Shostakovich, and Ravel. In its favor, this group contains no obvious ciphers—like the 1977 juror from the Philippines, a friend of Imelda Marcos (herself a friend of Van Cliburn), whom the contestants frequently put to sleep. But reading between the names, I infer a happenstance diversity: selections dictated by who happened to be available, or happened to be known to Van Cliburn or Richard Rodzinski. The Leventritt competition knew whom to get; its juries, dominated by Serkin and Szell, embodied a discernible point of view.

The jury changes, the contestants' faces are fresh; essentially, the rest of the Cliburn competition remains the same. As in 1985, it will last sixteen days, with two days off, as follows: the preliminary round, in two phases, occupies days one to five; the semifinals, consisting of a minirecital and a string quintet, occupy days seven to eleven; the finals, consisting of two concertos per finalist, occupy days thirteen to fifteen; the awards ceremony is allotted a day of its own. The Tokyo String Quartet will again take part in the chamber music round. The Fort Worth Symphony will again be the orchestra, again conducted by Stanislaw Skrowaczewski. There will again be a mandatory commissioned work by an American composer, this time William Schuman.

In 1985, applications were accepted from pianists eighteen to twenty-nine years old; for 1989, the upper age limit has been raised to thirty.* The cash prizes for the six top finalists have also been raised: from $12,000 to $15,000 for first place, $8,000 to $10,000 for second, and so on down the line. As in 1977, 1981, and 1985, the list of recital and orchestral engagements shows dozens of enticing

---

* Contestants—including the top prize winner of a recent major competition—have been known to falsify their birth dates in order to sneak under the age limit.

opportunities. And for the first time, some three dozen European, South American, and Asian orchestras are listed, including—the pièce de résistance—four Soviet orchestras, headed by the Leningrad Philharmonic. Ibbs & Tillett, a major London management, has been retained to oversee all winners' tours outside the United States and Canada. Such unprecedented international exposure reflects Rodzinski's eagerness to promote the Cliburn abroad. It also signifies new eagerness abroad to host and hear the Cliburn winners.

The uniqueness of the Cliburn's management function bears stressing. For two seasons, it books some three hundred recital and orchestral dates for its three top pianists. No other international competition does anything remotely comparable. Some, as Jeffrey Kahane found out in Tel Aviv, award virtually nothing but a check and a medal. It is quite common for competitions to lose track of past winners altogether. At the same time, the Cliburn has only slowly acknowledged that the results of its largess have proved problematic, and has only incompletely acted on that knowledge. No longer, as under Martha Hyder, does the foundation naively imagine that more is necessarily better. Richard Rodzinski emphasizes that "the letters of agreement we sign with presenters are agreements in principle only; they become contracts only once the winners are announced. The presenter retains the option to select the second- or third-prize winner. The main thing is to maintain flexibility, because we may have a winner who can't handle sixty or eighty concerts a year. And what if our winner already has a concert booked on a date we have booked for him in advance? Another thing: this time around, the Carnegie Hall recital is not five months after the competition; it's a *year* later. Similarly, we hope to be able to adjust the schedule so there are concerts outside the limelight, where a new concerto or sonata can be tried out. All this has to be done through very careful consultation." Rodzinski's young artistic administrator, Denise Chupp, is responsible for working out the details. As she is a trained pianist, she, too, understands the logic of prudent management. "Ideally, the gold medalist will play fifty to seventy concerts the first year," she says. "It's what's expected of a major artist these days. If he thinks that's too many, we'll work on reducing it. And I'd like to see the silver and bronze medalists get forty to fifty-five dates a season—though that won't be easy." The gold-medal dates pay $2,500 each; silver and bronze winners get $2,250 per engagement. The Cliburn Foundation does not collect a fee. American Airlines, as the Cliburn's "official carrier," provides free concert travel in the United States for the gold medalist.

Rodzinski and Chupp see further than Martha Hyder could in 1977, yet remain committed to booking dozens of major dates. Rodzinski's guiding assumption is that his judges will pick a winner to win.

The first, pre-preliminary round of the 1989 Van Cliburn competition takes place privately, beginning on February 19. There are 193 pianists, appearing not onstage but on a television screen. A special, four-member jury is impaneled to select thirty-five contestants from this group. The process lasts eight days.

Every big music competition must devise an initial method for whittling down the field. In the United States, more than abroad, applicants are required to submit an audiotape. This promotes a more private, leisurely, and, potentially, fairer winnowing process than "cattle call" competitions like the Chopin, where it may take more than a week to hear 125 contestants play for twenty-five minutes apiece. Yet audiotape screenings are notoriously unreliable, and not merely because applicants sometimes edit or falsify the tape itself. Any batch of taped auditions will reveal a bewildering variety of instruments, acoustical conditions, and crude or sophisticated recording equipment. Although choosing among dozens of absent pianists is tougher than picking from a smaller group one actually sees and hears, "screening" judges are typically less impressive than the full-fledged jurors who pass on the public rounds. When Mordecai Shehori, a forty-one-year-old pianist with refined Romantic instincts and an unusually plush, colorful sound, failed to survive taped auditions for the 1988 Concert Artists Guild competition in New York, the simplistic and contradictory written comments of the preliminary judges (who did not know the age or identity of the applicant) included:

[Judge 1:] Beethoven [*Appassionata*] has temperament but needs rhythmic stability—too many tempo changes. Seems to have potential but not ready for this competition. Wrong notes. Technical passages tend to be messy.
[Judge 2:] Beethoven—Opening a little rushed through. Rest of movement well-planned and well-played (although occasionally pounded). Chopin—Pounding again. . . . Bach—very old-fashioned musically—over-romantic, over pedalled.

Any of the three young, unremarkable finalists in the Concert Artists Guild competition that year might have benefited from lessons from Mordecai Shehori. The Kapell competition was another in which taped auditions resulted in an unusually weak field in 1988 (no first prize was given).

Characteristically, the Cliburn competition has spared no trouble or expense in striving to invent the fairest possible screening method. In early years, the Cliburn asked for no tapes of any kind. In 1977, a landslide of applications necessitated an impromptu "screening panel," which held a limited number of live American auditions in the course of limiting the contestants to 104—an unwieldy number to house and hear. For 1981, Anthony Phillips, as executive director, decided to try something new: videotaped auditions throughout the United States and Europe in pursuit of a smaller, more uniformly selected field. Each applicant was given an hour's studio time during which to record a twenty-minute recital. The tapes were then reviewed by a five-member screening jury, which chose only forty-two candidates. The same procedure was repeated in 1985. For the 1989 competition, over 250 applications were eventually received. Rodzinski and his staff were able to reduce this number to 193 on the grounds of insufficient repertoire and/or experience. The subsequent videotapings—in seventeen cities from Los Angeles to Helsinki to Tokyo—were somewhat different than in 1981 or 1985. Rodzinski sensibly decided to simulate concert conditions: audiences were invited, and each pianist played a fifty-minute recital. Three teams of videographers were deployed, rather than two. Applicants in the Soviet Union and Asia were videotaped for the first time.

Back in Fort Worth, the 193 candidates now appear in procession on a huge video screen, installed in a specially designed room. The judges are Maxim Shostakovich, Joaquin Soriano, and Ralph Votapek from the main jury, plus Minoru Nojima, a prominent Japanese pianist and Cliburn laureate. John Giordano, who will chair the Cliburn jury for the fifth time in a row, is on hand to break possible ties. The stationary video camera watches the players' hands, arms, and faces, imparting a concertlike impression (which cynics suggest helps identify which candidates are the most promotable). Every effort has been made to match conditions from city to city. Only three engineers have been used, all trained by the same producer. Uniform state-of-the-art equipment and uniformly close microphone placements have minimized acoustical differences among the seventeen locations. Also, the pianists are viewed and discussed six at a time, grouped by venue, so that a problematic instrument in Chicago is not directly juxtaposed with a better one in New York, or the opera studio of Budapest's Franz Liszt Academy does not compete directly with the acoustic opulence of the Sala Apollinee in Venice's La Fenice theater. Each candidate has chosen twenty minutes from his forty-five-minute recital; the tapes have already been edited accordingly. Less than half the jury's verdicts are unanimous; Giordano must break ties more than half a dozen times.

In short: the Cliburn has conducted a precompetition competition, arguably more crucial than the public rounds to come. In most cases, less than half an hour of playing is assessed, none of it live. Instruments, acoustics, and audiences vary significantly. It is a worrisome fact that in 1981 and 1985, some of the pianists most highly regarded at this preliminary juncture did not make it to the final round. Among the videotaped 1981 applicants who did not even make it into the competition was the highly regarded but controversial Andrei Nikolsky, who subsequently won the Queen Elisabeth. In less elaborate, less "scientific" competitions, a screening oversight is correctable—as when Lucy Mann prevailed upon her tape jurors for the 1983 Naumburg to change their minds and admit Stephen Hough, who arguably became the Naumburg's most impressive piano winner. The 1989 Van Cliburn screening audition is not without its surprises. Generally, however, both the judges and the foundation staff are pleased with the results. Ralph Votapek says: "The top fifteen or twenty performances I saw renewed my faith in young pianists and made me itch to get back to practicing"; he calls the 1989 field "definitely better" than in 1981, when he first served on the screening jury. According to Joaquin Soriano, the 1989 candidates show that "personalities are becoming more important—they are less afraid to express themselves with more freedom." Minoru Nojima agrees that there are "fewer cookie-cutter types." Richard Rodzinski says, in a March 2 press release: "We are grateful to the jury for their countless hours of profound deliberations. They have carefully and thoroughly selected one of the most outstanding arrays of extraordinary pianists ever brought together for any competition anywhere in the world."

Impressions of a strong array are buttressed by the decision to name forty contestants, not the anticipated thirty-five. Nineteen countries are represented.* The contingent of ten American citizens, including three born in the Soviet Union, is considered small, although many of the foreign contestants have studied in America. The Soviet group of four began as fifteen screened by the Russians

---

* See Appendix A.

themselves in Leningrad, of whom five were selected for videotaping by the Cliburn. The other biggest contingents are from West Germany, also with five contestants, and, surprisingly, the People's Republic of China, with three. Overall, the 1989 field is notably old: more than half the pianists are aged twenty-seven to thirty. It is also notably experienced. There are contestants who have already played with the Cleveland and Philadelphia orchestras, or the London Symphony, or the Leipzig Gewandhaus. There are former first-prize winners of the Geza Anda competition, of the Bachauer, the Busoni, the Clara Haskil, the Kapell, the Marguerite Long, the Montreal, and the Paloma O'Shea, as well as former second-prize winners from Brussels and Leeds.

All this argues that Rodzinski has succeeded in securing an impressive field. It also documents a situation of continued overcrowding. For the most part, the Cliburn's 1989 contestants are not fledgling artists still in school or recently graduated. Rather, they are toughened young professionals, with a slippery toehold on the career ladder they hope will rescue them from a vast talent pool in which many have sunk and many others barely remain afloat.

Backing up Richard Rodzinski are hundreds who work without pay behind the scenes. This is the Cliburn Foundation's grass-roots support group, its corps of women volunteers. In New York City, the Cliburn is known for its winners. In Fort Worth, this volunteer army ensures that the foundation's local impact transcends its quadrennial piano competition. Like the Cliburn Concerts, which maintain the foundation's visibility during noncompetition years, the volunteer corps makes a virtue of necessity: its women—of all ages, and representing a range of the city's white neighborhoods— promote community feeling and an unparalleled popular piano fervor. The army's spirit pervades even the Cliburn Foundation's headquarters, where the professional staff of twelve is, excepting Rodzinski, entirely female.

For the first competition, in 1962, there was no professional staff, no office space to speak of; volunteers addressed and stamped brochures at Boswell Dairies. Today's Cliburn Foundation has a full-time, paid Volunteer Coordinator: Mary Connor. A youthful mother of two, she first served the Cliburn as an usher a dozen years ago. Her six hundred volunteers, she says, "are the backbone of the competition—they do all the things the staff doesn't have time to do and probably wouldn't want to do."

The Cliburn's extramusical trademarks include lavish hospitality and administrative efficiency; its volunteers contribute vitally to both, and much else besides. Four months before the 1989 competition, forty of them address and stuff color-coded invitations to fifty luncheons, dinners, and receptions. Four thousand name tags must be lettered by volunteer calligraphers. Volunteers will tend the Cliburn Café and the Cliburn Boutique, with its tote bags, watches, mugs, and T-shirts. They will obtain flowers and fruit for Ed Landreth Auditorium and make sure the Worthington Hotel's Hospitality Suite is well stocked with beverages. They will be interpreters and translators, page turners, furniture movers, chauffeurs. They will lend their pianos and cars. And, as host families, they will house and feed, mother and father the contestants.

Mary Connor estimates that her volunteers work 93,600 hours—the equivalent of a one-million-dollar contribution. The foundation's four-year budget (1985–89) is $4.8 million beyond that. This is more than six times the budget for 1973–77—the last pre-Hyderization cycle. It also represents a modest increase over 1981–85, mainly reflecting increased costs for radio and television production: the PBS documentary and thirteen-week radio series will absorb $1 million. With ticket revenues of $230,000, the private, nonprofit Cliburn Foundation is 75 percent dependent on unearned income. Seventy percent of its income is raised locally. The biggest donors are the Tandy and Mobil corporations, which underwrite the entire million-dollar media expenditure, and Robert and Ann Bass, who underwrite the Tokyo String Quartet, among other things. The Amon Carter Foundation pays for Stanislaw Skrowaczewski, the Sid Richardson Foundation for the Fort Worth Symphony. Individual donations make up 14 percent of the budget. After the Robert Basses, Van Cliburn is the biggest individual donor. Public sources—the National Endowment for the Arts, the Fort Worth Arts Council, the Texas Commission on the Arts, and the City of Fort Worth—contribute only 6 percent.

Both the fund-raising effort and the volunteer army are overseen by the foundation's chairman, who works without pay. This is Susan Tilley, whose husband is chairman of the Fort Worth Chamber of Commerce and a longtime Cliburn board member. Mrs. Tilley first ushered for the Cliburn competition in 1966. Her friend Martha Hyder convinced her to be housing chairman in 1977. Tall, stylish, and slender, she was, I am told, Miss Dallas and graduated Phi Beta Kappa from Southern Methodist University. Mrs. Tilley, who is modest, tells me: "I've been around music all my life. My mother was a great fan of music. We always heard the Metropolitan Opera broadcasts on Saturday afternoons. She'd take us to the symphony, and to the Met when it came to Dallas. In those days, there was a good music program in the public schools. And I studied piano from the time I was in kindergarten until I graduated from high school. In fact, one of my teachers was Rildia Bee's sister's husband's sister." Mrs. Tilley initially "hated" asking people for money but has learned to "nudge and push" politely and effectively. "They say fund-raising is 99 percent cultivation. People give to people they know." She comes into the office five days a week, five to six hours a day. She also spends many hours with Van Cliburn as friend, adviser, and ex officio manager. The dazzle of the Cliburn competition still makes her eyes dance. Though most previous chairmen have presided over a single cycle, she is expected to continue through 1993. So is Richard Rodzinski. The foundation has needed this kind of continuity.

Mrs. Tilley is a much less dramatic chairman than Martha Hyder was. But she is a more comfortable public figure than her predecessor, Phyllis Tilley (their husbands are first cousins), whose behind-the-scenes fund-raising was appreciated by those in the know. "When Martha was chairman we had a three-person office," Susan Tilley comments. "And during the competition we'd hire part-time help. We didn't have as much money and couldn't afford a large staff—and so Martha did everything. My philosophy is, if you're going to have a professional staff don't be a dilettante, looking over their shoulders. I think I give more leeway to the professional staff than Martha or Phyllis did. You do find yourself being nosy when you shouldn't be. And Richard and I confer a lot. But I try to stay out."

The energetic application of volunteerism and local money can lead in perilous directions. Volunteers and donors must be paid off. The Cliburn competition's premium patrons—they pay up to $450 apiece—are 450 "Golden Circle" subscribers, who get to chat with distinguished visitors, and with Cliburn himself, at elaborate dinners and receptions. The volunteers, too, are entitled to rub shoulders. This can encumber socially disinclined jurors and contestants. Some participants in the 1977, 1981, and 1985 competitions found Martha Hyder or Phyllis Tilley intrusive or gauche. Susan Tilley operates with a lighter touch. "I think there's been too much entertainment at past competitions," she says of the parties. "Pianists have been 'strongly encouraged' to attend. The social side—that's not what they're here for. I think that should be done somewhat differently."

* * *

Benefit events account for about $340,000 per quadrennial cycle. For 1985–89, there are six: three Neiman Marcus "Catalogue Capers," a two-day "Festival of Music" at Van Cliburn's home, a Neiman Marcus Silver Anniversary party, and—the grand finale— the "Goldfingers" Gala Benefit concert and reception, so named because four Cliburn gold medalists take part. The foundation had invited all seven of its past winners to participate. Those who accepted were Steven De Groote and José Feghali—the two medalists with homes in Fort Worth; the 1962 winner, Ralph Votapek; and Vladimir Viardo, who will be making his third Fort Worth appearance since *glasnost* freed him to return to the United States in August 1988. With Martha Hyder's help, he has obtained a teaching position at the University of North Texas in Denton—thirty-five miles northeast of Fort Worth. He has also taken an apartment in New York and played at the Hollywood Bowl and Carnegie Hall.

I myself arrive in Fort Worth April 28—one day before Goldfingers, about three weeks ahead of the 1989 contestants. The piano fever is tangible. I read and hear about the "Western hemisphere's premier piano competition," "the world's most prestigious," "America's most important"—the sixteen days that make Fort Worth "the center of the music world," advertised as a mecca for leading musicians and "international celebrities." Peter Rosen is already at work on his television show. In the *New York Times*, Bernard Holland has begun his series "Playing to Win—a periodic view of the Cliburn competition." In fact, the Eighth International Van Cliburn Piano Competition figures to be one of the most extensively reported classical music events in memory. Journalists are expected from New York, Chicago, London, and Tokyo. The Voice of America is coming. So are *Vogue* magazine, *Town and Country*, the three national television networks, and CNN.

Goldfingers has the makings of an appropriately gaudy prelude. The four stars have never appeared together before; a certain amount of ego jostling has already complicated who will play what with whom. The foundation has in mind an evening of diverting shorter works—some for the unwieldy combination of four pianos, some for two pianos, some for piano duet. The tickets cost from thirty to two hundred dollars.

Goldfingers proves neither thrilling nor trivial. The program lists two-piano works by Ravel and Lutoslawski, and by Copland in transcription. The four-piano pieces are by Milhaud and, in transcription, Moszkowski, Handel, and Sousa. The four-hand pieces are by Schubert and Mendelssohn, plus some delicious Russian kitsch curated by Viardo. The performances are smart. The audience likes best Lutoslawski's Variations on a Theme by Paganini—and so do I. I sense no prejudgment of this unfamiliar work by a contemporary composer. For that matter, each piece is received on its own terms. The applause is never excessive, never insufficient. Compared to most New York concerts, Goldfingers is not pretentious or routinized but spontaneous. The hall itself—Texas Christian University's 1,235-seat Ed Landreth Auditorium, which is also used for all but the final-round concerts of the Cliburn competition—is surprisingly unassuming. With its plain walls and gray metal seats covered in red velour, it looks more like a high school auditorium than an impending celebrity mecca. And the acoustics are excellent.

After the hall has cleared, the four pianists are photographed on stage, arm-in-arm, beaming smiles. Then they attend a lavish reception at the City Club downtown. Half the audience seems already there, along with Van Cliburn and Rildia Bee and other local notables. Four days later, Cliburn holds a press conference to say he will perform in the Soviet Union. Three weeks after that, the Cliburn Foundation announces that, for the first time, the entire competition is sold out. But on May 22 a phone call from South Africa casts a sudden, incomprehensible shadow: Steven De Groote is dead. According to his Johannesburg physician, he has succumbed to "multiple organ problems," "tuberculosis of the liver, pneumonia and kidney failure." Though he had recently canceled some concerts owing to ill health, he was expected back in Fort Worth to give a master class May 26, the day before the competition would begin.

My impressions of Steven refocus in a rush. He mistrusted quick congeniality; most who met him casually found him cold. Fellow pianists knew him as an unusually rounded musician, a quick learner, a fabulous sight reader. Music businessmen who called him "faceless" and demeaned him as "another" Cliburn winner were half correct: with his probity and caustic intelligence, he wore no fancy faces. In cheerful Fort Worth, his actual face was complicatedly frank; he made no secret of disliking Martha Hyder; he could not endure the competition's hyperbolic self-image.

Some solo artists make their major contribution by the age of forty—after that, their novelty value wears off and there is little else to take its place. De Groote's novelty ceased when he was no longer the Van Cliburn winner. His major contribution only began, I think, as his career acquired a second wind in the year or so before his death. He had made a name in West Germany. He was to play in London with the Academy of St. Martin-in-the-Fields, with the Scottish National Orchestra in Glasgow, with the Guarneri String Quartet, with the Dallas Symphony. Two De Groote recordings— of the Bartók Quintet, with the Chilingirian Quartet, and of the Reger Concerto, with Michael Gielen—are scheduled for commercial release. He himself always insisted that he was never cut out to be the Van Cliburn gold medalist—which was true. But twelve years after winning the Cliburn, he was ready, at age thirty-six, to benefit from the gold medal itinerary, or something like it.

The *Fort Worth Star-Telegram* reports:

Martha Hyder, chairman of the Cliburn competition the year De Groote won, recalled him fondly.

"Just think of all that went into making a Steven De Groote, all those years of practicing and concertizing, and it's just gone," Hyder said by telephone from her vacation house in San Miguel Allende, Mexico.

Hyder, who decorated De Groote's studio at TCU, said that De Groote had always opened the studio for use by visiting guest artists and for use as a reception area after concerts. The studio will be used as a warmup room for contestants at this year's Cliburn. . . .

First
Preliminary
Round

THE EIGHTH VAN CLIBURN INTERNATIONAL PIANO COMPETITION BE-
gins at 9:30 in the morning on Saturday, May 27, and the audience
arrives early, because seating is unreserved. The stage of Ed
Landreth Auditorium is decorated with the flags of nineteen countries. More than half a dozen film and television cameras are ready
to roll. The jurors take their seats at three long tables covered in
black cloth; each member's place is marked by a decanter of water
and a miniature flag. Also on the tables are scores for all the music
to be heard today—a typical Cliburn touch, atypical of other piano
competitions. "This is the first round of what is going to be the
focus of the classical-music world," says Steve Cummins of radio
station WRR-FM, which will broadcast competition highlights
(Texas Christian's KTCU broadcasts the entire competition live).
Jury chairman John Giordano adds a word of welcome, then introduces "one of the most distinguished juries that has ever been
put together for a competition." Audience members crane their
necks and applaud as each of the jurors is named.

Two days before, the thirty-eight contestants (two of the original
forty having withdrawn) picked lots to determine the order in
which they would perform. Traditionally, "1" is considered the
worst slot, especially when, as at the Cliburn, it falls early in the

morning. But the Cliburn elaborately compensates; it holds two preliminary rounds, so that contestants who begin poorly have an opportunity to do better. And phase two of the preliminaries, in which the order of the players is retained, begins at an evening hour.

David Buechner of the United States has drawn the unlucky number 1, and this is ironic. Buechner's controversial early elimination in 1985 is remembered; the *Star-Telegram* goes so far as to call it "the seventh Cliburn's closest brush with scandal." For that matter, Buechner, at twenty-nine, is a competition veteran so easily agitated, disconcertingly outspoken, and vividly scarred—his rough, ruddy face is lined with worries—that he inherently carries controversy in his wake. At Juilliard, where he received six major awards and scholarships, he was twice hospitalized for bleeding ulcers. He is convinced that the 1981 Beethoven competition in Vienna, in which he placed fourth, was rigged. At the 1986 Tchaikovsky competition, his rehearsal time for the Tchaikovsky concerto was limited to five minutes; a television camera caught him despairing: "I'm withdrawing. . . . I just can't play tonight." He finished fifth. His failure to place in Leeds in 1987, he believes, helped break up his marriage—"I was very upset about my career after that; I withdrew into myself." He has said that the Cliburn will be his last competition and that if he does not do well he may move to Japan, where audiences are better, and interest in the piano keener, than in the United States. For all that, he has had professional management for five years and has played with more major American orchestras than any other 1989 Cliburn contestant. Surveying his long track record—which also includes ninth place at the 1983 Queen Elisabeth, first place at the 1984 Bachauer, fifth at Leeds in 1984, and fourth at Sydney last year— the *Star-Telegram* rates him 3 to 2 to make the finals, 6 to 1 to win the gold: "a perennial near-winner for whom this year's Cliburn is probably make-or-break. He almost always finishes in the money."

Catholicity of repertoire is a Cliburn trademark; its winners are expected to excel in Baroque, Classical, Romantic, and modern styles; in sonatas, chamber music, and concertos. Repertoire for the first preliminary round is the most restrictive in the competition. Candidates must select (1) a major work of Johann Sebastian Bach, (2) a Haydn or early Beethoven sonata, (3) a major work of Chopin, (4) a Chopin étude, and (5) an étude by Bartók, Debussy, Liszt, Rachmaninoff, Scriabin, or Stravinsky, or the Prokofiev or Schumann Toccata.* This choice is more liberal than the 1969 list, a monument to arrogance erected by jury chairman Ezra Rachlin (then conductor of the Fort Worth Symphony); every entrant had to prepare Bach's *Italian* Concerto, a Scarlatti sonata, one of two Mozart sonatas, one of five Beethoven sonatas, one of four Chopin études, a Brahms intermezzo, Schumann's *Symphonic Études*, and two of Liszt's *Transcendental* Études or his B minor Sonata.† At the opposite extreme, some competitions—the Kapell and Naumburg are prominent examples—invite contestants to play whatever solo repertoire they feel represents them best.

David Buechner's choice for the first preliminary round consists of Bach's B-flat Partita, Haydn's Sonata in E-flat, Hob. XVI:52, Chopin's Third Ballade and A-flat major Étude from Op. 10, and a seldom heard étude by Bartók. John Giordano has chosen approximately twenty-five minutes of music from Buechner's list; Buechner may play these selections in any order. And so the first music of the 1989 Cliburn turns out to be the most violently dissonant of the entire competition: Bartók's Étude, Op. 18, No. 1, a motoric study in angry ninths, in a suitably blistering performance. The opening and closing movements of the Bach partita—an utter non sequitur—come next. These are harpsichord or clavichord cameos, not intended for modern piano. Buechner opts for unabashedly pianistic readings, the Prelude mellifluously smooth and full-toned, the Gigue, forty-eight measures of uninterrupted triplets aflutter with light and shade. The Haydn sonata, even more than the Bach, is problematic on the modern piano: the final seven-note chord of the opening *Allegro* sounds thick and ill-defined. But Buechner's Steinway responds avidly to the Romantic surge and lavish textures of the Chopin ballade.

If the Cliburn craves an audience, it rewards its audience with respect. At other competitions, contestants are interrupted midway through an étude or a sonata movement, and the audience is asked to hold its applause. At the Cliburn, interruptions are avoided, applause is encouraged. Buechner's audience is unusually quiet,

---

* See Appendix A.

† For subsequent rounds, 1969 contestants had to prepare a piano trio; one of four works by Albéniz, Ravel, and Debussy; the Bartók or Prokofiev Sixth Sonata; the Chopin B minor or one of two Schubert sonatas; a work by a composer of his or her own country; the Beethoven Fourth Concerto, the Brahms D minor, the Rachmaninoff First or Rhapsody on a Theme by Paganini; and the Prokofiev Second, Bartók Second, or Barber Concerto. Ostensibly intended to secure a high-caliber field, Rachlin's requirements secured a tiny field from which most high-caliber players were excluded.

eager to appreciate every piece. Only the jury is undemonstrative. Did Buechner blunder playing Bartók for György Sándor? Will he be penalized for shading the Bach gigue with discreet applications of pedal (an accessory unknown in Bach's day) and for his interpolated crescendos and diminuendos (unavailable on the harpsichord)? Should he have used less sound in the Haydn (risking affectation) or rolled its final chord to mitigate the Steinway's thunderous bass (a Romantic innovation, contradicting the light-framed, light-toned fortepianos of Haydn's day)? Buechner's fate is left hanging.

While David Buechner bows, the applauding audience is suddenly illuminated for filming by Peter Rosen's cameras. The next performance onstage, already begun, is for pianos, not pianists. Two white-gloved handlers, dressed in white shirts and black pants, wheel Buechner's Steinway to the rear. Two more handlers, identically clad, push a fresh piano to the front, open its lid and keyboard, and stroke its white keys and black veneer with their cloths. This brisk procedure is so doting, so ritualized, as to evoke the deferential manipulation of Japanese Bunraku puppets by their cloaked human masters.

In all, the Cliburn offers eight proud instruments to choose from—probably a new international record. Two belong to the Cliburn Foundation itself: an American Steinway selected by Van Cliburn and subsequently rebuilt in Fort Worth, and a German "Hamburg Steinway," chosen by Cliburn in London. The remaining six are a third Steinway, from the firm's New York headquarters, plus a Baldwin, a Bechstein, a Bösendorfer, a Kawai, and a Yamaha. In short: the pianos hold a competition of their own. "For the pianists, a competition is the fastest way to become famous," says Yamaha's Yoji Suzuki. "For the manufacturer, if chosen by a majority of competitors, it's proof of quality."

According to Richard Rodzinski, piano manufacturers "pushed about twenty instruments," all free of charge, on the 1989 Cliburn competition. He limited the field to eight because that is how many fit on the Landreth Auditorium stage for the contestants to test and compare. In Warsaw and Moscow, pianists get a few minutes to choose from a more limited selection, and host-country entrants are sometimes given extra time to make up their minds. In Fort Worth, each of the thirty-eight pianists was allotted a full hour to pick a piano—a process taking up to seven days. Some contestants were cool, almost casual about it. For others, bobbing from one keyboard to another, sixty minutes did not seem time enough. When it was his turn, David Buechner asked that the auditorium's doors be locked and demanded that the photographers and television crews depart.

If some pianists undoubtedly fetishize their favorite pianos, the underlying pathology is understandable. Unless they are fabulously wealthy, pianists cannot travel with their own instruments, as vocalists and violinists do. And yet a pianist is as intimately bound to his Steinway as a fiddler is to his Stradivarius. Crucial differences separate even fine pianos of the same make. Some players prefer "light" to "heavy" action—that is, less resistance to the finger by the key. For some, an inherently "colorful" sound counts for less than a neutral sonority susceptible to coloristic manipulation. Instruments vary greatly in volume (what suits a Brahms concerto may pulverize a Mozart sonata), in registration (is the bass too dark? the treble too bright?), in duration (a "long" sound that sings versus a more rapid decay, promoting transparency). And there is the critical issue of upkeep: not mere tuning but expert "regulation" and replacement of parts. For an instrument subjected to repeated concert use, inherent quality may matter less than the quality of its long-term maintenance.

The pummeling action of thirty-eight young virtuosos at a sixteen-day piano competition inflicts special wear and tear. Six piano-makers have sent their own technicians to this year's Cliburn to ensure that their instrument makes the best possible impression; Kawai has sent *five*, including three from Japan. The foundation's two Steinways are serviced by Priscilla and Joel Rappaport—the official Cliburn technicians since 1980 and among the few credentialed master piano builders (*Klavierbaumeister*) in the United States. Both worked in Europe, at the factories of Bechstein and Bösendorfer, and trained with Steinway personnel from New York, London, and Hamburg. Their duties at the competition run the gamut from emergency repairs, completed onstage in a matter of minutes, to all-night sessions with tired instruments. At the highest level, the Rappaports' work is arcane and controversial: one man's piano guru is another's charlatan.

Steven De Groote was a confirmed admirer of the Rappaports. "They are very expensive and very good," he remarked four weeks before the competition began. "So it would be very nice if the manufacturers had shut up and stayed at home. Instead, Richard was put under intense pressure from companies in New York who insisted on sending their instruments to Fort Worth. So now we have our two Steinways plus one from New York and a Baldwin and a Bösendorfer and a Yamaha and God knows what else. That's an example of rampant commercialism. I think it's absurd to ask a contestant to try out eight pianos. A better number would be five. And they should be the best pianos a couple of pianists can find. Not what a bunch of businessmen can impose."

At the piano tryouts last week, some European contestants found that none of the offered instruments had actions as heavy as what they were accustomed to. The vast majority of the competitors—twenty-nine—chose one of the Cliburn Foundation's two Steinways, maintained by the Rappaports. Six chose the Steinway from New York. Three chose the Yamaha, one, after long consideration, the Baldwin. The Bechstein, Bösendorfer, and Kawai went begging.

After David Buechner comes Jürgen Jakob of West Germany, playing Bach, Beethoven, and Chopin; then Wolfgang Manz, also of West Germany, with his Bach, Beethoven, Chopin, and Liszt; then China's Lin Hai, with Bach, Beethoven, Chopin, and Stravinsky; then Victor Sangiorgio of Australia, and Bach, Beethoven, Chopin, and Rachmaninoff . . . a parade of fifteen pianists lasting until 7:15 in the evening, with a single break for lunch. The next day, a Sunday, ten pianists play from two-thirty to ten forty-five. The first round of the preliminaries concludes Monday, 9:30 to 6:30, with thirteen pianists. Impressions, sharp at first, blur and refocus intermittently. The mind wanders. The ears tire.

The repertoire—its numbing redundancy—is itself fatiguing. Ten pianists have listed Bach's *Chromatic* Fantasy and Fugue; John Giordano, who decides which offered pieces will be heard, has instructed each of the ten to detach and perform the seven-minute Fantasy—resulting in five versions on Saturday alone. Seven pianists play a movement from Bach's *Italian* Concerto. Giordano feels the First and Fourth Chopin Ballades admirably showcase the performer. The competitors agree: nine of them have offered the one, seven the other, and Giordano has in every case said yes. What is more remarkable: Liszt's Eighth *Transcendental* Étude, *Wilde Jagd*, is heard four times the first day—and it is by no means as subtle a showpiece as either of the Chopin works. To the consternation of certain jurors—who grow as inured to the hoofbeats of *Wilde Jagd* as I do—Giordano ignores the exceptional Twelfth *Transcendental* Étude, *Chasse-neige*, which three contestants have listed. And why has he asked Károly Mocsári, who offers Beethoven's *Moonlight*

Sonata, to perform only the first movement, which—in addition to being more ruinously familiar—consumes more time while revealing less than either movement two or movement three?

One certain outcome of these programming decisions, propagating the mainstream of a mainstream, is a fixation on performance; the music itself, ceaselessly recirculated, quickly tires and recedes from consciousness. The fixation is variously frustrating and engrossing. My peak frustration comes in certain stiff, careful performances of Bach—a composer most of these young players all too obviously would prefer not to play, and with good reason. It is not only that no one can tell them how Bach should sound on a modern piano (though some of the judges may try*). More crucially, Bach's music is based on notions of musicianship they do not embrace. Baroque keyboardists were expected to be able to improvise, to transpose at sight, to "realize" figured basses, with their skeletal instructions toward melody, harmony, and counterpoint. This eighteenth-century ideal, enshrined in Carl Philipp Emanuel Bach's once famous 1762 *Essay on the True Art of Playing Keyboard Instruments*, infiltrated the understanding of generations of pianist-composers. Mozart, accustomed to improvising ornaments and cadenzas, would sometimes play a new concerto with only a sketch of the piano part before him; Liszt, with his lightning fingers and equally nimble musical intelligence, was said never to play the same piece twice without extemporaneously embroidering it; Bartók altered rhythm and notes in performances of his own piano works; Ernö von Dohnányi improvised Mozart concerto cadenzas well into the twentieth century. Even for Bach, his *Chromatic* Fantasy—the one performed by more than a quarter of the Cliburn contestants—is a work unusually imbued with the spirit of improvisation. Some dozen measures of chords in half notes, marked *arpeggio*, invite the player to manipulate rhythm, tempo, and registration at will. Elsewhere, there are florid recitatives and long, unaccompanied runs whose spur-of-the-moment digressions defy a disciplining pulse. Moreover, to transfer this Baroque keyboard music to the modern piano doubles one's opportunities to illuminate its aura of spontaneous creativity. The potential result is a kind of Bach playing, almost unknown today, documented on a 1935 recording by Edwin Fischer. Fischer hauntingly shades the arpeggios to suggest light

---

* A case in point: the 1975 Leeds competition, at which jury member Rosalyn Tureck, a specialist in Bach, disapproved of the Bach style of András Schiff. Schiff (who tied for third) has since become a celebrated Bach exponent. He never won an international competition.

refracted through stained glass. Adding octaves, transposing to- ward the bass, pedaling through the bar line, he conjures the Gothic thunder of a great organ. His "speaking" recitatives are as articulate as any Bach Evangelist. The entire work is consumed by a Faustian creative fever—it really does sound composed on the spot. Fischer's recording is famous, but it seems doubtful many of the Cliburn contestants have heard it. Most are performance specialists of a different order. Their teachers consider today's young virtuosos notoriously less literate, musically, than their predecessors of even five or ten years ago.

Haydn also fares poorly at Fort Worth. Here is a composer who, for all his conditioned popularity, holds limited popular appeal. He is not a sufferer, a lover, a confessor, a combatant—all the personae we expect our heroic musical executants to embody. His knowing wit and repartee privately gratify the attuned interpreter. Inter- preters otherwise attuned—to a mass public, for instance—smooth away his subversive detail, transforming him into a cut-rate Mozart. This is the Cliburn norm.

A problematic exception is the Haydn of Eduardus Halim, whose Bach is similarly unusual. He is a twenty-seven-year-old Indone- sian who is already well known in New York, where he quietly studies with his hero, Vladimir Horowitz. Like an earlier Horowitz protégé, Byron Janis, Halim, with his sunken cheeks and thin, angular frame, his bow ties and ear-to-ear smiles, even *looks* like Horowitz. At the piano, his hunched shoulders and splayed, active fingers are, again, Horowitz trademarks. And like Horowitz, he strives for a maximum freedom of gesture, maximum color, maxi- mum sound. At the Cliburn, his Bach and Haydn are the most determinedly pianistic. In the Ouverture to Bach's D major Partita, he underlines the contrast between the sonorous, dotted-rhythm introduction and the mobile, contrapuntal *Allegro*, in which his suddenly racing, feathery articulation is a coup. His Haydn sonata is Hob. XVI:46 in A-flat, probably chosen for its dreamy *Adagio*— two of the most Romantically chromatic pages Haydn wrote. But John Giordano has chosen the opening *Allegro*, a much less inter- esting movement, which Halim enlivens with stabbing accents, streaks of pedal, *détaché* pointillism, and the like. The trouble with his Bach is that even if one accepts Halim's approach aesthetically, the D major Partita is not a fit *pianistic* vehicle for Romantic exec- utants. What Halim should be playing—what he is scheduled to play in the semifinal round, where Bach is not compulsory; what Horowitz himself plays instead of Bach—is Bach as transcribed for the Romantic piano—its seven octaves, its three pedals—by Ferruccio Busoni.* The trouble with Halim's Haydn is that its delights and surprises, engineered by Halim, are inferior to Haydn's own, which are obscured. Only when he comes to Liszt's *La leggierezza* is Halim gloriously in his element: in a prismatic performance, he *sprays* the chains of *pianissimo* sixteenth notes up and down the keyboard. It is nothing less than what Liszt asks for.

Other pianists—Buechner, for one—are less uncomfortable in Bach and Haydn, but the homecoming to Liszt—or Chopin, or Rachmaninoff—is characteristic. The Cliburn pianists are happiest when they can take off their gloves and play as loudly or softly as they please; when their fingers are kept busiest; when their nine-foot instrument itself is most fully utilized by the music at hand. After an hour or two, one takes for granted the marvelous speed and accuracy with which they dispatch the post-Beethoven war-horses. At the same time, few of them possess Halim's (not to mention Horowitz's) range of color and nuance. And even in Romantic repertoire, where they are freest, the projection of feeling is imprecise and predictable, volatile yet unfocused. Though the ballades and études catch fire, they sometimes seem as incomplete, stylistically, as the Bach and Haydn extracts.

Fortunately, finally, there are a handful of pianists here who transcend these generalizations—whose playing makes a gamut of music come alive. At first, they materialize singly from the pack. After three days, they add up. I count perhaps five such artists; the more the field blends in its uniformities of power and polish, the more they stand apart. One cannot say they shed new light on old repertoire; the competitive context—its fixation on performance—discourages purely musical intake. Rather, they redeem the performance fixation. They impress in Bach and Haydn. They make the Romantic war-horses matter. They command respect, admiration, amazement.

According to conventional wisdom, national schools of performance have disappeared in today's cosmopolitan concert mart, with its all-purpose literature and interchangeable celebrity instrumentalists and conductors. And yet, at Fort Worth, national schools sort out the international field, and distinguish, especially, the contrasting identities of those pianists who impress most deeply—as well as two incomplete talents that cannot be ignored. First, and

---

* After the competition, I learned that Halim's preferred version of the D major Partita is in fact the Busoni Edition, in which Busoni's protégé Egon Petri suggests octave doublings and fuller chording and registration. It is understandable—and even appropriate—that Halim experienced the Cliburn's Bach requirement as demeaning.

most conspicuous, are the Russians, two of whom, both students at the Moscow Conservatory, are instant candidates for the gold medal. Alexei Sultanov is a veritable wild child from Tashkent, in the shadow of the Himalayas. Small (five feet three) and compact under a shaggy mop of hair, he looks even younger than his nineteen years. In his white turtleneck, black jacket, white socks, and black shoes, he is magnetic, hot-tempered, a minidynamo. Even compared to thirty-seven other world-class competitors, all older than himself, he is the possessor—or possessed by?—tireless, piston-action digits. His musical intensity is of the relentless, all-purpose variety. Bach and Haydn simmer uncomfortably atop it. Chopin and Rachmaninoff, hammered and pounded into shape, absorb it bravely. The other Russian, twenty-one-year-old Alexander Shtarkman, is a finished artist, as civilized as Sultanov is savage. If Sultanov evokes the legacy of Anton Rubinstein, the quintessential "force of nature," Shtarkman evokes Sviatoslav Richter—to many, the outstanding Russian pianist of recent decades. His lean, penetrating sound is Richter's sound; his musical intelligence is sophisticated, incisive. Onstage, impassive and contained, he seems twice his age. His Bach—a toccata excerpt—is the most ruminative of any contestant's; the weighted hesitations imply introspective depths; the ample rubatos convey the illusion of maximum creative freedom. His Haydn is alert to the music's own quirks. He surveys Chopin and Liszt majestically, from a height. The pivotal stresses are keenly plotted. The virtuosity is inconspicuous but complete. If, like Richter, he is not a warm pianist, his interpretive sovereignty is precocious, precise, unaccountable.

None of the competition's four West Germans is on Shtarkman's level, but as a group they are strong, with a tendency toward stiffness. Their playing is serious, clear, concentrated, respectful. They eschew display. The best of them, twenty-eight-year-old Wolfgang Manz, was second at Leeds and Brussels eight and six years ago. Of the Americans, a more variable group, my favorite is Kevin Kenner, twenty-six, who has studied with Leon Fleisher since 1982. Kenner is a Gary Cooper type—tall, handsome, patient, wholesome ("Van!" exclaimed Ann Murphy of the Cliburn office when she first set eyes on him). Kenner's playing is spaciously paced and planned. His ringing *fortissimos* shake the piano but are never hard (like the equally tall Garrick Ohlsson, he capitalizes on the leverage of his long arms to apply natural body weight; he never forces the tone). His Haydn is genial, relaxed, anecdotal. The long line of his Chopin—the F minor Ballade—invites both inwardness and cumulative thunder.

French pianists, as a school, crave clarity and elegance. Traditionally, their technical schooling is grounded in *jeu perlé*—perfect, pearly evenness of articulation, achieved with a steady hand and wrist. Their concomitant disavowal of arm and shoulder weight is controversial: compared to many deep-toned Russians and Germans, the French produce a brittle, shallow piano sound. And their aversion to Teutonic subjectivity can make them seem impersonal. In America, French pianists—such as the late Robert Casadesus, or today's Michel Beroff and Jean-Philippe Collard—are an acquired taste. The 1989 Cliburn fields only a single Frenchman, but he is exceptional. Jean-Efflam Bavouzet, twenty-eight, is small and trim. His porcelain complexion and jet-black hair, his restlessness and charm, produce a striking resemblance to the actor Jean-Pierre Léaud. Bavouzet's reading of the Sinfonia from Bach's C minor Partita is stylishly light, buoyant, and rhythmic—rather like the pop version once recorded by the Swingle Singers. His Beethoven and Chopin will doubtless sound objectionably hard-toned to some on the jury, but few of the nineteen preliminary-round Chopin ballade performances capture the epic (and therefore impersonal) dramaturgy of these works as convincingly as Bavouzet's F major Ballade does in the whispered stillness of its close. His Schumann Toccata is spectacularly taut and clean.

Over the past decade, the percentage of American contestants in the Cliburn has dropped from 46 to 27. The percentage of Asians has more than mounted accordingly. They are the new wave, arising from countries where the canonized concert repertoire is as fresh today as it has grown stale in the West. They flock to American music schools and conservatories. At Curtis, where seventeen of twenty-one piano majors are non-Western, Gary Graffman observes a work ethic reminding him of his own Jewish family, with its roots in Eastern European poverty. "You see the same kind of drive you do in the Korean grocers all over New York City. Three generations work long hours in those stores so that the ten-year-old of the family can do something better. The pressure on the young is tremendous. When the Asian kids at Curtis get an A-minus they're terrified of how to explain it to their parents. A silver medal at a competition is considered a loss. I have to tell these students that there is more to life than practicing twelve hours a day." How successfully do they assimilate Bach, Beethoven, and Brahms? My own, tentative impression is that Eastern pianists are mainly of two types: emulators of scant sustained personal identity, and more complex assimilators, whose outsider status catalyzes an unforced originality. At Fort Worth, I find the eight Asian-born pianists a

relatively bland group. Eduardus Halim—the Horowitz protégé—
is an exception. The Asian who excites the most comment is South
Korea's Ju Hee Suh, who at twenty-one has already placed second
at Leeds, acquired major management, and performed with the
New York Philharmonic. Some like her best. The piano transforms
her from the most girlish contestant, tiny and shy, into a demon
doll. In Liszt's A minor *Paganini* Étude, her hands and arms are
literally a blur; like Alexei Sultanov, she displays—overdisplays—a
natural keyboard mechanism of awesome rapidity. Bernard Holland of the *New York Times* asked her why she had entered, and
reported: "She smiled quietly and with her small, sweet voice answered, 'I want more.' " Both Holland and I find the most remarkable of the Asians to be Tian Ying, a twenty-year-old Chinese who
studies at Boston's New England Conservatory. Every measure of
his playing is articulate; every rubato, every nuance, tells. He is a
refined colorist, with an impeccable ear. And he is possessed by an
eerie poise that at some level becalms everything he touches. His
tinted *Chromatic* Fantasy is the only one to suggest familiarity with
Fischer's recording, or something like it. His Haydn—a composer
deeply understood by his teacher, Russell Sherman—ceaselessly
explores the hovering hesitations and darting resolves of the C
minor Sonata, Hob. XVI:20. His Schumann Toccata is as clean as
Bavouzet's; rather than working up a lather, however, it acquires a
serene gloss. With his deadpan demeanor and smooth temperament, Ying (who, conforming to American practice, puts his sur-
name last) is no crowd pleaser. But he delights and amazes the
connoisseur.

Finally, there is the competition's most idiosyncratic, most un-
classifiable pianist. He is Pedro Burmester, twenty-five, of Portugal. With his long, gaunt face and limp limbs, brooding Latin
features and padded pin-striped suit, he is instantly different. He
bends so far over the keys that his high fingers nearly graze his chin.
With Tian Ying, he has the most sophisticated ear of any competitor, alert to tint and half-tint, nuance and timbre. Unlike Ying, he
also possesses a restless, meddlesome musical intelligence. He is the
one contestant whose Bach—fearlessly ornamented, voiced, and
pedaled; deeply immersed in its own, evocative world of feeling and
sound—suggests an essential affinity. His finespun, suddenly robust Haydn is a model of ironic intelligence. His mandatory étude,
by Scriabin, is irrelevant.

Richard Rodzinski summarizes the crucial attributes of the
Cliburn's sought-for gold medalist with the words "charisma" and
"communication." I favor another word: the pianists I prefer sub-

jugate or intoxicate with a wizardry of knowledge or instinct, technique or interpretation, I find "uncanny." The Van Cliburn of 1958, documented on recordings, is such an inexplicable artist, to whom I eagerly submit. So may be Pedro Burmester, and Alexander Shtarkman, and possibly Tian Ying. I have high hopes, as well, for Jean-Efflam Bavouzet and Kevin Kenner. I am nearly as impressed by several others. The consensus in Fort Worth, following the first preliminary round, is that the 1989 field is the strongest at least since 1977.

Second Preliminary Round

A DINNER BREAK, AND THE MARATHON CONTINUES. DAVID BUECHNER begins the second preliminary round at eight o'clock Sunday night, some ninety minutes after Ju Hee Suh finishes round one. This time, Buechner's program consists of a movement from Mozart's A minor Sonata, Scriabin's Fourth Sonata, and Liszt's *Spanish* Rhapsody. The Scriabin is a two-movement work progressing from reverie to ecstasy. The truest performances yield a white-hot, visionary intensity—the pulsating chords of the final pages throb like strobe lights. Buechner's reading, if not visionary, achieves a convulsive physical excitement that is highly satisfying. In the *Spanish* Rhapsody, he goes for broke. Bernard Holland writes in the *New York Times*: "David Buechner's playing of the Liszt Spanish Rhapsody . . . had an air of desperation, radiating an almost frantic virtuosity that seemed to cry out for acceptance. Mr. Buechner is . . . at the outer age limit for most major competitions." The *Fort Worth Star-Telegram* critic Wayne Gay, who is individually reviewing every one of the competition's 106 performances, likes Buechner more; he calls him "a pianist of magnificent technique and romantic emotion." The *Star-Telegram* also reports, in a separate story: "American David Buechner led off the second phase last night. The workaholic pianist, who has spent little time partying and even less schmoozing with the media, shined for 25 minutes. . . . He departed immediately afterward, refusing comment and raising a leather briefcase to eye level when a photographer tried to snap his flushed face." In Fort Worth, thirty-eight pianists are the local movie stars or celebrity politicians; they attract attention even by rejecting it.

The three-day schedule for this segment of the Cliburn is at least as concentrated as for phase one: 8:00 to 10:45 P.M. Monday night; 9:30 A.M. to 10:45 P.M. Tuesday; 9:30 A.M. to 9:45 P.M. Wednesday. Contestants must offer repertoire in three categories, of which the first is "Mozart: any sonata." Categories two and three are less specific; the former, with a choice of ten composers from Beethoven and Schubert to Tchaikovsky and Rachmaninoff, is roughly "Romantic"; the latter, listing twenty-two composers ranging in style from Albéniz and Ravel to Boulez and Webern, is "twentieth century."* This time it is the jury's job—not John Giordano's—to whittle down the offered repertoire to a twenty-five-minute program: competitors are told the day before which parts of their submitted pieces they will have to play.

The phase-two repertoire is so generalized that the list of composers seems both arbitrary and incomplete; a free choice would make more sense. Mussorgsky, for instance, is not included; and yet Edward MacDowell (whom Van Cliburn favors) is, and so is Karol Szymanowski (new this year; Richard Rodzinski's father knew and performed this interesting Polish composer). Category three lists Samuel Barber and Aaron Copland but not Charles Griffes, whose 1918 Piano Sonata is one of the best by an American.

The contestants' programs are varied if conservative. Of the composers in categories two and three, thirteen—Albéniz, Boulez, Falla, Granados, Grieg, MacDowell, Messiaen, Shostakovich, Stockhausen, Szymanowski, Tchaikovsky, Villa-Lobos, and Webern—find no takers. The most popular pieces are sonatas by Chopin, Mozart, Prokofiev, Scriabin, and Rachmaninoff. Only one pianist, Leonid Kuzmin, picks something by Schubert (whose music otherwise goes unheard for the duration of the competition): the *Wanderer* Fantasy. The jury asks for movement two, which has no ending; and Kuzmin, rather than interpolating the cadential chord the ear demands, leaves it that way—a bizarre and vulgar moment. The Mozart requirement is predictably problematic—his keyboard

* See Appendix A.

music is even harder to make "pianistic" than Bach's or Haydn's. Most of the thirty-eight Mozart sonata movements sound unnaturally subdued (no dynamics past *mezzo forte*); others are more individually falsified.

By the competition's fifth day, the jury is fighting off fatigue. Some jurors, experienced in the techniques of listening stamina, consciously tune out those pianists they already discount; others struggle to hear everything afresh. I exercise the former strategy by sitting out half a dozen performances. In general, however, this second preliminary round is more satisfying than the first. The repertoire is not as redundant. To the degree that the pieces are less imposed, the playing tends to be more interesting. The selections are longer. Perceptions of personal favorites, and of the reputed front-runners, expand and sharpen—and not only as a function of what is heard and seen onstage. The competitors are a pervasive presence: in the auditorium and its lobbies, at parties and meals, in the homes of their hosts and of their hosts' friends. With the famous exception of David Buechner, they are regularly interviewed, taped, photographed, and filmed for newspapers and magazines, radio and television programs. No other piano competition is so open, so public. Friendships are quickly established—between the competitors, between competitors and the Cliburn staff, or the Cliburn volunteers, or the neighbors next door. The host families look forward to visits from members of the press. The dazed pianists, each an overnight star, in many cases accept Fort Worth's blanket curiosity and congeniality as an irresistible comfort. In its daily four-page supplement, the *Star-Telegram* reports that Seung-Un Ha arrived from New York with thirteen pairs of shoes and has already purchased four more; that Andrew Wilde showed up at Landreth Auditorium wearing a checked jacket and checked shirt, black pants, white shoes, and yellow socks; that Alexander Shtarkman, Veronika Reznikovskaya, and Elisso Bolkvadze were poolside guests of Rosalyn and Manny Rosenthal, whose Cliburn house-guest, Ju Hee Suh, was visiting another house to practice.

Before long I feel personally acquainted with some dozen competitors—either vicariously or as the result of formal or informal conversations.

ALEXEI SULTANOV AND ALEXANDER SHTARKMAN

Russia's human cannonball finds more music in the slow movement of Mozart's K. 330 Sonata than I would have thought possible after his assaultive Chopin and Rachmaninoff in round one. But he reads Liszt's *Mephisto* Waltz as if he had never touched a book: its programmatic richness (a wedding feast is interrupted by Mephistopheles' fiddling and Faust's wild dancing) is ruthlessly canceled. That his supercharged performance, superfast and superloud from the start, leaves nowhere to build is a point as obvious as the interpretation itself. Even the piano objects: midway through, a string snaps. Prokofiev's Seventh Sonata furnishes another exercise in barely controlled violence. But if Alexei Sultanov is primitive, he is also elemental: his small body fuses with the instrument. Even his curt, unsmiling bows, his wincing skyward glances, and the sudden pelvic thrusts that shake his mane seem wholly unpracticed.

I pass on interviewing Sultanov; the portrait that emerges from stories in the *Star-Telegram* is perfect. When, as an infant, he received a violin from his parents, he furiously smashed it—and so became a pianist instead. The day before the 1986 Tchaikovsky competition, he broke a finger opening a piano lid, but he competed anyway; he survived the first cut before the jury insisted he quit. He studied kung fu for three years and owns a black belt. He arrived at the Dallas–Fort Worth airport with a Bruce Lee pin on his lapel. "Other than piano, the only passion he's expressed in Texas is for some kung fu videos [he reportedly rents up to three a day], cigarettes, pizza and shashlik—provided it is prepared correctly." One day he discovered two black snakes in the backyard pool of his hostess, Susan Wilcox.

"They were no little, no big," Sultanov said. Nonetheless Wilcox "was very afraid, yes."

But not Sultanov.

"I don't afraid of snakes, no."

Accustomed to handling cobras in his native Tashkent, the pianist reached his hands into the depths and pulled out the serpents.

"I take it to her and she scream, yes, very."

Offstage, Sultanov is a likable-looking fellow, with his compacted energy and unpretentiously earnest, boyish face. Many in the audience adore him. The pianists I talk to react with horror or admiration; there is no middle ground. Before the competition, the *Star-Telegram* rated him the "pre-competition favorite," if there was one. It is assumed that he will make the finals.

Sultanov's antithesis, Alexander Shtarkman, continues to impress. Only one American, Shari Raynor, has offered an important American work—Aaron Copland's Piano Variations; she tells me she feels unusually close to this music as if the affinity surprises her. Shtarkman confidently anchors his second preliminary recital with Rachmaninoff's Second Piano Sonata and Stravinsky's Three Movements from *Petrushka*. His identification with these two big Russian works is sure and true. Clarifying Rachmaninoff's dense chordal thickets, his synthesis of technical resource and mediating intellect is spellbindingly poised. He always sits comfortably, with loose hands; the pronounced leftward tilt of his swaying head (*away* from the audience) suggests the ironic amusement he finds in the first movement of Mozart's K. 332 Sonata, or in Stravinsky's fairy-tale narrative. His bows—even after the cascading six-octave glissando with which *Petrushka* closes—are tiny and expressionless; he stands *behind* the piano bench.

Musically, Shtarkman is a consummate pilot. He takes nothing for granted. He accelerates and retards at will. As has become apparent, he is not a colorist, and as his *fortissimos* lack fullness, he cannot contour the loudest dynamics. Instead, he relies on the calibrated hesitations musicians call agogics to achieve minute differentiations of stress. Even the filigree of Chopin's G minor Ballade speaks; and its blistering coda is expressive in every bar. Shtarkman's organizational acumen depends on countless unpublicized technical feats: where another pianist (say, Britain's Andrew Wilde in Liszt's *Wilde Jagd*, which Shtarkman also plays) dramatizes a huge downward leap by pausing suddenly at the precipice, Shtarkman leaps fearlessly, dramatizing the larger landscape.

From a distance his erect carriage, thinning hair, mustache, and beard stress the illusion of ripeness. Up close, his unlined twenty-one-year-old face is startlingly youthful. But he retains a dignified reserve. He is, as he explains to me through an interpreter (though his English is quite good), the product of a concentrated musical upbringing. His father, Naum, is himself an eminent pianist (he finished third to Van Cliburn in the 1958 Tchaikovsky competition). He began piano lessons at five. From an early age, he was told "that when I'm seated at the piano, I'm already a grown-up person." His current teacher at the Moscow Conservatory is Sergei Dorensky—the Soviet representative on the 1989 Cliburn jury (who therefore cannot vote for him). "He encourages you to work by yourself and develop your own point of view. He teaches you, but in such a tactful way that you don't notice it."

Dorensky himself studied with Gregory Ginzburg, an assistant of Alexander Goldenweiser, who studied with Alexander Siloti, whose teachers included Nikolai Rubinstein and Liszt. Shtarkman appreciates this lineage; he "of course" considers himself a perpetuator of the "Russian school." He admires Richter for his "out-standing understanding of form," Gilels for the "depth" of his last performances, Sofronitzky for his "poetry" and "Romantic sensi-bility." In Fort Worth, he has purposefully programmed as much Russian music as possible. According to Vladimir Viardo, among others, the Russian piano school is fading as links to past glories grow tenuous. But Shtarkman feels confident the Russian school will continue "as long as there are pianists and teachers to sustain it." He has previously competed at the Tchaikovsky, Leeds, and Oslo competitions. He has already performed with orchestra "about fifty times."

KEVIN KENNER

His round-two picks—Alban Berg's fin-de-siècle Piano Sonata and Rachmaninoff's Sonata No. 2—are decadent fare for this wholesome American. But his patience and easy power, the long, arching lines he plots, do take effect. If the Berg Sonata seems purged of its neuroses, the prairie spaciousness of Kevin Kenner's interpretation makes Berg's evaporative parting gesture—a loving backward lapse into nineteenth-century tonality—magically still; the audience holds its breath before applauding. At the same time, Kenner projects a lingering bashfulness. Shtarkman's Rachmani-noff, heard the day before, was more firmly molded, more power-fully projected. Kenner's slightly stooped carriage and slightly crooked bows likewise convey a quality of "Aw, shucks" self-effacement. He is a more assured performer than when I heard him at the 1988 Bachauer competition; but, at twenty-six, he falls tan-gibly short of his full potential.

Up close, he is even taller—six feet four and a half inches, he tells me—than he looks onstage. His features are sharp and clean, his jaw is strong, his hair dark-blond and curly. He is earnest, open, courteous. I have heard he was a Mormon and ask him about it. "For me, music is part of my religion," he replies. "My religion is perhaps the most important thing to me. My entire perspective on life is encompassed by my sense of an underlying divinity." He was born in Coronado, California, south of San Diego. He attended the San Francisco Conservatory before moving on to Leon Fleisher at Peabody. "Then I took time off. I found I had a lot of questions about life. Having grown up in the Church, I went to Brigham Young University and studied philosophy and religion there. Then I did my service in Vienna. I returned to Peabody, and Fleisher, in 1985."

"Service," in Mormon parlance, is a missionary period abroad. Kenner's service in Vienna lasted a year and a half. "I interrupted my studies; I didn't practice. I think it had its benefits. I remember the freshness of feeling the piano again. At first, it was like visiting a stranger—I felt so much more sensitive to everything. Sometimes when you play a lot you feel a crust. It's nice to take a bath. So my service was a good experience. It gave me perspective. It's wonderful to be a musician—and I appreciated my music more, having been away from it—but there's a lot more to life than sitting down and playing the piano."

JEAN-EFFLAM BAVOUZET

Of four renditions of Prokofiev's curt, violent Third Sonata, Jean-Efflam Bavouzet's is on every level the most gripping. The *Allegro tempestoso* main material is both superpowered and precisely sardonic; the bittersweet *Moderato* second subject is the more poignant for remaining taut. In two movements from Schumann's F minor Sonata, Bavouzet confirms what his phase-one Schumann Toccata intimated: if his crystalline sonority is not conducive to an idiomatic tenderness, he conveys this composer's psychological instability with unusual authority, and also a paradoxical Gallic poise. His playing is mercurial and elegant, forceful and specific.

In conversation, Bavouzet again evokes the actor Jean-Pierre Léaud. He is small, pale, and fine-featured; clever, quick, and sincere. The main surprise is his eyes, which are huge and lucid under high, dancing eyebrows. A shock of black hair falls over his forehead, à la Napoleon. He can juggle and imitate the sounds of cars. He knows about miniature trains. His rapid, animated English is charmingly misaccentuated.

"My first teacher, Ventzislav Yankoff, was a student of Marguerite Long. For me, he is the old French school, which is based on *jeu perlé* and a very clear sound. The modern French school is for me Pierre Sancan, with whom I studied at the Paris Conservatory. He advocates more arm weight and is influenced by the Russian school. Definitely, the Russian school is by far the best. I really believe in the Russian school."

But Bavouzet idealizes the "cold passion" of Richter, Maurizio Pollini, and Pierre Boulez. And his favorite music is by Haydn, Beethoven, Schumann, Bartók, and Ravel. He also likes Stockhausen and Ligeti, and Chick Corea and Soft Machine. He plays jazz and "was at one time, to the despair of my mother, more interested in jazz than in classical." At the Cliburn, he has chosen the astringent Bartók Second as one of his concertos—even though he has never performed it. "I consider it one of the most important piano concertos of this century, with maybe the Ravel left-hand. I know it is a completely crazy idea for a competition. But I thought: The day I will play it will be one of the best days of my life."

Bavouzet is married to the Hungarian pianist Andrea Nemecz, who accompanies him to Fort Worth; they are expecting their first child in October. Like Eduardus Halim, he is on the roster of New York's Young Concert Artists, which means he is assured a number of American dates. Competitions have helped him: he met his wife at Spain's Paloma O'Shea; he got to play with the Gürzenich Orchestra of Cologne as a result of winning a Beethoven competition there; his good reviews at the 1987 Leeds resulted in European management and an upcoming London debut recital at Wigmore Hall.

"If I have one comment about competitions, it is: Why is it obligatory that there be only one first-prize winner? And why is it that you have to decide who is first, second, third, fourth, fifth, and sixth? What makes the difference between the fourth- and sixth-prize winner? Can you say when you hear two performances of the Liszt Sonata that you give the second prize to Pollini and the first prize to Richter, when there are quite different artistic visions? I think the first prize is done for commercial reasons: a first-prize winner is definitely more easy to sell. So I prefer what Young Concert Artists does: to choose a certain number of winners, *without* ranking them."

TIAN YING

When Daming Zhu arrived in Fort Worth in 1981 as one of the first two Chinese to compete in the Cliburn, he spoke almost no English and had played with orchestra two or three times. He had chosen the Schumann Quintet for the chamber music round because it was the only piano quintet for which he could locate music. Having never heard a decent performance, he "rehearsed" by spending an entire day playing along with a recording by Arthur Rubinstein and the Guarneri Quartet, supplied by his host family. His piano education had been interrupted for ten years by the cultural revolution—during which he worked on a farm, then played accordion in a traveling ensemble that entertained troops. He had entered the Beijing Conservatory in 1979 at the age of twenty-seven. Though the Cliburn was his first international competition, he finished sixth and became a local hero.

Today, Daming lives in Fort Worth as artist in residence for the local junior college district—and is, of course, an honored guest at this year's Cliburn competition. During a lunch break, he explains to me how Western classical music first came to the attention of the Chinese public in the 1920s, how Chinese music students first studied abroad in the thirties and forties, how Li Mingqiang—on this year's jury—was one of the first Chinese to compete internationally, finishing fourth in Warsaw in 1960 before the cultural revolution interrupted his career. The Beijing Conservatory, he continues, now occupies a new sixteen-story building, including a splendid record library and a less splendid collection of books. "A lot of people in China really love Western classical music," he says. "But the rate of assimilation will be different from Japan because of the economic situation. People won't have the same consumer power to buy records, tickets, CDs. You have to eat first." Looking back to 1981, he considers his preparation to have been strongest in Romantic repertoire. "Oriental music is monotonic, melodic. There's no harmony in Chinese traditional music. In the big Western Romantic pieces, the melody is important. But Classical and Baroque music is harder to assimilate, because the harmonic language is so critical. You know, music is a part of culture; you have to look at it in terms of the sister arts—architecture, painting, literature. So the more chances you have to experience another people's culture, the more you can understand their musical language."

In 1988, Salt Lake City's Bachauer competition was won by a nineteen-year-old Chinese, Kong Xiang-Dong, whose main preparation had been at Shanghai. The 1989 Budapest International Conducting Competition was won by En Shao, who studied at the Beijing Conservatory before acquiring a scholarship to the Royal Northern College of Music in Manchester. Tian Ying, the most remarkable Asian talent at the 1989 Cliburn, was born in Shanghai in 1969—which means he was only eight years old when the cultural revolution ended. He has lived and studied in the United States since 1983. Compared to Daming Zhu eight years ago, he feels comfortable with a gamut of Western composers: in round one, his Bach, Haydn, Chopin, and Schumann were uniformly satisfying. His second-round performances of Scriabin's Fifth Sonata and Rachmaninoff's *Corelli* Variations confirm that Ying is a pianist of uncanny refinement. As he never flaunts it, his instrumental gift is not instantly apparent: everything comes easily; he never sweats. But there is also the growing suspicion that his musical understanding may be, more than distilled, somewhat denatured. Perhaps his long, impassive face, with its glasses and cropped hair, contributes to my impression that his "Eastern" serenity inhibits Scriabin's sexual-religious rapture, or Rachmaninoff's Slavic morbidity.

Ying himself will have nothing to do with this kind of thinking. "Everybody makes music," he tells me. "Who cares where you're from?" Offstage, he is a tall, smooth-skinned twenty-year-old whose friendly manner, if soft-spoken and reserved, cancels his onstage severity. Though he is no conversationalist, he emphatically denies that his musical education was especially "Chinese." "Tons of students study Western music in Chinese conservatories now. But you cannot make a concert career staying in China, dealing with the student unrest and political changes." Ying's own first teacher was his mother. At fifteen, he attended the Interlochen Arts Academy in Michigan. He has studied with Russell Sherman, at the New England Conservatory, since 1986. "He's so fabulous. Most big-name professors just tell you how to play the piece: a *forte* here, a *piano* there. Mr. Sherman is a one-of-a-kind pianist. And he encourages his students to think." He has entered the Cliburn competition "simply because Mr. Sherman looked at the catalogue and said, 'You've got all the repertoire they ask for.' But I wouldn't have done it if I didn't have to. I mean, if you want to make a concert career, unless you study with a powerfully connected teacher, it's not going to happen by itself. In general, I don't think that for me, at twenty years old, it's such a good idea to be in a competition like this. My main plan for the next three, four, five years is to study with my teacher and learn as much as I possibly can."

Though he retains Chinese citizenship, Ying has not been to China since 1981; four years ago, his parents moved to the Ivory Coast. The occupation of Tiananmen Square by protesting students, which coincides with the Cliburn, does not distract him. In fact, his coolness under pressure amazes people here. A month before the competition, he told the *New York Times* he did not intend to prepare for twelve hours a day: "That kind of work ethic is built into the Japanese and Korean cultures. The Chinese are a little different." Whereas other contestants disappear to practice or rest, he regularly turns up at parties, or in the audience at Landreth Auditorium. "I don't practice a lot," he tells me. He also says: "I think there are two kinds of pianists. Some are passionate and reach out. I love to play for people. But I am more the second type, which asks the listener to come to him."

PEDRO BURMESTER

He opens his phase-two recital with four movements from Schumann's *Kreisleriana*—as persuasive a performance of this music as I have ever encountered. Where Schumann rushes forward, and then writes "still faster," Pedro Burmester is a wild man. Elsewhere, Schumann's whimsy, and the speaking stillness of his Romantic solitude, are equally realized; how exquisitely Burmester weighs the broken chords, each note a different color! For Mozart, he offers a pellucid, unpatronizing account of the first movement of the C major Sonata, K. 545—the one every beginner learns. He closes with a different kind of novelty: Leonard Bernstein's little-known transcription of Aaron Copland's *El salón Mexico*, whose call to attention is a series of roof-rattling G major chords—eight major triads followed by a triple exclamation mark. Burmester sings the borrowed Latin tunes with native insouciance. He wafts the popular aromas and nails the syncopations of the big dance numbers. The folk sources, vivid imagery, and rhythmic bite of Copland's Mexican holiday suggest a New World Three Movements from *Petrushka*. For the first time at the Cliburn competition, I feel newly drawn to a composer or piece of music.

Collapsed in a chair in the book-lined study of Leon Brachman, his Fort Worth host, Burmester remains a presence. His black hair is long and shiny atop his elongated face. His dark eyebrows meet. His eyes are smiling and ironic. He wears a gold earring in his left ear. A cigarette dangles from his lips, which are sensuous and full. He comes from a wealthy Spanish-Portuguese-German family and speaks five languages. He has studied in Portugal and the United States, with Portuguese, American, and Russian teachers. "I don't like to stay with the same teacher for a long period of time. I think it's dangerous."

Burmester took second prize in Portugal's Vianna da Motta competition in 1983. He subsequently failed to survive the first cut in Warsaw ("It was a shock to me—I never played Chopin after that") or the second cut at Leeds two years later. Even in New York's Concert Artists Guild competition, which is not a world-class event, he failed to make the finals. ("We got to see the comments of the jury. One jury member wrote, 'This guy has a beautiful sound'; another said, 'My God, how he pounds.' ") He plays "90 percent of the time" in Portugal, where he is well known. (He once hosted a radio show that programmed "everything from Palestrina to Prince"; on another occasion, he performed popular music on an electric piano at an "open-air mostly rock concert.") "Since January, I've played about thirty times, including nine performances of the *Moonlight* Sonata for a ballet company. It made me realize how boring it would be to tour with the same pieces. By the third performance I was asking myself, 'What can I do with this music to make it more interesting?' Once I learn something, I don't want to play it again unless I let it sit for a few years." He has only appeared with orchestra some fifteen times. "What happens with a concerto is you have one or two rehearsals to check the trouble spots. There's no time to discuss anything else. And most concertos are just piano versus orchestra, and in my opinion not very interesting."

He is undismayed by his recent disappointments on the competition circuit. "Look, it only means fifteen people didn't like what they heard. I don't take it that seriously." He blames competitions for contributing to a worldwide "standardization" of performance. "But I think this is changing now. People care if they hear something personal, something that doesn't repeat itself."

His musical hero is Glenn Gould—not for his playing so much as for his point of view. "It was a late discovery. I like the way he makes you forget the piano as an instrument to show off with. He throws out the bible of clichés about how to play Bach, how to play Mozart, how to play Schoenberg. And I understand perfectly why he stopped playing in public. Competitions, playing all over and all the time—this comes with a big career. I don't care about it much, but I can't afford not to. I don't want a career performing a hundred times a year. And establishing a career when you're very young can be a step toward this." For Portuguese EMI, Burmester made a recording of the Bach E minor Partita, plus Bach transcriptions by Busoni and Myra Hess. À la Gould, he produced it himself. "Each track uses a different microphone placement. For the Toccata and Fugue in D minor, I put two very powerful mikes *inside* the piano. For the partita, the microphones were *underneath* the piano. That came off best, I think." What would Burmester do if he won the Cliburn competition? "I can't say I'm against winning it. It would be presumptuous of me to say this at twenty-five."

He originally split the Cliburn screening jury 2–2. His ultimate fate here is anybody's guess. No other competitor challenges conventional wisdom as directly. In his Bach partita movement, he used at least three basic tempos where Bach shows one. In his Haydn sonata movement, he made no attempt to temper his nine-foot Steinway; and he rolled the final chord from the outside in—a stroke of truly Gouldian individuality. In *Kreisleriana*, he (quite sensibly) did not omit all the repeats, as the jury had requested. He also reconceived some *pianissimos* as *fortes*, and in places redistributed the notes between the hands (a practice many pedagogues abhor). He regrets that he was not asked to play the slow movement of his Mozart sonata, which he liberally ornaments.

He unquestionably has a following. Members of the Cliburn staff adore him. So, quietly, do Robert and Ann Bass. Leon Brachman, who has hosted four losers since 1962, and who once was concert-master of the Harvard University orchestra, knows Burmester is special—and dares to speculate that he might just win.

The
Jury
Speaks

CHARLES EDWARD RUSSELL'S *The American Orchestra and Theodore Thomas* celebrates the feats of a Pied Piper among conductors, a self-made musician who came to America from Germany as a child; whose itinerant orchestra followed the railroad tracks north to Minneapolis, south to Mobile, west to California; who later led the New York Philharmonic and founded the Chicago Symphony and Cincinnati Festival. A classic statement of the early impact of Old World music upon New World innocents is this third-person reminiscence from Russell's 1927 book:

> In 1877, Theodore Thomas came to the town where the boy lived. . . . The playing of [Schumann's] Traumerei seemed something unbelievable. Theodore Thomas had orchestrated the piano score and united with it as a trio the Schumann Romanza. Only the strings were used without the basses. At the end, the beautiful melody grew softer and softer, slowly fading until it seemed to be drifting in the air. . . . With all intension, rapt, leaning forward, the listeners were following it. Of a sudden they awoke to the fact that Mr. Thomas had laid down his baton and there was no sound. For the last minute there had been none. The violinists had continued to move their bows without touching the strings, but so strong was the spell, these thralls had believed they still heard that marvelous elfin melody. A strange gasping noise arose as two

thousand people suddenly recovered their breath and consciousness, and then looked at one another to see if all this were real.

Evidence still exists that to all impressionable persons hearing that concert, life was never the same afterward. It was not alone that they had heard something beautiful; there had been shown to them things and potentialities they had never suspected.

Sixty years later, Leon Brachman had his own symphonic epiphany. "I grew up in a small town in Ohio. I had a good musical education there. We had our civic music series, but no symphony orchestra—that was beyond the budget. And so before going to Harvard in 1938 I had heard orchestras on the radio once in a while, but I'd never been close to one. I went to the opening Boston Symphony concert of the season, and it just overwhelmed me. I remember they played Debussy's *La Mer*, which I'd never even heard of before. I sat there with my eyes closed, imagining everything, the play of the waves and so on. It was so exciting that when I got back to the dorm that night I wrote a seventeen-page letter to my violin teacher in Marietta. I've been in love with the sound of a symphony orchestra ever since."

While at Harvard, where he majored in astronomy, Brachman married Faye Rosenthal of Fort Worth (whose father, a Jewish cowboy, was once ticketed for driving too many cattle down a Dallas main street). He settled in Fort Worth, went into the chemical business, retired, grew restless, and started a computer company. He also has a business in Haiti, flies his own airplane, and is chairman of All Saints Hospital. Though he no longer plays the violin, he is a leading supporter (and past president) of the Fort Worth Symphony and sits on the board of the new Fort Worth Chamber Music Society. With his round, ruddy face and crinkly eyes, he is an infectious optimist, a believer in limitless personal possibilities. Like Charles Edward Russell, he embodies the New World's occasional capacity for sincere, substantive, and yet genuinely popular appropriation of elitist Old World culture.

At the 1989 Van Cliburn competition, newcomers to classical music cannot be expected to listen as innocently as Russell could in the pre-phonograph, pre-radio 1870s, as impressionably as Leon Brachman could in the pre-television 1930s. No one any longer predicts, as Russell did, that the continuing dissemination of an American concert culture will prove morally regenerating, a "scourge of materialism." And yet here is Gray Mills, a tall, gentle-faced insurance man, attending piano concerts for the first time in his life and saying: "I really didn't know what to expect. I suppose

I thought that I'd be bored out of my mind. My background is in athletics—football at TCU, baseball, golf. So I didn't think I would care for classical music; I didn't think I would understand it. But the competition has been very interesting, very enjoyable. One thing I find myself appreciating is how fast and smooth their fingers are, moving across the keys. I'm so impressed that their hands can almost glide across the keyboard, and the next moment, they'll strike it hard. And by now I've heard so many different pianists that I'm beginning to know what pleases me." Mills and his wife, Nelda, are hosting Predrag Muzijevic, a superb Yugoslavian pianist who studies with Joseph Kalichstein at Juilliard. They agreed to house a pianist because this year's housing chairman is a close friend and talked them into it. Muzijevic practices in their living room, on a borrowed piano provided by the Cliburn Foundation. He and several other competitors sometimes swim in the Millses' pool. "Nelda and I are very impressed with Predrag and Eduardus [Halim] and the others—as people. They've opened up a new world to me—the pressures of their profession, the hard work they put in, the politics of it all." The Millses expect to attend recitals and symphonic concerts in Fort Worth next season—for the first time.

Leon and Faye Brachman can remember when, shortly after World War II, the Dallas Symphony would give six concerts a year in Fort Worth in the three-thousand-seat Will Rogers Auditorium, and about two hundred fifty people would attend. They remember the first year of the Cliburn competition, when tickets for the early rounds were free and the hall was never more than half full. Fort Worth's own orchestra now plays six pairs of subscription concerts (plus more than a hundred other "services" in and out of town). And the Cliburn sells over $200,000 in tickets. "This is a community, not a big city," Leon Brachman tells me. "This is a place where people like to be involved. Look: if I were to move to New York City, how many generations do you think it'd take for my family to get on the New York Philharmonic board? If you were to move to Fort Worth, I could get you on the board of the Fort Worth Symphony the next day."

The audience at the Eighth Van Cliburn International Piano Competition confirms Fort Worth's burgeoning cultural appetite: for five days, it has listened with steady concentration and mounting partisanship. The number of empty seats—naturally, few ticket buyers can attend morning, afternoon, and evening—is diminishing. During the daytime, the listeners are mostly women of all ages. At night, more men appear. There are also impressive numbers of young people, seated with their siblings and parents. Of the host families, some—like the Brachmans, who house Pedro Burmester— come mainly to hear their guests. Others sample the field. Sultanov and Andrew Wilde drive the audience to its feet. But every pianist—including some who are simply dull—is heard with sympathetic attention. Even Schoenberg's atonal Op. 11 Piano Pieces and Aaron Copland's angular Piano Variations inspire hard, silent listening. The lobbies hum with conversation. I hear no talk of golf, or Tiananmen Square, or the dramatic resignation of the Speaker of the House, Fort Worth's own Jim Wright. "I didn't think you'd want to do this," one man tells another. "Sure, I always like to try something *different*," his friend replies.

Then, suddenly, a new mood—of excitement suppressed or deflected—displaces the hours of consolidated attention and spontaneous enthusiasm. It is 10:00 P.M. Wednesday night, the two preliminary rounds have just concluded, and yet most in the audience do not go home. They sit, or drift in and out, or stroll outside in the Texas heat. Conversation grows muted, tentative, fitful. All this betokens the new factor. Previously inconspicuous, or a benign social presence, the jury has retired to determine which twelve contestants will survive the first cut.

Every music competition makes jury rules intended to ensure fairness and thoroughness. Should there be discussion before the vote? Should a first prize necessarily be given? Should jurors be disqualified from voting for students or former students? Should the ballots be open or secret? There are no easy answers.

Are competitions sometimes "rigged"? At the 1965 Chopin competition, five Russian and seven Polish pianists took part in the semifinals. At this point, all five Russians were given low marks (on a scale of 1 to 25) by the seven Polish judges (on a jury of twenty-one). As a result, no Russians advanced to the final round. The Polish judges had intended to limit the possibility of a Soviet winner, but this more drastic outcome went too far. The jury secretary proposed that the list of finalists be expanded from six, as provided for in the rules, to eight—but this would have looked even worse. The six finalists were then announced to the public, which responded with outrage and consternation.

"Bloc voting" of this kind is alleged to taint the Tchaikovsky and Chopin competitions, with their heavy concentration of Soviet and East European jurors, some of whom arrive with instructions from their governments. In fact, political, national, and personal loyalties are an inevitable factor in the behavior of any jury. And jurors with strong opinions will always seek allies and underlings. Sometimes a majority of jurors will conspire to change its mind for appearance' sake. Even when no juror violates his first impression, or his conscience, vagaries of the system can nullify or magnify his vote. At the 1986 Tchaikovsky competition, a scale of 0 to 25 was used, with any scores more than three points above or below the average thrown out as a safeguard against favoritism. One juror, Daniel Pollack of the United States, later reported:

> what clearly seemed a fair system backfired when jury members, out of enthusiasm for a given talent, would give the contestant a 23 or 24, let's say, and the average turned out to be 19. That vote would then be thrown out, thereby lowering the contestant's score. If there were three or four such votes, it could possibly even eliminate a top talent. It took quite some time, especially for the Western jury members, to adjust their numbers strategically so that all their choices would count. Since there was no discussion, one could only guess at what the average might be. I am afraid that some talents could have fallen away in the first round because of this system.

Not all such inequities are inadvertent: clever and experienced jurors can outsmart dissident colleagues in any system that tampers with the raw vote.

One response to these well-known problems of musical adjudication is to adopt more complex tallying procedures intended to weigh each vote with subtlety and precision. Some years ago, the Rubinstein competition of Tel Aviv considered an unusual tabulation method devised by a computer analyst—and then decided not to employ it. The Cliburn competition, among others, has moved to the simplicity of a pass/fail system, dispensing with numbers altogether. According to John Giordano, who has served as the Cliburn's jury chairman since 1973 (in which year the jury rules had to be improvised, as no jury handbook yet existed): "We have decided to abandon numerical voting—in which jurors rate a contestant on a scale from, say, 1 to 100, after which the highest and lowest scores are eliminated. We've found that most jurors find it difficult to work with—you just can't put a numerical value on a musical performance. A pass/fail system is both more valid and much easier to use."

The Cliburn competition's 1989 Handbook for the Jury stipulates, for example, that each juror will vote to pass twelve competitors into the semifinal round. Any pianist who gets a passing vote from all the jurors advances automatically. The remaining semifinalists—to simplify somewhat—are those with the next-highest totals. All twelve slots must be filled. The same procedure dictates the selection of six finalists. The method for choosing among the finalists is a succession of single votes—for first place, second place, third place, and so on—with each juror voting for one competitor. The chairman does not vote except to break a tie— although he may choose to uphold the tie instead. Inevitably, certain jurors teach or have taught certain contestants. The handbook says: "Any jury member having or having had at any time a familial, teaching or professional relationship with a competitor must declare such relationship, and, if asked to do so by the Jury Chairman, abstain from voting on that competitor's performance." Though jurors are required to keep their deliberations secret, secrecy does not prevail in the jury room. Some competitions disallow discussion in order to equalize exhortative and timid voters. Others permit discussion in order to promote common standards and criteria (and, incidentally, to expose incompetent jurors). The Cliburn sanctions discussion at any time during the deliberations. And all ballots are signed.

In 1985 (as we have seen), Andrew Raeburn did not require that the jury award a first prize—in effect, imposing an ongoing standard of excellence that all gold medalists must come up to. This year, the rules mandate that a first prize be given. Richard Rodzinski believes that "no first prize is a *bad* idea. Everybody down the line feels castigated. *All* the contestants feel they've been slapped. I think competitions should make it very clear to themselves, to jury members, and to their boards what their purpose is and whether they can realistically expect to find somebody to fulfill that purpose. In our case, we're looking for a winner who's not only talented but also competent to take on a career, right away. Because of our international efforts to rouse the best contestants, and because we have a prize that is really significant, it would be very strange if we couldn't come up with one or two people capable of fulfilling that goal. Smaller competitions like the Kapell, which takes place every year, can't realistically expect that. But we can." (It is less curious than significant that Rodzinski is unaware that the 1985 Cliburn rules did not require a gold medalist; whatever the handbook may say, a winnerless Cliburn competition *is* presently unthinkable.)

Rodzinski is singularly responsible for another change—one that typifies his tenacity. The most notorious outcome of music competitions is the "consensus" winner, who least excites yet least offends. In a pass/fail system, he would be the pianist who falls within every juror's group of twelve or six, yet who is no juror's first choice—and so advances to the final round over those pianists several jurors like best and others cannot stand. Rodzinski has therefore instructed a local computer expert to devise a means of "Acknowledging Controversial Contestants":

> During the first vote of the Preliminary and Semifinal rounds . . . the Jury members . . . are requested to identify their top three choices (in no particular order). In tabulating the vote, the computer will flag any competitor who gets more than three such top votes, but does not pass on to the next round. These names will be brought before the Jury members for discussion and a possible re-vote.

The first paragraph of the jury handbook expresses the same priority as follows:

> The Eighth Van Cliburn International Piano Competition is seeking to discover and recognize those pianists who, in addition to being first-rate musicians, have that extra something special—something to say, and the ability to communicate it through strength of personality, charisma, conviction. In short, we are looking for artists, and not just proficient technicians who play everything correctly, but who ultimately say little or nothing.

Notwithstanding the simplicity of its procedures, the jury takes a long time to whittle the field of thirty-eight to twelve—or it seems to. At 11:00 P.M.—about an hour after the jurors retired—the audience is summoned to return to Ed Landreth Auditorium. The contestants are asked to sit together in the first rows. But the wait continues. It eventually becomes apparent that, in fact, a verdict has already been reached and that Peter Rosen and his television crew have been apprised of it; in the jury room, they are filming the jurors' comments. Some of the waiting pianists begin to fume.

It is past midnight when a battery of television lights is switched on, blinding the audience—a sure signal that the show will start. The ensuing half-hour ceremony is aimed at the microphones and cameras; the four hundred remaining audience members, including the contestants, are reduced to bystanders at a media event. First, Van Cliburn strides to the podium. Peering into the cold brightness, he begins: "This has been a very exacting competition. It's been one of the highest levels that we could ever envision." In orotund tones, he repeats the story he always tells at this juncture: how his father wanted him to become a doctor; how he came to accept his son's musical aspirations; how he built a piano studio in the garage; how he began a tradition of "little envelopes" of appreciation. Now Van Cliburn will give each of the contestants an envelope in memory of his father. "It is not much. The value is nothing. It's only the thought. . . . Every one of you who has dedicated yourself to classical music are really soldiers for beauty. . . . When you think of the potential audiences for classical music all over the world, there are not even enough pianists." Next, Bernie Appel, president of Radio Shack (a division of the Fort Worth–based Tandy Corporation), announces he has a portable compact-disc player for each competitor. The thirty-eight pianists are called, one by one, each to receive an envelope from Van Cliburn (it contains $100) and a CD player from Bernie Appel, each to be applauded and photographed with Van Cliburn and Bernie Appel and the envelope and the CD player. Finally—it is twelve-forty in the morning—John Giordano rises to announce the lucky names. Looking haggard, he confides: "I'm half crazy for those whose names I'm not going to call out, and I'm half crazy for those whose names I *am* going to call out. . . . This was a very difficult and very opinionated and strong-willed jury." He lists Jean-Efflam Bavouzet, Elisso Bolkvadze, Pedro Burmester, Angela Cheng, José Cocarelli, Kevin Kenner, Lin Hai, Benedetto Lupo, Kayo Miki, Alexander Shtarkman, Alexei Sultanov, and Tian Ying. Meanwhile, newspaper and television cameras fasten on the faces of the winners and, especially, the losers. David Buechner is a portrait in frozen dejection. Next to him, Eduardus Halim, whose ever-present smile has been his signature, stares into space; the scrutinizing cameras crave Halim's tears but find none. While a daze overtakes the crowd, radio, TV, and newspaper reporters rush to interview as many pianists as can be corralled. The Cliburn staff hustles the twelve semifinalists onstage for an official photo session, leaving behind those losers who care to linger. They are wry, or confused, or angry. John Nauman is red-eyed. "Look at that group," he says, pointing to the stage. "I'd kill . . . No, I wouldn't kill. . . . But for eight months, this was all I did." Predrag Muzijevic is sorry he did not stage a "walkout" during the Radio Shack presentations—"Who's this event for, the media or us?" Some losers read collusion into the survival of the third Russian, Elisso Bolkvadze. Others note the coincidence of judges and semifinalists from Brazil, France, Japan, and China, of neither judges nor semifinalists from West Germany (with four pianists in the field). The audience, gathered in knots, does not clear the hall for an hour and a half. Leon Brachman looks around and observes:

"Twenty-five years ago when they announced the winners people thought the gods had spoken." This year, people are perplexed and ask questions; or are indignant and render opinions. It speaks volumes for Fort Worth's growing sophistication that the jury has been demystified.

My own reaction is a mixture of satisfaction and stupefaction. Bavouzet, Burmester, Kenner, Shtarkman, and Tian Ying are still in the running. But the remaining seven selections seem almost arbitrary. I side with Eduardus Halim, who is already twenty-seven, lives on a tight budget, shares a tiny Manhattan apartment with his wife, and plays only fifteen times a year. I worry about Predrag Muzijevic, whose native Yugoslavia offers no career base for a pianist of his caliber and who has been denied an opportunity to continue studying with Joseph Kalichstein at Juilliard. I feel for David Buechner, who lacks nothing in diligence, experience, or intelligence, and who thought he might win. None of the three remaining women seems to me on the level of another Yugoslav who studied at Juilliard (with juror György Sándor): Rita Kinka. And where is Wolfgang Manz? One of the older eliminated pianists confides great unhappiness he came to Fort Worth, where he feels "like an animal on display." "The temptation was too great—I couldn't resist it." He is distraught that his participation will be documented for an international audience in Peter Rosen's video, that his failure to please the jury will be interpreted as an artistic failure. He will have trouble putting his "digression" behind him.

Wayne Gay of the *Fort Worth Star-Telegram*, whose daily reviews are already a source of controversy (at least one contestant has threatened to quit because Gay finds him an unexciting "mainstream" player), surveys the carnage and writes for Friday morning's paper:

> For months, the management of the Van Cliburn International Piano Competition—and the Cliburn jurors—have adamantly and publicly avowed the cause of personality, warmth and individuality.
>
> Other competitions may end up with bland winners, they said. . . .
>
> Not us, they said. We're going for the communicator, the original presence, the warm human being who reaches the crowds. And then, early yesterday morning, the jury picked the safe, the correct, the bland for the semifinal round.

Now Richard Rodzinski is furious. When the *Star-Telegram* refuses to permit him a rebuttal, he allows a reporter, Christopher

Evans, access to the Star Chamber. Evans writes for Saturday's paper:

> Rebutting popular and critical disapproval of their semifinal choices, several members of the Cliburn jury suggested last night that their detractors had been moved by what they could see, and not by what they could hear. . . .

In choosing the semifinalists, three jurors said, they had rejected what the public had not—style without substance.

Incredibly, the angriest person in town turns out to be a juror: Britain's John Lill. Though, according to the handbook, "Jury members will not discuss with any person whatsoever outside official Jury meetings their opinion of competitors' performance or any other aspect of their adjudication responsibilities," Lill is so unnerved by the elimination of Ju Hee Suh, the Korean demon-doll, that he cannot restrain himself. He tells the *Star-Telegram*: "There has been a great, great injustice done, particularly to one great pianist." He tells the *Philadelphia Inquirer*: "There's a tremendous amount of mediocrity on juries today. It's a reality that must be talked about." He believes that at least four of the eliminated pianists are victims of partisan or literal-minded pedagogue-jurors. He says he is so "disillusioned" that he can participate further only as a bystander. He is considering packing his bags and going home.* Another upset juror is György Sándor, who tells the press: "The jury is the problem here, and we are all to blame. We made a big mistake, which could result in no first prize being given. Now, even one of my colleagues who voted against Ju Hee is saying, 'Maybe we shouldn't give one.' " But other voters are pleased. Ralph Votapek comments: "I have no reservations about the people we've chosen to go on. I think we've done our job. Not all of [our choices] have personality, but some of them do. Myself, I've heard some pianists who do too much, they have too much flair. I don't like that."

The morning after the vote, one juror asks me if I can explain what criteria he is being asked to apply. It is an unanswerable

---

* The best-known resignation-in-protest from a piano jury was that of Martha Argerich, who deserted the 1980 Warsaw jury when Ivo Pogorelich failed to advance to the finals; Louis Kentner resigned from the jury earlier in the same competition, citing inequities caused by the unwieldy selection process (jurors voted 0 to 25, with no discussion). Arturo Benedetti Michelangeli resigned from the jury of the 1955 Chopin competition when Poland's Adam Harasiewicz was named the winner over Russia's Vladimir Ashkenazy. Arthur Rubinstein, on the 1960 Warsaw jury, gave one of the losers, Michel Block, his personal prize. Rubinstein was frequently, and publicly, at odds with the jury of the Tel Aviv competition begun in his name in 1974.

question. Does promise matter more than present accomplishment? Should the ruthless Cliburn itinerary be taken into consideration? Does enterprising repertoire count? What about platform manner? Popular versus elite appeal? Dependability versus spotty inspiration? What makes an artist "best" or "better"?

It says a great deal about the Cliburn competition that it absorbs the shock of this ordeal within a day. In public and in private, disappointed or disillusioned young pianists are fed and feted, distracted and—sometimes—consoled.

Its many lavish parties are a Cliburn tradition—evoking traditions much older than the Cliburn. Franz Liszt, in his early years, was petted by aristocrats, in whose salons he only sometimes felt like a degraded accessory. As he complained in an 1837 letter: "I was overcome by a bitter disgust for art, which had been reduced in my view to a . . . diversion for polite society, and I would sooner have been anything in the world than a musician in the service of the Great Lords, patronized and paid by them as on a par with a juggler or the performing dog Munito." A century later, New World millionaires not only imitated the high-cultural accoutrements of Old World wealth but were encouraged to collect art and artists by the negative example of governments: America eschewed public arts subsidies.* In today's Fort Worth, the collected artists are usually pianists—who both enjoy and resent their extramusical celebrity much as Liszt did. Their wealthiest patrons and party hosts harbor no such ambivalence. For its fashion-conscious readership, *Town and Country* magazine characterizes the Van Cliburn competition as "the perfect opportunity for [Fort Worth's] most influential and socially prominent citizens to show their visitors what Texas-style hospitality really means"—the "perfect excuse" to give a party. In Westover Hills and Rivercrest, the finest families compete for the privilege of entertaining the glamorous visitors—including "legendary figures of the music world who serve as jurors and the specially invited star guests." Naturally, it is a frustration that the competition's sixteen days can accommodate only a limited number of parties. Many competitors, as Fort Worth has learned, want privacy. Even past jurors have politely complained of receiving more invitations than they can comfortably accept.

---

* In a 1932 speech honoring the fiftieth anniversary of the Berlin Philharmonic, the conductor Wilhelm Furtwängler tellingly stressed the difference between indigenous and imported arts institutions by likening American orchestras to "pet dogs" (*Luxushunden*).

According to Mildred Fender, chairman of the entertainment committee, the schedule for the 1989 competition includes twenty-odd official parties. With menus ranging from La Ballottine de Dindonneau Farcie des Pistaches Sauce Madère to fried chicken and corn bread, champagne to beer, some are black-tie sit-down dinners, others Western cookouts. No paid management could organize these events more thoroughly than the Cliburn volunteers: there are maps showing where to drive, valets to park your car, name tags to tell people who you are. Only the pianists go home early. Among this year's social highlights: a buffet dinner for the jury at Van Cliburn's place; dinner in Gordon and Beverly Smith's terraced backyard, with its potted hibiscus, hanging baskets, and fans in the trees; and an alfresco luncheon at Martha Hyder's featuring a mariachi band, with kilim rugs and lace-trimmed umbrellas adorning the stoa.

The temptation to caricature is both deserved and misleading. As unmistakably as the Cliburn parties serve to satisfy social needs and ambitions, their unmistakable friendliness is a balm for anxious or unhappy competitors. Moreover, the guests are mainly humbler folks—members of the volunteer army, for whom personal contact with pianists, jurors, and other interesting out-of-towners is a just reward for hard work. Another beneficiary is the press corps, which is plied with good things to eat and drink. At the Worthington Hotel, reporters and critics even enjoy access to the Hospitality Suite, where they carouse with outspoken jurors—until Richard Rodzinski expels them to a smaller hospitality room of their own (which they refuse to use).

Behind the scenes, the host families are the truest, most enduring source of hospitality. Notwithstanding their often opulent homes, these are appreciators, not collectors, of artists. Even pianists who do not endear themselves to the Cliburn Foundation retain close ties to their onetime Fort Worth hosts. In fact, the city pays year-round attention to its past and present visiting artists. After Daming Zhu came from China to finish sixth in the 1981 competition, Martha Hyder arranged for him to audition at the Juilliard School— and he was accepted. Van Cliburn himself helped secure his participation in Texas's Round Top music festival. The 1985 fifth-place winner, Károly Mocsári of Hungary, studied with Jorge Bolet in Paris on a scholarship subsidized by Fort Worth families. His hosts also saw to it that his teeth were fixed while he was in Texas.

This year, the chairman of the housing committee is a round, bubbly, and loquacious woman named Sharon Martin, who tells me: "I first advise the host families: 'I cannot begin to tell you what you've taken on. And you don't know what you're getting, either.' I mean, sometimes these people are very demanding—you know, take me here, take me there. In 1985, there were probably three to five families that were real glad to see that person leave. I tell host families to remember the strain and pressure that these kids will be under. I tell them this is basically a surrogate-parent situation: you serve the meals and you do the washing and you hold their hands during the tense and sad moments. This year, I had fourteen smokers and four vegetarians. Not that many homes want a smoker, so I took care of them first, not realizing I would get into terrible trouble with the pets. A larger number of competitors this year are allergic to cats and dogs. And you know we can't get these kids *sick*—they have to play the piano. And if they have to go to another house to practice, I have to check the practice house for cats and dogs, as well."

The 1989 Cliburn hosts include nine doctors, five attorneys, and eighteen businessmen. All of the guest pianists have their own room, and most have their own bathroom. All have access to a grand piano, at their host's or someone else's home. Jean-Efflam Bavouzet and his wife have an entire suite to themselves in Betsy and George Pepper's palatial Park Hill home, which once served as the Historic Preservation Council's Designer Showhouse. Konstanze Eickhorst stays in a guest cottage at the more modest Arlington Heights home of Renie and Sterling Steves, who have hosted competitors three times before, with mixed results. Their 1981 guest "took advantage," says Renie Steves. Sterling Steves amplifies: "He was what I would call a professional competitor. He knew all the ropes when he was here. The primary thing he was interested in, after he was eliminated, was talking to some of the jurors who were favorable to him, trying to arrange some concerts for himself in the United States. He was drinking cognac at ten, ten-thirty in the morning. If I lived in Romania I might also have a drinking problem. Anyway, he seemed rather bitter about being cut. He would never go to hear another contestant or to any of the parties. Then we went away for a weekend and he drank us out of house and home—including a 1938 Chateau d'Yquem, which is a premier sauterne. He also had a fetish about taking back medications to Romania—he would have us drive him from drugstore to drugstore, trying to coerce the pharmacists to give him prescription medicines."

The Steveses' 1977 guest was Alexander Mndoyants of the Soviet Union. According to Renie: "Alec was an ultrasensitive person, full of loving and caring. Having him as our guest was a whole-family experience. We learned to be quiet when he needed quiet. And it was noisy and fun when we needed to be noisy. We'd have all the Russian guys to dinner here, and they'd go next door to swim at the Fishers', which was a big deal for them. And when Alec was practicing in our living room, the neighbors would ask us to open our windows so they could hear. And we balanced his meals, trying not to get his stomach upset—you know, meats, grains, vegetables. He loved the food. He loved the family. He loved Fort Worth—the spaciousness, the friendliness. And it was all in sign language, because he didn't speak any English. Before he left, he went around taking pictures of the whole house, every room." When Mndoyants returned to the Soviet Union, he sent the Steveses a letter, which they had translated and typed by a friend. Then they framed it and hung it on the wall. It reads:

> From the first day of parting I have missed you very badly. The only thing that gives me any comfort is the slides which incidentally came out very well and which I look at almost every day. All my relatives and friends are ecstatic over your family and glad I stayed with you. No one will believe that Renie is the mother of three children. . . . Those two days I spent with your family I will remember all my life. . . .
>
> > Kisses and hugs to you all,
> > Alex

Four years ago, the Steveses visited Alexander Mndoyants in Moscow and met his mother, brother, wife, and child. "We would not have gone to Russia otherwise," says Sterling Steves, who, as a leading local attorney, was Fort Worth campaign manager for his friend Lyndon Johnson in 1964, a presidential elector in 1968, and a candidate for mayor in 1973. "We only went there to see Alec and his family."

Thursday night—about seventeen hours after the early-morning announcement of the semifinalists—Jo and Holt Hickman host an outdoor dinner at their colonial mansion, fifteen minutes northwest of town. Each of the house's four levels has a deck overlooking Eagle Mountain Lake. The two hundred guests help themselves at long tables of food and drink. Konstanze Eickhorst is there with Wolfgang Manz. Faye and Leon Brachman bring Pedro Burmester.

Nelda and Gray Mills share a table with their poolside contingent of Predrag Muzijevic, Eduardus Halim, Rita Kinka, and Victor Sangiorgio. Peter Rosen circulates with his cameras and microphones, asking the losers what they think of the jury. Van Cliburn, who arrives over two hours late, poses for photographs with some of the guests. Burmester and Muzijevic admire the Hickmans' fifty-five-foot yacht and try to figure out how to steal it. The yacht's name is *Why Not?*

Semifinal Round

"IT IS IMPERATIVE THAT THE MEDALISTS SELECTED BE OF SUCH A caliber, so completely prepared in every way so as to carry out the rigorous concert schedule as outlined in the Official Program Book," says the jury handbook for the 1989 Van Cliburn competition. But China's Lin Hai, who begins the semifinal round, is an unformed, inexperienced twenty-year-old. The centerpiece of his program is *Pictures at an Exhibition*—a reading innocent of every Victor Hartmann picture Mussorgsky describes. Scanning the audience, I see Predrag Muzijevic, whose highly detailed, tautly organized *Pictures* was the high point of the 1987 Naumburg competition.

The Cliburn semifinals include two distinctive twists: every contestant performs a commissioned solo work and takes part in a piano quintet. The Cliburn commissions always go to an American composer; the past recipients are Lee Hoiby, Willard Straight, Norman Dello Joio, Aaron Copland, Samuel Barber, Leonard Bernstein, and John Corigliano. This year, the commissioned composer, proposed by Van Cliburn, is the seventy-eight-year-old William Schuman. It is a typically nostalgic, sentimental Cliburn gesture. When he studied at Juilliard in the early fifties, Schuman was its president (in Cliburn's words: "the great man on the throne"). He later became president of Lincoln Center for the Performing Arts. As much as any American composer of his generation, he embodied centrist, official culture; he received the first Pulitzer Prize in music (1943) and was the first composer to be commissioned by the United States government (1955). His best-known music dates from the forties and fifties. Over the past decade, his production has dropped precipitously. As the "dean" of American composers, he is honored for past service.

And so it falls to Lin Hai, as the first semifinal recitalist, to give the premiere of Schuman's *Chester:* Variations for Piano. It adapts a 1956 overture for band, itself based on the third movement of the 1956 *New England Triptych* for orchestra. Lin's performance ignores Schuman's evocations of church choir and military band. But the greater problem is the piece itself. As piano music, it is unidiomatic. It poses no engrossing issues in interpretation. The purpose of the commissioned work is twofold: to enrich the contemporary literature; and to challenge the contestant to acquire and shape music he has never heard played. The Cliburn contestants consider *Chester* a naive imposition.

The Cliburn was the first international piano competition to require a chamber music performance. This "musicianship" test, too, was an inspiration of Van Cliburn himself (though he never played chamber music). In its early years, the Cliburn usually asked for a piano trio. Since 1977, the chamber music round has consisted of quintets with the Tokyo String Quartet. These alternate with the semifinal recitals. Listening to Kayo Miki's thin contribution to Brahms's F minor Quintet, I thumb through the program book to see which eliminated pianists would have performed the same work: Muzijevic and Eduardus Halim; Thomas Duis, a forceful German born to play Brahms; John Nauman, an erratic American powerhouse.

What began as a piano festival has become truly a piano contest, a battleground of winners and losers. It is all but impossible to listen to Lin Hai and Kayo Miki without second-guessing and finger-wagging. "Judgment . . . sits heavily on these proceedings," writes Bernard Holland in the *Times*. "The preliminary rounds were long and wearing, but we miss their innocence."

According to Shmuel Tatz, a physiotherapist whose patients have included Bella Davidovich, Barry Douglas, Jeffrey Kahane, and Vladimir Feltsman: "I am always telling pianists that for competitions, musical preparation is not enough. You need psychophysical training. You see, for a pianist, the pain usually comes *after* a concert. At a competition, he must play for a longer period, which means the body is still working during the time it needs to recuperate. A pianist may take aspirin before a concert to deal with neck tension, or lower-back pain, or a hand problem. Then, after a couple of days, the body starts to express this pain. That is why the treatment before a long competition—the physical preparation—is so important. You know, the famous Russian piano pedagogue Heinrich Neuhaus said that a pianist's body must be as trained as a dancer's body. It has to be strong and coordinated. He would send his students to a body trainer."

Seven days into the Cliburn competition, stamina is a palpable factor. Privately, the semifinalists are practicing intensely and rehearsing with the Tokyo String Quartet. Publicly, they are playing four times in the space of eleven days. And the psychological tension—the pressure of expectations—builds as the field narrows. In recent Cliburn competitions, fatigue and pain conspicuously hampered Santiago Rodriguez, Jeffrey Kahane, and José Feghali. In 1989, some front-runners are already beginning to fade.

Significantly, the three remaining Russians—beneficiaries of the most elaborate precompetition regime—are exceptions. Like Lin Hai's, Alexander Shtarkman's recital is anchored by *Pictures at an Exhibition*—a performance as strong, clean, and stirring as his preliminary recitals promised. The unpredictable pauses between sections are calibrated to perfection. The trembling, *pianissimo* modulation to the major in *Catacombs* is nothing less than sublime. Alexei Sultanov offers hackneyed repertoire—the *Appassionata* Sonata and the Chopin B minor—in the thundering style we have come to expect from him. At least the *Appassionata*'s inferno of feeling welcomes his raging energy: the massive chords and swirling arpeggios boil up from inside his coiled body and bind it to the keyboard. But the shattering volume and rattling fingerwork of this performance are squandered; Sultanov pays so little attention to balances, voicing, and pedaling—to the rudimentary refinements of piano playing—that the music's pointed violence is generalized and dispersed.

Jean-Efflam Bavouzet plays a disappointingly ordinary program —the Liszt Sonata and Ravel's *Gaspard de la Nuit*, plus the mandatory Schuman—disappointingly. He sounds tired and flat. And the competition's Hamburg Steinway—Bavouzet has switched from the Yamaha he used in rounds one and two—is itself tired: his *fortissimos* shatter its earlier dark luster. (The Rappaports have it sounding fresher the next day.) Kevin Kenner's performance of the first movement of Chopin's B-flat minor Sonata is uncharacteristically tight. He fails to project the scenario of grief and consolation in the same sonata's famous Funeral March. Tian Ying's poised, speaking Mozart—the A minor Rondo—achieves a disembodied pathos. His Ravel—another *Gaspard*—is typically polished and sophisticated, and yet the work of a distinctly less accurate, less acute player than the preliminaries revealed. His Liszt—two *Transcendental* Études—is a giveaway: what I miss in Ying is Romantic ego. He impels concentration. He freshens and purges. But the sweep of Liszt's F minor Étude, its vicissitudes of personal suffering and ecstasy, elude him.

Pedro Burmester, as always, is a special case. Of the semifinalists, he has chosen the most personal program: in addition to *Chester*, the Busoni transcription of Bach's organ Toccata and Fugue in D minor, Beethoven's Sonata in E-flat, Op. 7, and Liszt's transcription of the *Liebestod* from Wagner's *Tristan und Isolde*. There is no "strategizing" here—Burmester is simply picking pieces he adores. The Liszt transcription, of music for heroic soprano and large orchestra, is hard for any pianist to bring off. The Beethoven sonata does little to showcase the performer (only pianists appreciate its patches of awkward fingerwork); the slow movement, fraught with weighty silences, welcomes a subjectivity nurtured by age and experience. Like Bavouzet, Burmester has switched pianos: to a louder instrument that shouts his unstinting *fortissimos*. As with Bavouzet and Ying, his confidence or concentration seems to dip in this round: there are wrong notes and memory slips. He is, in any case, not as polished a player as Ying or Shtarkman; and his fingers are not as spectacular as Sultanov's or Ju Hee Suh's. I like him more than ever.

The opening movement of Beethoven's Third Sonata, Op. 2, No. 3 in C, includes a page of arpeggios and rapid passagework just before the coda—in effect, a quasi cadenza inviting soloistic display. At Fort Worth, four pianists treat this eruptive page with such misguided respect—as if Beethoven's notation were as self-sufficient as Stravinsky's—that the intended impression of spontaneity is sacrificed to "textual fidelity." Burmester's Op. 7 risks a truer fidelity; his details of dynamics and articulation supplement the evidence on the page. The result, if undeniably spotty, at least takes the measure of this big sonata. The rondo finale, in which he "breaks hands" to heighten the lyric impetus of the principal tune, is memorably songful; near the close, a daringly prolonged fermata (indicating a pause) amplifies the Schubertian clairvoyance of Beethoven's wayward search for closure.

*   *   *

If the semifinal recitals are the most stressful portion of the competition to date, the chamber music round is a relaxant. For the first time, the contestants do not walk onstage alone. The repertoire itself—in addition to the Brahms, the piano quintets of Dvořák, Franck, and Schumann are played—invites collegial rapport. The semifinalists I talk to regard the chamber music requirement as a pleasure.

For the Tokyo String Quartet, however, the Cliburn is a marathon. Year round, the quartet—among the busiest and best-known in the world—gives some 120 concerts. In Fort Worth, it must give twelve performances, and rehearse twelve times, in six days. The rehearsals last ninety minutes; there is also a thirty-minute "warm-up" with each contestant before going onstage. The quartet must counsel the pianists, guide or submit, soothe or goad. In concert, it must give its best—the contestants are fighting for survival—regardless of qualms or fatigue. A week before the competition, I met with the quartet members and asked why they do it.

KAZUHIDE ISOMURA (viola): It's tough work.

KAKUEI IKEDA (second violin): But quite interesting. You'd be surprised how different the approaches of the different pianists can be. One fellow actually came to the rehearsal with a piece of paper on which he'd written all the rubatos and tempo changes we were expected to make.

SADAO HARADA (cello): Physically, it's very tiring. We are fighting with this gigantic instrument that makes a tremendous amount of sound. Also, mentally, it's very pressured. One reason we like it is the excitement of discovering an exciting young pianist. Quite honestly, the last time we were a little disappointed. And rather often, the pianists we like best don't even advance to the finals. We keep saying, "This is it, this is the last time."

ISOMURA: Backstage some of the contestants are almost ill, which can make us very nervous.

PETER OUNDJIAN (first violin): It's actually much more fatiguing than playing twelve concerts running. But it's so different from what we do the rest of the time. I mean, there's nothing quite like the adrenaline of a competition. You have to pace yourself very carefully. Which is difficult, because each pianist is giving 110 percent.

HARADA: We feel a great responsibility.

IKEDA: I remember when we did the Dvořák quintet with Jeffrey

Kahane in 1981. I was so exhausted. But when we began to play, we felt we were breathing fresh air.

OUNDJIAN: Kahane was definitely the most memorable. Jeffrey, as a chamber musician, was already completely rounded. He fit in so easily. He made us laugh, and he also moved us. I do feel that chamber music exposes the general musicianship of a pianist. Even in a concerto you can ignore a pianist's tendency not to listen very well, or not to stay together with the orchestra. I think it exposes a tremendous amount.

But it can also go awry. At the 1988 Bachauer competition, the three local string players furnished for piano quartets were so weak that the strongest contestants had to play either down to their level or over their heads. In other instances—especially in piano *trios*, which can demand tighter integration than the piano-plus-string-quartet configuration—a contestant may find himself hopelessly at odds with his enforced collaborators. At the 1989 Van Cliburn competition, the most striking, most surprising feature of the Tokyo's performances—of four Brahms Quintets, three Schumanns, four Dvořáks, and one Franck—is variability. A relatively timid or blunt pianist makes the group sound lumpy and lackadaisical. At the opposite extreme, Alexander Shtarkman and Jean-Efflam Bavouzet challenge the Tokyo at every turn.

Shtarkman is the lone competitor to choose the Franck. It is a quintet the Tokyo does not know well. Even if this were not so, the players would be unprepared for Shtarkman's understanding of this long, sensuous piece, whose erotic luxuriance of texture and mood can seem self-imprisoning; they must defer to him as to a senior colleague. Wafting floating particles of sound, or smoking the keys with his burning *fortissimos*, he fastens with trancelike rigor on Franck's characteristic alternation of torrid impulse and voluptuous languor. Trying to match his controlled intensity, the Richter-like suddenness with which he turns the heat on and off, the Tokyo sounds out of control.

But the Schumann Quintet with Bavouzet is a complete chamber music experience. The rapport between the players is already apparent in rehearsal. In the slow movement's C major episode, Bavouzet asks the quartet for bigger swells and diminuendos: "*Yes*—and then no." Kakuei Ikeda critiques his own rippling accompaniment as "too static"; the instant result is a looser, more rhapsodic, more shapely rendering of the score's dreamiest pages. Bavouzet's instinctive response to Schumann's interior agitation animates the movement's second contrasting episode, in F minor. "It must be more urgent," he tells the Tokyo. "You should even make me accelerate." In the *Scherzo*, which other pianists find frolicsome, he has everyone stress and sustain the sudden *pianos*, heightening Schumann's weak-beat accents. The Tokyo, in turn, counsels from experience: "You have to listen to the cello here." "You're rushing your triplets." To Bavouzet's amazement, Kazuhide Isomura and Sadao Harada (though they have performed this work dozens of times) take time out to refine a question-and-answer viola-and-cello dialogue. The performance, the next day, is flexible, alert, a model of spontaneous give-and-take.

Has Bavouzet redeemed himself? More likely, his disappointing semifinal recital will remain his undoing: chamber music is notoriously irrelevant to the competition's outcome. Jeffrey Kahane confirms: "If you have a player with a lot of chamber music experience, who loves the repertoire and knows how to get along with people, you can put together a wonderful performance in one rehearsal. It's quite possible. But I can't imagine a situation in which the chamber music round would be taken into consideration as a deciding factor. I think the judges get tired of it."

The semifinals end with Benedetto Lupo's 9:30 recital Tuesday night. The jury retires to choose six finalists at 11:45. The audience is invited to return to the hall. The television lights go on at 1:15 A.M. The pianists are corralled; the gate is shut. For the first time, the jury appears onstage. Van Cliburn's address is sonorous and surreal: "This has been such a wonderful phase. We always look forward to the semifinals because musicians always love the literature to be found in chamber music." But the crowd is edgy. There are announcements: The Robert Basses are thanked for underwriting the participation of the Tokyo String Quartet. Tandy will give all the contestants headphones for their new CD players. RCA will add a batch of Van Cliburn compact discs. Then John Giordano reads the names: Elisso Bolkvadze, José Cocarelli, Benedetto Lupo, Alexander Shtarkman, Alexei Sultanov, Tian Ying.

In the lobby, minutes later, someone is denouncing the proceedings as a "meat market." Members of the Cliburn staff, among whom Jean-Efflam Bavouzet and Pedro Burmester were favorites, do not hide their disappointment. Predrag Muzijevic, an Eastern European fatalist, is for once visibly distressed. Victor Sangiorgio of Australia is caustically amused. A third pianist who did not advance past the first cut, Ireland's Hugh Tinney, has already listened to the tapes of his preliminary-round performances and is "angry." He will be a jury member at next year's Santander competition—alongside Joaquin Soriano of the 1989 Cliburn jury. In my program book, I scan the concerto performances we will not be hearing this week: Bavouzet's Bartók, Halim's Rachmaninoff, Kenner's Chopin; Brahms by Burmester, Duis, Nauman, Muzijevic. Even Ju Hee Suh's Rachmaninoff Third begins to look inviting.

The Cliburn unties this knot of letdown and frustration with a private rodeo the next evening. It has been scheduled to take place at Texas Lil's Diamond A Ranch. But rain falls heavily all day, until Lil's dance floor is submerged under three feet of water and the rodeo arena looks like a lake. So she loads ten trucks with horses and food and relocates her Wild West Show to the Cowtown Coliseum, beside the stockyards on Fort Worth's North Side. Four hundred guests guzzle beer from the can and pile their paper plates with barbecued beef and potato salad. All the jurors have cream-colored straw cowboy hats. Strapping Sergei Dorensky and svelte Cristina Ortiz wear theirs with style. Abbey Simon's seems huge shading his stubby body. Li Mingqiang seems merely unfazed.

The jurors, the pianists, the press, the Cliburn staff, board, and volunteer army, sit as one on the coliseum's wooden benches. Banners and signs surrounding the dirt arena read: DODGE TRUCK, MILLER LITE WELCOMES YOU, HOME OF TARRANT COUNTY SHERIFF'S POSSE. An amplified band warms up the crowd with country tunes. A spandex gladiator races around the arena astride two horses. A mother-and-son team tumbles and does handstands on horseback. Redskins and gunslingers enact the History of the American Indian. A solemn Civil War tableau ends with fallen soldiers and steeds. The patriotic spectacle is a history of . . . Texas. There are rope tricks, dancing girls, gunfights galore. The audience of pianists and reporters, bankers, attorneys, and housewives hoots and hollers. Bernard Holland of the *Times*, whose musical education in Vienna made him a diehard American, puts down his beer can to marvel: "This is what I love about this country. It's so vulgar. It cheers me up so much. I feel so much at home."

After an hour or so, we leave the coliseum and drift across the street to Billy Bob's. It is "the world's biggest honky tonk," with forty-two bars and live bull riding. While Jean-Efflam Bavouzet hustles me through a game of pool, Cristina Ortiz two-steps across the dance floor with Victor Sangiorgio, whom the jury trimmed from the field of thirty-eight two long weeks ago. At the Queen Elisabeth competition, dour Belgians segregate even the jurors from one another and secrete the finalists in a "music chapel" without radio, TVs, or telephones.

Is there any place bigger than Texas? The horizons stretch to infinity. The populace speaks in a drawl so easy you pick it up in a day. The men, with their calm Texas eyes and soft Texas voices, ambush you with their hidden intensity. The women knock you over with gusts of Texas friendliness. Big Dallas flaunts its sophistication; the skyline looks as new as Star Wars. Little Fort Worth exudes personal history. Its lonely skyscrapers cannot dwarf its frontier courthouse and prairie downtown rimmed by telephone poles and railroad tracks. Its cowboys drive pickup trucks and pick fights on the North Side. Its oil and cattle fortunes are old enough to sit comfortably within the vast homes of Westover Hills. Its wealthiest residents adore its cowboy roots; at the Will Rogers Coliseum and the Kimbell Museum, they wear Stetsons and boots with their black ties and jackets. It is not Texas provincialism but Texas pride that spurs them to do things bigger and better. As a state of mind, Texas may seem a naive newcomer to Old World art. But it is not a snobbish newcomer, or insincere, or small. It absorbs Beethoven and Brahms, Van Cliburn and Martha Hyder, Europeans, Russians, and Chinese, without blinking. Its cowboys and horses, barbecues and beer, lift the spirits and drown the sorrows.

Final Round

THE LONGEST BREAK DURING THE SIXTEEN-DAY VAN CLIBURN COMPE-
tition occurs following the announcement of the finalists on Tuesday night, June 6. The music does not resume until the concerto
round begins Thursday night. It is an opportunity to recuperate,
regroup, reflect.

I had hoped to meet with the Tokyo String Quartet about its
piano-quintet marathon, but all four players have already left town.
An article in the *Star-Telegram*, however, says that Alexander
Shtarkman and Jean-Efflam Bavouzet were the group's own favorites among the twelve semifinalists. Shtarkman "was *very* demanding," Peter Oundjian told a reporter. "We had a hard time believing
he was twenty-two years old." (Actually, Shtarkman is twenty-
one.) Of Bavouzet, Oundjian said: "I think we were most comfortable with [him]. He had the quickest response, and there was a real
give and take."

Bavouzet himself feels happy with his performance of the Schumann Piano Quintet and ashamed of his semifinal recital. Today,
his large, lucid eyes are very sad. "That was something that can
never have happened to a Russian contestant with my skills. There
would have been somebody pushing him and saying: 'I have heard
you play the Ravel *Gaspard* and the Liszt Sonata and you play them

both very well, but you have never played them together, and so I will listen to you play them together, three times.' You need that. You need a coach, I am sure."

Pedro Burmester, too, acknowledges that his semifinal recital hurt him. "Probably I should have played *Kreisleriana* instead of the Beethoven, and the vote might have come out differently. But I love that sonata. Perhaps I'm a little bit careless, which makes me vulnerable. I cannot say I was eliminated for no reason. I don't agree that I deserved to be eliminated. But I understand. What's funny is that if I were to be a jury member—which I hope I will never be—I would never judge on the basis of one moment but on the basis of everything, of every round. About future competitions, I try to keep an open mind. They try to be fair. The juries try to be fair. I think I'll go on doing them, because there is actually no other choice these days. And I'm glad I came here. People got to know me; I got to know people. I'd rather come here than stay at home and be the best pianist on my street."

I catch Kevin Kenner just after he has attended a brunch for jurors and eliminated contestants. He is earnestly perplexed. One juror feels his playing, with its long lines and expansive rubatos, lacks "pulse." But the others "all seem to like it." "Pianists my age are still learning, taking chances," he tells me. "I took a chance with my Chopin sonata. I consider it a very dramatic work. The first theme is marked *agitato*. So I took a very quick, compressed tempo. It didn't work. I'll never do it again. Also, the slow movement, the Funeral March, kind of exasperates me. I haven't lost too many loved ones. If I had, I could perhaps understand this piece a little better. For now, I can imagine what it's supposed to feel like—but that's not enough. I think competitions like the Cliburn would be good for artists in their forties, who are experienced in life, and ready for the spotlight, and don't have to experiment so much. But somehow there's this notion that when you reach age thirty time's up. My feelings about competitions change every day. I got into this competition thinking I could win if I really put my mind to it. Then, in the semifinals—as the papers started to mention my name more frequently, and the audience started to warm up to me—I became rather nervous. It was as if I had lost my self-esteem. I found it hard not to think about impressing the jury. And I was physically fatigued. I had intended to just go out and enjoy the semifinal recital. But it was actually pretty scary."

Kenner will shortly be going to Germany on a scholarship, to study with the prominent piano pedagogue (and competition juror) Karl-Heinz Kämmerling. He also plans to enter the Kapell competition next month, the Chopin competition in 1990, and maybe the Tchaikovsky the same year—"although hearing the Russians here, I don't know; they're tough." He has recently joined the roster of Affiliate Artists, which he finds "better for pianists than competitions. You don't make as much money; but in other ways, their idea of offering a service for two weeks, giving recitals locally and getting to know the local conductor—it's wiser for a young musician than going from city to city, getting shot down by people who expect perfection from a competition winner. It would be so nice if we could just work on the music we find interesting. But there's always the business aspect. For me, right now it seems best to go to Germany and study. But there's no time for new repertoire; I'll be preparing for Warsaw, or for the Tchaikovsky. Sometimes I think I'm not going to be very successful at pursuing a concert career. Because I'm not a pushy kind of person. Anyway, I'm happy this thing is over. I'm tired. I'm really tired."

Another pianist still in Fort Worth (most have left) is Rita Kinka, whose airplane ticket does not return her to Yugoslavia until after the finals. She had impressed me as the female contestant most likely to succeed.

The fate of women at the Van Cliburn competition is controversial. By reputation, the Cliburn is a kind of slugfest. Except for Cristina Ortiz, all the winners have been men. Of eighty-nine finalists since 1973, only *two*—including this year's Elisso Bolkvadze—have been women. The percentage of female entrants, over the same period, is 31.

In fact, the concert world at large is not notably hospitable to women who play the piano. The leading female pianist of the nineteenth century was Clara Schumann—whom her hovering father treated like a son, and whose sustained success challenged, but did not diminish, reigning conventions situating women at the parlor piano, not onstage. Only in our century has the parlor piano, and its genteel practitioners, disappeared. A list of the prominent women pianists who died between 1960 and 1980 is not inconsiderable: Gina Bachauer, Clara Haskil, Myra Hess, Marguerite Long, Elly Ney, Guiomar Novães, and Maria Yudina are all names to reckon with. Curiously, today's list is shorter: Annie Fischer, Alicia de Larrocha, and Martha Argerich, players of great reputation, are as active as they care to be. Mitsuko Uchida, born in 1949, seems on the verge of enduring international prominence. Bella Davidovich has a following on both sides of the Atlantic.

The relative inability of women to advance as solo instrumentalists—or as composers, or musicologists, or music journalists—is a topic deserving a study of its own, whose starting point would be the insularity of classical music in the late twentieth century. As the musicologist Susan McClary remarks: "Women have been admitted as professionals into classical music in relatively large numbers only in one area: singing. Since we no longer have castrati, biology dictates that you need women to sing certain roles. One factor contributing to discrimination is the Anglo-American prejudice that identifies music as women's work or as an amateur endeavor. Most males have experienced the anxiety that if they're musicians, that must mean they're sissies. So on the professional level, music—like cuisine or clothing design—necessarily becomes *men's* work. This has been especially true with the piano because of its strong traditional association with women. Which means that if you want piano playing to be a respectable male profession, you have to agree that it's something women can't really do. The harpsichord, which was once the province of Landowska and Sylvia Marlowe, has also been appropriated by the real—that is, male—professionals. What's left is teaching, and we have had premier piano pedagogues such as Rosina Lhévinne or Adele Marcus. But that's a space that women have always been allowed to occupy—it's associated with nurturing."

Among women pianists of my acquaintance, some make no excuses; gender, they say, is as irrelevant to their chances as to their artistic identity. There are some whose professional ambitions are simply less concentrated, less egotistic, than those of their male counterparts. Some decry the premium on heroic repertoire, performed with huge orchestras in huge halls, or the priorities of presenters and managers who fear women "won't sell" or might prove unstable ("maybe she'll have a kid"). Some perceive blatant prejudice: the belief that women simply are not as good as men.

One outspoken critic of gender bias in the piano business is Lydia Artymiw, whom the reader may remember as a finalist in the 1976 Leventritt competition. She also finished third at Leeds in 1978. Still only thirty-six, she enjoys a reasonably robust career, with fifty to sixty dates a season, including frequent engagements with the Guarneri String Quartet. Yet she believes that "being a woman, it's much harder. If I were a man, I'd be much further along. Especially in Europe, there's this chauvinistic attitude: they tell you you've played well and pat you on the head. It's a myth that women pianists are weaker, that they don't have the stamina that men do. Look at X. He's a wonderful pianist, with a wonderful career, but when it comes to sheer muscle, sheer power, I'm sure he would be the first to admit that I can produce more sound than he can."

Can the Cliburn competition's Rita Kinka play "like a man"? The question is subverted by her beauty. Tall, poised, she appears onstage in a simple black skirt and red satin blouse. Her long, curly blond hair is bound by a clip. Her rippling arms, which have no elbows or wrists, are a model of relaxation; swaying from the waist, she draws power easily from the piano. Her music-making is vivid, fluid, and unforced, all curves and no angles. In the second preliminary round, she seemingly tries too hard and pushes. The stride of her "March of the Davidsbündler," from Schumann's *Carnaval*, is rangy and free. Earlier in the same piece, however, there are hard sounds and patches of wrong notes.

Without rancor—her blue-green eyes laugh constantly—Kinka tells me she feels she played well enough to have advanced. "I never wanted to try the Cliburn competition, because it has a reputation for being antifeminine. But then I went to America for a year, to study at Juilliard, so I entered. I felt my program was ready. My first reaction when the semifinalists were announced was that many of my favorites didn't pass. It was so strange that I actually felt happy to remain in their company: David Buechner and Eduardus [Halim]. And all those German pianists: you can like them or not, but they are really highly accomplished. The Cliburn is supposed to demand so much physical strength, such great sounds: that's what I always heard. But it's interesting: [juror] Ralph Votapek told me, 'You have *too big* a sound.' I wanted to make big contrasts.

"In Brussels, there are always many more women in the finals than here. I can't explain; there are so many strange things. There are more little girls that learn the piano than little boys—which is also interesting to consider. I think you can judge only whether a pianist is 'weak'—you can't say who is a woman, who is a man. Because you don't have to have physical strength to produce a big sound—there are other factors in technique. Speaking with different people here in America, I feel that, not only for musicians and pianists but also in other areas, the women have fewer chances. We're always told that America is the land of equality. But when they can choose between a man and a woman, people will choose the man; women have to work much harder to be recognized. It's not my opinion about America—it's what American women tell me."

At twenty-seven, Kinka has won prizes at the Munich, Schumann, Sydney, and Viotti competitions. She plays forty to fifty times a year in Europe. She is married to her former teacher at the University of Art in Belgrade. She "of course" intends to have children. "I can't say that it will have no impact at all. But many pianists have children. It only makes a big difference when there is no equality in a marriage. I have friends who manage this very well."

Like Predrag Muzijevic, she is in the United States because Yugoslavia is confining and there is little money. She had to pay air fare to the Cliburn out of her own pocket. She is hoping for American management.

"I have always the feeling that I can communicate with the public. But I dislike playing in competitions. Even recordings are hard for me—when there is only you and this microphone. Competitions where there are only judges, and no audience, are particularly hard: you can only think about how they are listening. Playing at the Cliburn was much more like a concert. The audience was great—although it seemed to prefer very fast, very loud performances. At the Tchaikovsky competition, the audience was the best. They know even little professional details. The audience at the Cliburn likes everyone; they only clap more, never less. In Moscow, only the best pianists are treated with total admiration and respect. Here, it is such a premium that we have come and they can hear us. People feel proud to have such an event in this city: everybody is waiting for four years. That's why I feel sorry when their expectations are not fulfilled, when so many of the most interesting pianists are eliminated. Because they are so well prepared and organized, and spend so much money, and care so much."

Some pianists leave; others arrive: gold medalists Vladimir Viardo and José Feghali; Philippe Bianconi, who finished second in 1985 and who visits Fort Worth as often as he can. Over the past four seasons, Bianconi has given a Cliburn Concerts recital, appeared twice with the Fort Worth Chamber Orchestra, and performed in a dozen other Texas cities. He has also played for first and second graders in the Fort Worth schools. He and his wife invariably stay with his 1985 hosts, Jay and Ann Murphy, who intend never to host another competitor because they could only be disappointed.

Though his career has not always been easy—he switched American managers not long ago—Bianconi made crucial headway with the help of his Cliburn silver medal. "Naturally, I didn't get nearly as many engagements as José [Feghali] did," he tells me. "Frankly,

I think he got too many. I got about forty, which was very good. It kept me busy but left time to relax and to learn new repertoire. And of course, it brought me back to Fort Worth. We really like it here; Southern hospitality is no myth. It's incredible, when we come, how many people know us. And they are so proud of the competition, and of its winners. Especially this time, being able to just watch is a fascinating experience. It's almost nonsense that you have all these pianists playing one after another and have to choose one over the others. Look at Burmester and Shtarkman: they are a world apart. I can't imagine being a member of a jury and thinking: Okay, this one is the first, this one is the second, this one is the third, and being completely convinced that this is the order and there is no question. There are always questions, because this is art—questions of taste, culture, of so many different things."

The Cliburn medalist with whom I had most looked forward to pondering the meaning of the 1989 competition was Steven De Groote; he was to have arrived from South Africa in time for the finals. Instead, I attend two memorial concerts, neither of which evokes his memory. The first takes place during the gala dinner the night before the competition begins. Van Cliburn eulogizes De Groote as a "courageous spirit" in the context of a honey-voiced paean to "beautiful music." ("The great things carry . . . the theme of the eternal. . . . When all of us in this room are but a memory, the great works of art will still be heard and seen.") Cliburn has chosen a program including selections by the choir of his Broadway Baptist Church (whose choristers he has outfitted in black on this occasion at his own expense); Tchaikovsky's "None but the Lonely Heart" and Rachmaninoff's "Vocalise," rendered by a soprano and a pianist who, as he tells us, "sang at mother's birthday"; and Aaron Copland's crashing, brass-and-percussion *Fanfare for the Common Man*—after which he requests "a moment to reflect on the life and talent of Steven De Groote." One of De Groote's friends privately remarks that "Steven must be turning over in his grave," but this is surely wrong: he is grinning knowingly.

The second memorial concert takes place the day before the final round begins. It is organized by De Groote's friend and collaborator Robert Davidovici, the splendid concertmaster of the Fort Worth Symphony. Davidovici has envisioned a program of Schubert, because Schubert was De Groote's favorite composer: the F minor Fantasy for piano, four hands, suavely performed by Ralph and Albertine Votapek; the slow movement from the *Unfinished* Symphony, stiffly performed by John Giordano and members of the Fort Worth Symphony; three movements from the A major

Sonata for Violin and Piano, feelingly performed by Davidovici and Philippe Bianconi. Van Cliburn has added a couple of songs—*Ave Maria* and *An die Musik*—heard in churchy renditions Schubert would not have recognized. And he contributes another eulogy, including poems by Lord Byron and William Cullen Bryant, delivered in slow, meaningful tones.

Tributes in the Fort Worth and Dallas papers are equally off course. I ask Robert Davidovici to remember Steven. He says:

"We began playing chamber music together in 1983. He grew up in chamber music. It was always his first love. It reminded him of good times touring with his family. He yearned for a semblance of family life—if not actually living again at home, at least being in the kind of warm, cultivated environment he grew up in. I think it's significant that he didn't have a 'Jewish mother' to push him. By that I mean there were no ulterior motives for his vocation in music: no parents living through the success of their child, which is the East European mentality I grew up with. Music was simply a natural part of his family life. In fact, he once taught our children and said if they don't want to practice, don't make them practice. He was of the opinion: if they're not curious enough, forget it.

"Steven's airplane accident made his joy in playing the piano more palpable. There was some kind of metaphysical experience in having such a close brush with death. I remember he said: 'Wouldn't it be nice if we could advertise in *Musical America* that we will play for free—just for expenses? How much freedom we would have. We could play whatever music we pleased. And people would know we weren't doing it to make money.' We actually toyed with that concept for a time.

"There was no nonsense with Steven—no frills, no effects. It is fairly unusual to encounter people of his integrity in music. It's a business, full of businessmen who are not musicians: promoters, presenters, managers with their 20 percent cut. And artists are artists. Or some artists are artists."*

*　　*　　*

---

* A true Steven De Groote memorial, months later, was a majestic, fifty-three-minute recording of Brahms's Second Piano Concerto, issued as part of a two-CD set of "Romantic Piano Concertos," with De Groote in live performance with the Cape Town Symphony, under David de Villiers, in 1987 and 1988. The other concertos are the Beethoven Fourth and Rachmaninoff Second. Manufactured in Europe as Fidelio 1881/1882, these CDs document the important artist De Groote had become ten years after his premature exposure as a Cliburn gold medalist.

By design, the final round with orchestra—required for membership in the World Federation of International Music Competitions—is the capstone of any international piano competition: the occasion for peak arousal, peak public profile, peak "money" repertoire. At the 1989 Cliburn, the audience increases from 1,235 to 3,065 at this juncture. Peter Rosen's cameras double, from three to six. The press corps expands.

Actually, the competition is caught in a downward spiral, and not merely because the jury has seemingly squandered a strong field. The new venue is the cavernous Tarrant County Convention Center Theatre, whose air-conditioning system is unacceptably loud and whose acoustics make music sound pale, dry, and soft. For the first time, television lights illuminate the audience during the performances. The audience itself is a new factor: much better attired, much less attentive than at Ed Landreth Auditorium.

Of the leading American competitions, only one—the Naumburg, which does not care to join the World Federation—dispenses with a symphonic finale: as at the old Leventritt, contestants play portions of concertos, with a second pianist standing in for the orchestra. The Kapell competition employs the National Symphony, the Bachauer the Utah Symphony—with the incongruous result that the accompaniments are usually more accomplished than the soloists. For years, the Casadesus competition, which draws its orchestra from advanced students and graduates of the Cleveland Institute of Music, restricted its concerto repertoire to Mozart; although the 1989 competition also admits the first two Beethoven concertos, growing pressures to popularize and dilute this event—and to push the finals toward the ubiquitous Romantic warhorses—have so far been resisted.

The orchestra for the Cliburn has always been the Fort Worth Symphony. Since 1985, the conductor for the finals has been Stanislaw Skrowaczewski, currently principal conductor of Manchester's Hallé Orchestra. Since 1973, two concertos have been required: one with chamber orchestra (usually by Mozart), one with full orchestra (often by Brahms, Rachmaninoff, or Tchaikovsky). For the 1989 competition, the first category has been expanded, at Van Cliburn's suggestion, to include the F minor Concerto of Chopin—which also happens to suit category two ("a major piano concerto composed in or after 1800"). The finalists' choices dictate three long programs: Thursday night, Mozart and Prokofiev by Alexander Shtarkman plus Chopin and Beethoven by Tian Ying; Friday night, Mozart and Saint-Saëns by Elisso Bolkvadze plus Chopin and Rachmaninoff by Alexei Sultanov; Saturday night, Chopin and Brahms by José Carlos Cocarelli plus Chopin and Rachmaninoff by Benedetto Lupo.

Compared to the best-played sonatas and quintets of the semifinals, the level of these performances is not high. The rehearsals—about seventy-five minutes per concerto—are pressured and hasty. The orchestra is crippled by an improbably sour, imbalanced woodwind choir. The intimate repartee of the Mozart concertos is sacrificed altogether. Only in Chopin does Skrowaczewski manage to shape his accompaniments with a point of view. At Salt Lake's Bachauer, the excellent Utah Symphony, led by its own conductor, Joseph Silverstein, contributes much better work than this.

Twenty-two-year-old Elisso Bolkvadze looks lost on the vast stage. A prolonged memory lapse in the Saint-Saëns G minor Concerto seals her fate.

Italy's Benedetto Lupo is what Tian Ying's teacher, Russell Sherman, calls a "generic pianist." He will offend no one. His musicianship, taste, and tenderness make him impossible not to like. At the same time, his pianistic resources are undeniably limited in the high-powered company Fort Worth provides. Lupo's version of Schumann's G minor Sonata, in the semifinals, was monochromatic and tight compared to Predrag Muzijevic's in the second preliminary round. His Rachmaninoff Second Sonata sounded clotted beside Shtarkman's Rachmaninoff. His concertos are not bland but plain.

Brazil's José Carlos Cocarelli, too, seems a less distinctive artist than Burmester, Shtarkman, or Tian Ying. From day one, he has been strong, steady, and thorough. He has already won the Marguerite Long and Busoni competitions. His teachers include Merces de Silva-Telles, a disciple of Claudio Arrau. I see and hear Arrau in Cocarelli's high elbows and twisting, rotating arms; in his round sonority and two-handed textures; in the stretched harmonic tensions of his deliberate rubatos. But Cocarelli tends to evoke Arrau at seventy, and he is only thirty years old. His epic Brahms F minor Sonata, which lasts over forty minutes, is more completely plotted than any chess game. I find his Chopin concerto—his penultimate performance of the competition—much more convincing; its more modest involutions probe a sustained reverie. He is a pianist I have underestimated.

Alexei Sultanov's Chopin is, of course, hot. Its barely tempered accelerandos and crescendos—Sultanov is always straining at the bit—generate a kind of excitement. In the Rachmaninoff Second, he breaks the harness: even the simple crescendo of the opening measures heaves out of control. Tian Ying's Chopin is a marvel of poetic refinement. In his Beethoven Fourth, the composer's embattled ego is missing. And the orchestra is needlessly, problematically big, extra players apparently having been hired to impress us out-of-towners.

The surprise of the finals is Alexander Shtarkman. The clean lines and calculated proportions of his playing dilute to blandness. He sounds burned out.

The Cliburn allots a separate day to the awards ceremony, which this year takes place Sunday, June 11, at 5:00 P.M. Like the venue change from TCU to the convention center, or the chamber music round, or the double preliminaries, this makes the competition, if not necessarily better, bigger. There is also the understandable desire to give the jury more time to make up its mind. Less understandable is why this most stage-managed event of the competition must represent it as style without substance.

In 1985, the Cliburn for the first time hired a celebrity master of ceremonies to present its awards: F. Murray Abraham, the star of *Amadeus*. This year the celebrity MC is Dudley Moore, whose films include *Arthur* and *10*, and who happens to be an accomplished pianist and composer. The flags and floral settings onstage, and tuxedos and gowns in the audience, also make this event media-ready. Peter Rosen is sure to incorporate it in his documentary. And unlike any other portion of the competition, it is being broadcast live on national public radio.

Richard Rodzinski, in a brief address, thanks the jury: "We asked them to seek out the genuine communicators. . . . I believe the jury has succeeded." Susan Tilley thanks the organizations and individuals who have lent financial support. John Giordano introduces the jurors. Van Cliburn says: "Today, as never before in the world, we need classical music. . . . The number of people who are beginning to realize this great, deep-seated spiritual need, and the nourishment that classical art gives in a person's life—that number is growing constantly. For the *potential* audiences around the world . . . there are not even enough artists." Dudley Moore, who is being paid $10,000 this day, is ill-prepared—a situation he salvages only by making fun of his own mistakes. Then, one by one, he opens ten envelopes handed to him by Richard Rodzinski. The winners, who mount the stage as their names are called, are:

- of the Steven De Groote Memorial Award, for Best Performance of Chamber Music: Jean-Efflam Bavouzet, José Carlos

Cocarelli, Kevin Kenner, and Alexander Shtarkman (who receive $1,000 each).
- of the $1,000 award for Highest Ranking Pianist of the United States: Kevin Kenner.
- of the award for Best Performance of the commissioned work by William Schuman: Benedetto Lupo (who gets a gold watch).
- of the Jury Discretionary Awards for nonfinalists: Pedro Burmester, Kevin Kenner, Wolfgang Manz, and Andrew Wilde ($1,000 each).
- of Sixth Prize and $2,000: Elisso Bolkvadze.
- of Fifth Prize and $3,500: Tian Ying.
- of Fourth Prize and $5,000: Alexander Shtarkman.
- of Third Prize, $7,500, concert tours, and a compact disc recording: Benedetto Lupo.
- of Second Prize, $10,000, a New York recital, concert tours, and a compact disc recording: José Carlos Cocarelli.
- of First Prize, $15,000, a Carnegie Hall recital, concert tours, and a compact disc recording: Alexei Sultanov.

In the audience, Sultanov leaps to his feet, his fists clenched, his arms straightened in a V—just like (as everyone says and writes) Sylvester Stallone as Rocky. Radiating pleasure, he marches to the stage, his arms swaying. He dutifully shakes hands with the other finalists. He thrusts his trophy high. Steven De Groote and André-Michel Schub had been awkward in this moment of victory. José Feghali's winning smile was tempered by the warmth of the long hug he gave Barry Douglas. Sultanov's smile is gleeful.

In 1981, Schub had to play études on live television within moments of receiving his gold medal. In 1985, Feghali, Philippe Bianconi, and Douglas played concerto movements following a break. These impromptu performances, problematic for the pianists, are a popular necessity. This year, there is an intermission, after which each finalist performs an encore or two. Shtarkman's elegiac interpretation of a Bach/Busoni organ prelude is a solitary moment, interrupting the festivities. Sultanov dispatches Chopin's E-flat major Waltz, then the C minor Étude from Op. 10, delivered full blast from beginning to end.

The last party of the 1989 Van Cliburn International Piano Competition, immediately following the awards ceremony, is a black-tie dinner in the Grand Ballroom of the three-block-long Worthington Hotel downtown. Fourteen hundred guests, including the privileged "Golden Circle" patrons, attend. The menu includes suckling roast pork, black-eyed pea relish, fried catfish, and fresh berry shortcake.

Tian Ying, looking relaxed for the first time in a week, is "very pleased" to have finished fifth. His Beethoven concerto, he concedes, had been underprepared—he had not expected to advance to the finals. And he does not yet feel ready to tackle anything like the gold-medal itinerary. "I still have much to learn from my teacher," he says.

Though his dignity is hard to penetrate, Alexander Shtarkman seems drained and dejected. At the ceremony, hours before, he had been courtly, acknowledging his ovation with a short, somber nod, bowing deeply before kissing the hand of Elisso Bolkvadze. A jury member comments to me that Shtarkman "will be in trouble if he doesn't stop acting so old." Shtarkman himself says: "At this moment, I don't have any certain feelings."

Alexei Sultanov is cavorting with Philip Viardo, the twelve-year-old son of Vladimir Viardo, who had coached Sultanov in the latter stages of the competition, even (to Stanislaw Skrowaczewski's extreme consternation) during his orchestral rehearsals. Martha Hyder, who hovers protectively in Sultanov's vicinity, escorts him to a podium, where four bottles of champagne are decapitated with a saber. The first glass goes to Sultanov, who gulps it down whole. The jurors have this to say about him to local reporters:

MAXIM SHOSTAKOVICH: He is a great musician, a great artist, a real talent—unique. I listened to three bars and I was sure he must be the gold medalist.

RALPH VOTAPEK: His style works because he's not dishonest. He does sometimes outlandish things, but I personally don't think we could have gone any other way. He's not a flash in the pan.

ABBEY SIMON: A lot of complaints have been made about contest winners—and they've all been true. They all sound alike, bland. But with Mr. Sultanov, we have a fearless independent player who can be criticized in all sorts of ways, but we all can be criticized. If you are looking for a pianist with charisma, a pianist who is brilliant, I think Mr. Sultanov with his wonderfully poetic gifts fills the bill beautifully. . . . I'm sure he is an original.

Richard Rodzinski and Susan Tilley also seem very pleased. John Lill, according to the *Star-Telegram*, praises the winner but delicately questions "whether the gold medal [will] weigh too heavily on a performer as young as Sultanov, still not out of conservatory, still not fully formed artistically and yet to learn a breadth of repertoire." Votapek, during a panel discussion following the verdict, comments that "the Cliburn puts a bomb in your lap when you win it. . . . I think I would want to win second prize if I were entering the Cliburn." György Sándor, talking to Lesley Valdes of the *Philadelphia Inquirer*, calls Sultanov's victory "a tremendous scandal . . . he should have been given a scholarship [for further study]."

Rumors about the deliberations are, of course, rampant: that the jury was swayed by the public; that before the competition W told jurors X, Y, and Z that he wanted to see a Russian win; that the jury resisted placing two Russians in the first three slots, "demoting" Shtarkman; that Cocarelli and Lupo finished high partly because of their professional seasoning and large concerto repertoires. True or false, these stories point to the fact that people talk, and in talking influence one another: the opinions of the audience, or of the Cliburn board, or of the jurors expressed to one another, are neither determinant nor irrelevant.

I add two observations of my own: that when it came time to vote, impressions of the final- and semifinal-round performances were fresher than those of the preliminaries; and that—concomitantly—the two finalists whose stamina never faltered placed first and second.

Aftermath

BACK IN MY ROOM IN THE SAME VAST, MODERN WORTHINGTON HOTEL whose Grand Ballroom holds the Gala Closing Reception six floors below, I command a television, two radios, two telephones, twenty-four-hour room service, and a panoramic view of the sleeping city to the north. My bed could comfortably accommodate four. The furnishings are sleek, spotless, and well-meaning. I open a book of essays by Joseph Brodsky and read:

> I remember [Leningrad] right after the war. Gray, pale-green facades with bullet and shrapnel cavities; endless, empty streets . . .
>
> Those magnificent pockmarked facades behind which—among old pianos, worn-out rugs, dusty paintings in heavy bronze frames, left-overs of furniture (chairs least of all) consumed by the iron stoves during the siege. . . . —a faint life was beginning to glimmer. . . . I must say that from these faces and porticoes—classical, modern, eclectic, with their columns, pilasters, and plastered heads of mythic animals or people—from their ornaments and caryatids holding up the balconies, from the torsos in the niches of their entrances, I have learned more about the history of our world than I subsequently have from any book. Greece, Rome, Egypt—all of them were there, and all were chipped by artillery shells during the bombardments. And from the gray, reflecting river flowing down to the Baltic, with an occasional tugboat in the

midst of it struggling against the current, I have learned more about infinity and stoicism than from mathematics and Zeno.

Brodsky casts Old World shadows on my Fort Worth stay. What is self-expression without self-awareness? What is self-awareness without history? What interior spaces of the mind, what profound cultural alcoves has any young artist investigated during these six-teen intense, ritualistic days? My complicity alarms me: my callow enthusiasms and antipathies, my combative judgments of "better" and "best."

According to Alfred Brendel, whose career started quietly: "A pianist has to be thirty-five years old before you can tell if he can play a slow movement. Violinists, by comparison, all seem to have made their careers by the time they're thirty. But playing the piano is more complex than playing a single line—it takes longer to mas-ter. Conductors, who must deal with the problems of controlling many musical lines, and also with all those people in the orchestra— conductors take the longest to mature; look, for instance, at those conductors who only become special in old age." At twenty-five, Brendel could already play twelve recital programs but was not performing with any great frequency. The pianists whom he heard, and whom he most admired, were fifty years old and older. "My image of an important pianist was of an old person—a Fischer, a Cortot, a Kempff. I felt in no hurry." He competed three times: in the Geneva and Marguerite Long competitions, in which he got nowhere, and in the Busoni competition, in which he finished fourth in 1949, when he was eighteen. Today, he refuses to judge competitions, partly because "they take up too much time," partly because "I don't believe in them."

Distancing myself from my two weeks of listening, I reflect and discover what I have missed: for one thing, the subjective probes of a really introspective slow movement; for another, a worldly hu-mility or charm that—like Brodsky's Leningrad facades—grows wise with fatigue. Away from the piano, too, even the competi-tion's most worn-out contestants remain—unlike, say, Steven De Groote at thirty-six, or Alexander Toradze at thirty-seven— unworn.

I decompress.

The Cliburn trails a series of fractured mirrors: the media events it covets. No less than Brodsky's ruminations, they add perspec-tive. The downturn that began in the barnlike convention center—

the twelve mainly pallid concertos; the TV clichés of the awards ceremony—continues and bottoms out. Already, there has been an impromptu backstage press conference with the three medalists. The first question for Alexei Sultanov was "How tall are you?" He tells the cameras and reporters: "In this competition, I wanted the first prize or nothing"—a remark that makes its way into *Time*, whose story, headlined "Martial Music," begins: "Yiah! The diminutive kung-fu student attacked the Steinway hands on."

The day after collecting his gold medal, Sultanov is on an airplane to New York. He appears on television's "Today" show the next morning. His youth—he looks to be no more than fifteen—and his guileless smile are winning. Jane Pauley asks, through an interpreter, whether he felt "young" or "ready" to compete with pianists ten years his senior. "I felt myself as I am," he replies. He begins to amplify, but there is no time. "Well, would you play for us?" Jane Pauley requests with harried courtesy, interrupting a stream of Russian. The rapid efficiency of Sultanov's Chopin étude perfectly suits the "Today" show—two minutes, and he is done. Jane Pauley says: "Alexei Sultanov: the beginning of a brilliant career. We'll be back." Eight days later comes the "Tonight" show. "Will you please welcome *Alexei Sultanov*," says Johnny Carson. "Alexei?" This time it is the E-flat major Chopin waltz, sped up like a Keystone Kops chase. The audience responds with loud whistles and cheers. "Have you learned any American phrases since you've been here?" Johnny Carson asks. Sultanov replies in careful English: "Mostly I learned 'I need more practice' and 'I like Texas very much.' " The Texans in the audience whoop it up. Carson continues: "Let me ask you—I'm sure you get asked this a lot: now, you're nineteen, you're a good-looking young man—How about the American girls?" Sultanov answers: "Ummmmm. Nice! I like them. But I didn't meet anybody because no time." "Did you find America the way you wanted it? Any surprises in America?" "Ah yes. For me, surprise is anything—no, *every*thing. The biggest surprise for me is winning the competition." "Well, I can see why you won it. You're marvelous." A third talk-show appearance, on "David Letterman" July 27, backfires when Letterman plants people in the audience to yawn and fidget while Sultanov plays Prokofiev.

The Cliburn competition is also the subject of a thirty-minute "Nightline" segment, aired June 19. Forrest Sawyer, sitting in for Ted Koppel, begins: "Contestants train all their lives and plan their performance strategies like wartime generals. Imagine the pressure on a young pianist when all those years of training and study come down to one night. A single slip of the fingers, and you've failed.

Tonight we're going to take you inside that high-pressure world with a trip to the most important American piano competition, the Van Cliburn." Correspondent James Walker, who was in Fort Worth, fastens on the usual analogy: the pianists are like athletes. He concentrates on John Nauman, because Nauman is a former competitive swimmer. He is also tall, muscular, and blond. "Night-line" shows Nauman training in a New York gym, lifting weights, then cuts to Nauman training at the piano in a sleeveless athletic shirt and jeans. A later segment shows him performing Scriabin at the Cliburn competition. This is followed by John Giordano, an-nouncing which twelve pianists have survived the first cut. The camera frames, side by side, Eduardus Halim, whose smiling eyes go blank; Nauman, registering disgust and anger; and David Buech-ner, whose left hand supports his sagging, motionless head. Walker narrates: "John Nauman's name is never called—he's out of the Van Cliburn. And so disheartened he says he may never compete again." Next, there is Kevin Kenner, the "highest-ranking American," live from his parents' home in Coronado, California. Sawyer poses two carefully plotted questions: "I've been reading that [contestants] find out who's on the jury, they try to psych them out, to find out what their tastes are—you don't do that?" And: "The people who criticize . . . say these music competitions reward not the most original, or the most creative, but those who follow in those careful steps and who are the most virtuosic. Is that true?" Kenner man-ages a couple of concisely incomplete answers. Now the music part. "Give me an idea what a jury member will actually be looking for," Sawyer asks. By way of replying, Kenner cites a Fort Worth critic's distinction between "pros," who play what is written, and "artists," who transcend mere competence. Sawyer hurries forward: "Well, show me what you mean by that. Give me an example." At his parents' piano, Kenner twice plays the opening measures of Chopin's F minor Ballade, juxtaposing "what's on the page" against "what an artist would do—taking certain artistic liberties." Sawyer makes a final point: "The other thing people talk about is 'You've got to be a crowd pleaser.' . . . What would be [that] kind of thing?" Kenner complies with the closing seconds of Rachmaninoff's Sec-ond Sonata. "You know, you do have to have chops," he concludes. "I think you had pretty good chops there," Sawyer says, "and if you'll hang on with us for just a second, Kevin . . . You got a sense of the kind of music that he can play, he really is an extraordinary pianist. . . . When we come back, Kevin Kenner will play for us." A commercial break, and then, to close the show: "Kevin, if you would, just a little music." Kenner delivers two minutes of Chopin, abruptly cut short by the "Nightline" logo.

The program exudes confidence that its terse interview format suffices: that piano competitions, or any topic, can be simplified, schematized, comprehended. More insidious than this naïveté, I think, is an implied ambivalence toward sacralized high culture. The artist is a freak and yet a regular guy, a mysterious genius and a salable commodity. He must be praised and revered, humiliated and cut down to size. Nauman and Kenner are cameo performers—the one used to exemplify the pianist as athlete, the other to demonstrate how to and how not to. These observations are sharpened in conversation with Jean-Efflam Bavouzet and his wife, Andrea Nemecz, with whom I watch "Nightline" 's version of the Cliburn competition. Bavouzet, who has never heard of "Nightline," is exploding: "What do you mean? It is over?! It cannot be! There was so much lacking! The subject was so badly treated, I'm sure something went wrong. They couldn't find the right people. Or the person responsible for this program was ill. I'm sure. It was so unprofessional." Andrea, who once studied at Juilliard, is wiser: "You know, they can really do good things—when they cover politics. But the moment it comes to any kind of art, they become like children—they are so awestruck. They look at you as if you just dropped down from Mars." Bavouzet: "And at the same time, for Kevin, it was very cruel." Nemecz: "They made a fool of him. And the tone of it! You don't have to tell people: 'Oh, what a great artist that is!' The interviewer who knows something stands eye-to-eye with the artist and is not amazed. Here, it's either from too high looking down, or from too low looking up." Bavouzet: "When a program is made like this in France, it's made by a musician—somebody who knows music, who knows the music business." Nemecz: "In Europe, people are much more free to decide. Here, people have to *sell*. I think in Eastern Europe it is best—television is not commercial yet. On Hungarian TV, there are programs with the pianist Zoltán Kocsis, discussing very specific issues. No one *ever* says: 'How wonderful you are! Oh, I can see you are a great artist!' Nothing like that! Oh, this got on my nerves! And I was so much looking forward to it!"

I telephone Kevin Kenner the next day. He is typically earnest, well-intentioned, befuddled. "I felt kind of silly," he tells me. "Because the guy wasn't a musician. He wanted to simplify and pigeonhole everything. It certainly wasn't accurate. But I think for the public at large it was necessary to simplify. He said, 'Kevin, I want you to sit at the piano and play something two different ways.' And when we talked about technique, he wanted me to play something technical. It was very difficult. I figured, Look, it's better in my position to at least get something across to the general public. But I was angered when I saw the shot of Eduardus Halim, John Nauman, and David Buechner, learning they were cut. I had a terrible pain in my chest when I saw that. Those people are very fine pianists. In fact, this whole experience of the Cliburn has made me reevaluate: What am I doing here? What is it I'm really looking for? I really don't know anymore."*

What Dwight Macdonald called the "genius act"—the public's "strange ambivalence" that stresses the personal genius of the performer and yet demands, as a "rebate," that he "distort his personality to suit [mass] taste"—demands that Toscanini, that Horowitz, that Van Cliburn, be people just like you and me. It demands talk-show chitchat from Alexei Sultanov, weight lifts from John Nauman, and glib answers to "tough" questions from Kevin Kenner. It ruthlessly imposes its terse TV formats. Is the Cliburn competition, which eagerly facilitates this "exposure," itself a rebate, forcing high culture into an alien mode?

The Cliburn's media flagships are the radio series and television documentary for which the foundation itself has raised one million dollars. Ostensibly, these are autonomous journalistic undertakings. But their essential promotional purpose is easy to read. Evans Mirageas of Chicago's WFMT, whom the Cliburn has chosen to host and produce its radio shows, summarizes: "The foundation has no editorial rights. But I would be stupid if I did anything to offend them."

In a Cliburn Foundation press release, Mirageas calls his series, "Victory at the Keyboard," a "once in a lifetime opportunity to explore piano literature and the mystique of pianism." There are thirteen programs, heard over one hundred American radio stations. The topics include the social history of the piano, the legacy of Liszt, the "new" Russian school, the music business, and the fate of competition winners. But this impressive framework is crippled by details of format: as on the "Today" show, the "Tonight" show,

---

* A month after the Cliburn competition, Kenner competed in the Kapell competition. He and Kong Xiang-Dong, winner of the 1988 Bachauer, were considered heavy favorites. Neither survived the first cut (which is to say: neither got to play more than twenty minutes of excerpts). Kenner's fate mystified many musicians in attendance.

and "Nightline," brevity and speed are mandatory. In radio terms, that does not mean talking fast; it means talking less. For several decades, encroaching television mores have pushed "classical music" radio away from the leisurely interviews and live rehearsals it once welcomed. Mirageas's Cliburn shows are mainly music: excerpts from the competition, and recorded performances by jurors, past winners, and other pertinent pianists. These are stitched together with morsels of conversation: "sound bites" typically less than a minute long. Some of the material is strong, but the atomized presentation, in which every remark becomes a tenuous lead-in to an étude or a sonata movement, wastes it. Mirageas permits himself no sustained commentary or argument. Words, in this harried context, seem always in a rush to finish. The only exceptions are useless: the speeches of the awards ceremony, which are broadcast live; and the advertisements, which smoothly extol not only Mobil Oil and the Tandy Corporation but the Van Cliburn competition: "One of the most distinguished and celebrated events in the music world," featuring "the world's most talented pianists." Mirageas's invariably upbeat delivery seals the package: "Victory at the Keyboard" is itself an ad, if not a particularly tidy one.

Peter Rosen's ninety-minute PBS documentary, "Here to Make Music," is broadcast some four months after the competition, on October 18. He has previously produced numerous performing-arts specials, including "Rubinstein Remembered" and "Toscanini: The Maestro," both seen on PBS, and once did arts stories for the "McNeil/Lehrer NewsHour." He has promised the Cliburn Foundation "a different approach," focused on "the music itself. Why does one person win and not another? If we succeed, the viewers will be prepared to answer that question themselves." And yet his format is even more restrictive than Mirageas's: sound bites plus tiny *music* bites, constantly preempting one another until it becomes quite arbitrary whether the camera shows a talking head with background piano music or shows a pianist whose playing is silenced with talk. The particles of speech and music are scattered like so many scraps of paper—a strategy intended to keep jaded home viewers feverishly passive and therefore disinclined to switch channels. The show's lowest-common-denominator approach is also meant to facilitate maximum distribution outside the United States.

Is it necessary to aim this low? Mitchell Johnson's 1981 Cliburn documentary directed deeper, more consolidated probes at a limited number of contestants. Bill Fertik's 1985 documentary was scattershot but stylish. Rosen's flotsam drifts upon a sea of clichés: competitions are like combat; the judges' job is tough; charisma is elusive. His lack of musical sophistication discourages an informed rapport with his subjects; like Forrest Sawyer, he asks "hard" questions as if by rote. Benedetto Lupo's showcase is the closing two minutes of the Chopin E minor Piano Concerto, in which he sounds exhausted and underprepared. Elsewhere, the machine-gun pacing fractures much solider playing. Ninety-five seconds of Pedro Burmester's Bach—the longest, most arresting solo-piano excerpt—is tracked by four nervously panning cameras; and sidetracked by a cutaway to Burmester in Leon Brachman's living room. Frederick Wiseman, whose documentaries are one of American public television's proudest achievements, would be the ideal film maker for "Piano Competition." But Wiseman, who denounces PBS as a "bloated and engorged bureaucracy," does not fashion de facto advertisements for client/subjects. Where is the quality control that would question the necessity for such Peter Rosen sound bites as: "When music was written, when it was performed, it basically stems from something very human, and that human element has never changed. It's always been the same, continues to be the same, and will always be." And: "The right articulation, the right sound—it's almost like making love, you know. I cannot make love in front of people." And: "It's more of a challenge to play works that demand more emotional input." And: "Chamber music is the exchange and the interplay between artists. And that means that you capture an idea that someone else plays and you play with that idea and work together. And the melodic lines go from one instrument to another." And: "To play something new with the music, you must let it pass through you. You must be touched by the music." And: "It's a magical moment that happens to you on the stage. When you play in concert the way you want to play, it's then that you have special contact with the audience." And: "Everything is very different. Recital is different, chamber music is very different, orchestra is very different. These three different elements can show very well the personality and abilities."*

---

* In the opinion of PBS's Jeffrey Gabel, who attended part of the 1989 Cliburn competition, "Here to Make Music" was "a fine documentary" for a "general broadcast audience." Gabel, who oversees children's and music programming, comments: "Right up front I know the Van Cliburn piano competition is an important cultural event in this country and deserves national air time. And I know that the documentary-maker is someone of a high level of skill and consistency. So I'm quite willing to accept his film, unseen, and guarantee a prime-time place in the schedule." Is "Here to Make Music" self-promotional? PBS's conflict-of-interest guidelines, according to Gabel, are much "grayer" for cultural than for political programs. "And the hard fact is that the only way these [cultural] programs get produced is with special-interest funding. Some terrific things get done out of special interest. On the other hand, we reject cultural programs that are blatantly self-promotional

Sadly, this business-as-usual pabulum passes perfectly for high-cultural television fare.† According to television critic John J. O'Connor of the *New York Times*: "Peter Rosen is too astute and responsible a film maker to produce merely a glossy celebration. . . . He gets beyond the immediate glitter." The most indignant reviewer is Alan Rich of the *Los Angeles Herald-Examiner*, who calls "Here to Make Music" a "shallow, cliché-ridden, ponderous sack of tired camera tricks and hoary verbal gambits." As for the Cliburn itself: "this touted-to-the-moon quadrennial fraudulence . . . has actually sped more promising talent toward obscurity in its twenty-seven-year existence than kindness allows me to name . . . [a] degrading, talent-negating dumb display of ivory-ticklin'." Richard Rodzinski, who toys with the idea of a lawsuit, is of course enraged—yet is himself partly to blame. As with its broadcast awards ceremony, the foundation—which has kept watch over Rosen's editing—has misportrayed itself. The logic, as ever, is populist. And it is true that a more sophisticated show would probably have attracted a smaller audience. But the logic of maximum possible popularity harms the competition more than Rodzinski realizes. By reducing the Cliburn to a jumble of manipulated sound and music bites, "Here to Make Music" tarnishes its reputation and demeans its young pianists even while attempting to praise them.

In the aftermath of the Eighth Van Cliburn International Piano Competition, I collect a couple of sound bites of my own: from Richard Rodzinski, upon having administered the Cliburn competition for the first time, and from Andrew Raeburn, upon having for the first time attended as an outsider. Rodzinski says: "I do pretty much stand by what I said before we began: by and large the cream does tend to rise to the top. Which is not to say there aren't those who didn't get to the top—who for one reason or another were not selected—who still show strong potential for great careers." Raeburn says: "Looking back at 1985, the ranking might have been totally different with different jurors. This year, there might have been a completely different set of twelve after the first cut. The whole thing—like so many things in life—is partly a question of dumb luck."

---

and have no inherent artistic or entertainment value." PBS conflict-of-interest guidelines for funding focus on the underwriter (e.g., Tandy and Mobil), not the initiator (e.g., the Cliburn Foundation). In this regard, Tandy and Mobil are viewed as having no compromising "special interest" in music.

† In March 1990, Peter Rosen was named Best Director in the television Documentary/Actuality category by the Directors Guild of America for "Here to Make Music."

* * *

The members of the Tokyo String Quartet, with whom I meet in late October, retain vivid memories of the 1989 Cliburn competition. As in 1985, they found the level of the semifinalists disappointing—at least in chamber music.

KAZUHIDE ISOMURA: I think the attitude "Who is ready for a major career?" is wrong. Because this should be a beginning only. All the major talents find strength and creativity only gradually.

PETER OUNDJIAN: The problem is: how many times can you expect to find a major artist at a piano competition?

SADAO HARADA: I think there should be two types of competitions: one for relatively older, established artists, and another one for beginners—people just finishing their studies.

OUNDJIAN: And there should be three or four winners.

KAKUEI IKEDA: After two years of hectic playing, the major competition winners always go down. The prize is so big it's like the end of your life—you can never grow from it.

OUNDJIAN: Right. It's almost stifling for the winner. They don't have any time to grow. They just travel and try not to make fools of themselves.

IKEDA: Look at Pollini. He stopped for several years after winning the Chopin competition.*

For the first time at the Cliburn, the quartet was invited to meet with the jurors and share impressions. The semifinalists the Tokyo liked best were Jean-Efflam Bavouzet, Benedetto Lupo, and Alexander Shtarkman (Bavouzet and Shtarkman shared the chamber music prize with José Carlos Cocarelli and Kevin Kenner). Those quartet members who watched "Here to Make Music" were surprised by some of the performances. They were unprepared for the apparent ineffectuality of Shtarkman's Prokofiev Third Concerto. They were stunned by Pedro Burmester's Bach and bewildered by his failure to advance to the finals.

OUNDJIAN: Burmester was an inexperienced chamber musician. But he has a really wonderful sound. And he communicates.

IKEDA: He's very different. He's original. He could never win a big

---

* Maurizio Pollini played relatively few concerts for a period of years following his 1960 Warsaw victory at the age of eighteen. He reentered the public eye as an advocate of contemporary music, workers' concerts, and other causes outside the mainstream.

competition, in my opinion. He had brought such an old, old copy of the Schumann quintet—because it was his grandfather's. There was absolutely nothing written in it.

OUNDJIAN: He's the type of person you really cannot imagine practicing. He just plays the piano. And his playing is always fascinating to listen to.

I asked if there were any new thoughts about the Cliburn's chamber music requirement.

ISOMURA: Chamber music is good for a pianist. Because pianists are always quite isolated from other musicians. Especially young and ambitious and gifted pianists: they sit in the practice room for many hours, working on solo repertoire. Chamber music can be a very good experience for them.

IKEDA: But should they have to play chamber music in order to win a competition? Suppose they don't care to. It's almost like saying that all the winners have to be the same. For instance, I have never heard of Van Cliburn playing a piano quintet. And to me that's OK.

ISOMURA: I must say that for us it doesn't get any easier to rehearse and play twelve performances within a week.

IKEDA: Maybe it would make more sense to play only one or two movements with each pianist and really concentrate on it.

ISOMURA: I think that's a good idea.

OUNDJIAN: We can tell from the first ten seconds of a rehearsal what kind of musician we're dealing with. We can almost tell before they begin to play. If the judges are sensitive, one movement should be enough.

By now, Alexei Sultanov has been on the road for four months. His American debut recital at Pasadena's Ambassador Auditorium, the day after the "Tonight" show, split the critics. Daniel Cariaga wrote in the *Los Angeles Times*: "Unlike the last three Cliburn winners . . . Sultanov conquered immediately—and unequivocally. . . . The impassioned, articulate and sensitive playing that flows from his arms and fingers with the naturalness of a lion's roar or a bird's cooing expresses something more—much more—than mere good training . . . It expresses a successful bonding between performer and listener." Alan Rich wrote in the *Herald-Examiner*: "At this generally dreadful concert—easily the worst debut recital I've attended since the last Cliburn winner earned his obligatory Ambassador engagement—I heard the workings of an impressive piano-playing machine run by an unimpressive musical conscience . . . great gobs of notes at breakneck speed, with no shaping of events." A week later, Rich wrote: "It becomes tragically clear that a win at Fort Worth—or at Leeds, Moscow, Warsaw, Brussels, Sydney, and the other major stations along the competition trail—is no longer a guarantee of success. It is, if anything, a curse. . . . In normal times, [Sultanov] would now, having made his mark, retire from the limelight, find himself a good teacher of art history and aesthetics . . . and come back as a musician—not just a piano player—in four or five years." Though John Ardoin of the *Dallas Morning News* did not care for it, Sultanov's October 3 Cliburn Concerts recital was a local triumph. Without question, he has developed a larger, more excited Fort Worth following than Steven De Groote, André-Michel Schub, or José Feghali ever enjoyed. He sold out Ed Landreth Auditorium—which Vladimir Ashkenazy, Alicia de Larrocha, and Murray Perahia had not done.

No one considers Sultanov "bland." His strength and stamina are not questioned; his ripeness is. In the Soviet Union, he has a reputation for instability. "We've been quite careful," Richard Rodzinski says. "The concerts aren't one on top of the other. And his schedule includes good breaks; three weeks here, a month there. Some of the dates were last-minute things we couldn't turn down: recitals in Amsterdam and Lucerne, both of which were extraordinarily successful. And some are not Cliburn dates." Prior to the 1989 competition, the Cliburn eagerly signed letters of agreement with more than two hundred orchestras and presenters, most of which were certain to expect the gold medalist.* The result, so far, has been some 120 requests for Sultanov—far more than he can safely accept. The Cliburn, which must be tired of hearing warnings and predictions that Sultanov is unready, has tried to accommodate as many requests as possible without completely ignoring his need to practice, rest, and reflect. Twenty weeks since his Cliburn victory, he has played twenty times in Finland, France, Great Britain, the Netherlands, Poland, Switzerland, the United States, and West Germany. He continues to provoke a contradictory response—London is a debacle, Amsterdam a triumph leading

---

* The letters do not commit either party to the first-prize winner. Rather, they "serve to confirm our agreement in principle that one or more winners of the 1989 Van Cliburn piano competition will perform with XXX on a mutually agreeable date in the 1989–90 or 1990–91 concert season." Invariably, some orchestras and auspices on the Cliburn's list of promised engagements choose not to engage any Cliburn winner—which can make the list quite misleading.

to dates with the Concertgebouw Orchestra. His total bookings for 1989–90 number about sixty—fewer than Steven De Groote, André-Michel Schub, or José Feghali played as Cliburn winners, but still too many for him to maintain continuity in his studies at the Moscow Conservatory. Feghali, reflecting on his Cliburn tours, had observed: "The hardest part . . . is not the music but the other 95 percent." Now twenty, Sultanov remains a stranger in the United States. Even compared to previous Cliburn medalists, he confronts his winner's regime of airports and hotels, microphones and cameras, as a new experience. He plays only eight concertos. In the opinion of Ernest Fleischmann, executive director of the Los Angeles Philharmonic, Sultanov's Cliburn itinerary is "ridiculous for such a young artist, totally stupid"—and Fleischmann is right.*

The Cliburn promotes itself as a "safe bet," a valid and acknowledged "screening process": according to one puff: "the winners are guaranteed engagements and appearances with almost every major orchestra on international concert platforms." But the major American orchestral managers have adopted a wait-and-see attitude. (When I ask the Cleveland Orchestra's Thomas Morris if he is considering booking Sultanov, Morris replies: "Considering *who?*"—and this is no wisecrack; the name does not immediately register.) Generally, the post-1984 Cliburn itineraries suggest a pattern of diminishing credibility. Sultanov's best American orchestral dates are in Atlanta, Detroit, Milwaukee, and Rochester. He also plays a couple of outdoor concerts with the Philadelphia Orchestra and Pittsburgh Symphony—summertime bookings under separate auspices. De Groote, as the 1977 gold medalist, did better; he played prestigious regular-season dates with Cleveland and Philadelphia. Schub, four years later, appeared with the orchestras of Boston, Chicago, Cleveland, and Philadelphia—none of

---

* In subsequent months, Alexei Sultanov canceled concerts due to visa problems arising from homesickness, then to a hand injury sustained while operating a window. Presenters and journalists seem to find him likable—fresh, sincere, self-critical—but very inexperienced. It was widely predicted that Sultanov's Carnegie Hall debut recital would be clobbered by the New York critics. Though the Cliburn Foundation considered presenting him in a single concerto instead, the recital took place as scheduled on May 3, 1990. Sultanov's performance—of a warhorse medley by Mozart, Beethoven, Scriabin, Prokofiev, and Liszt—suggested he had acquired certain self-conscious refinements since his victory in Fort Worth. Donal Henahan of the *New York Times* found "some evidence [Sultanov] has the gifts necessary to build a respectable career given time to mature. In this program his thoughts about the music he chose to perform seemed unexceptional. . . ." Peter Goodman of New York *Newsday* thought Sultanov showed "barely an inkling" of the music's "deeper meanings." Bill Zakariasen of the *New York Daily News* called the recital "disastrous." Peter G. Davis of *New York* magazine heard "shallow, jangly, mechanical performances that lack even the most rudimentary musical impulse."

which engaged 1985's José Feghali. The Los Angeles Philharmonic and New York Philharmonic have never engaged a current Cliburn gold medalist. The present managers and conductors of these "big six" orchestras prefer to invite young talent on their own—or to engage middle-aged soloists passed over by the music businessmen.

Perhaps, as in years past, the gold medalist will not be the Cliburn competition's prime beneficiary. José Carlos Cocarelli, a seasoned thirty-year-old, plays about fifty times in the United States and Europe during the 1989–90 season, including appearances with the Atlanta Symphony and Buffalo Philharmonic that fell his way when Sultanov was needed in Moscow. Benedetto Lupo—who, like Cocarelli, knows nearly twenty concertos—has about forty dates, including two with the Rochester Philharmonic. Denise Chupp, Rodzinski's hard-working artistic administrator, has found a dozen concerts for Tian Ying. Elisso Bolkvadze has recitals in Pasadena and Washington, D.C.

Other nonmedalists are also sure to benefit. "Nightline" has showcased John Nauman and Kevin Kenner. "Victory at the Keyboard" and "They Came to Make Music" will win friends for Pedro Burmester and Alexander Shtarkman, among others. In fact, both Burmester and Shtarkman perform in October 1990 at the 92nd Street Y, one of New York's leading concert halls. As an invaluable service to all thirty-eight contestants, the Cliburn Foundation has handsomely recorded the entire 1989 competition and provides cassettes, without charge, to interested managers, presenters, and journalists. The Burmester and Shtarkman cassettes sell themselves. As the Y has made no prior commitment to the Cliburn Foundation, there is no risk of "upstaging" Sultanov, Cocarelli, or Lupo in the same hall. Other presenters who hear the tapes are trapped, however. "We'd love to do something with Pedro Burmester," says Catherine Fitterman, director of cultural programs for the University of Colorado at Boulder. "I think he's fantastic. But we've already contracted with the Van Cliburn Foundation to put on a winner. And my audience expects to hear the gold medalist. I felt the same way about the last Van Cliburn. I guess it's the American way, to think there's just one winner, whether it's piano or hurdles."

IV

CONCLUSION: A BETTER WAY

MY FRIEND RADOS MAINTAINS AN UNASSAILABLE ANTIPATHY TO MUSIC competitions.

He is a distinguished teacher of chamber music at the Franz Liszt Academy in Budapest, whose former students include the best-known young Hungarians—the pianists Zoltán Kocsis, Dezsö Ránki, and András Schiff; the members of the Takács String Quartet. They honor him as a strong mentor, and as a warm and trusted friend. He is both clever and reflective. His speech is grave and gentle. He smokes a pipe. His small flat is cluttered not with records, tapes, and scores (he does not own a phonograph), but with books. The door is always open to visitors. "As my time is worthless," he explains, "I can afford to spend it in this fashion."

Rados's droll, affectless manner; his curious way of peering upward while dipping his chin; the slight play of mirth on his compressed lips—all this projects a mixture of teasing intellect and fatalistic marginality mainly to be found in Eastern Europe. The mixture is combustible: at any moment, Rados may submit to gusts of laughter which shut his eyes, jerk his head back, and yank open his jaw, revealing a gaping hole where there once was a tooth. His shuffling walk and careless attire are also deeply characteristic.

Born in 1934, he is old enough to remember the Nazi occupation, and much else. He harbors no illusions.

Rados's collection of turn-of-the-century postcards is unique. There are more than a hundred of them, and all deal with music. Here are paintings of "innocent" ladies and "inspired" gentlemen playing or listening, miming "feeling" with their skyward glances, sometimes directed at angels with harps. One music lover buries his head in his hands, another weeps uncontrollably. There are also postcards of monks, nuns, and grizzled priests playing the violin, usually before a tombstone or shrine. Rays of light stream from on high; "the Transcendental," Rados explains. And there are composers. Daydreaming Schubert is teased by the girls. Beethoven, with his square chin and stern countenance, inhabits a landscape of storm clouds and lightning. Haydn, to Rados's delight, is a hopeless case— the postcards cannot depict him. But Rados has collected more than half a dozen renderings of "Chopin's Last Chords"; the haggard composer, slumped in a cushioned chair, fingers the keyboard with thin, infirm fingers. "Now do you *understand* Chopin?" Rados asks me.

If reprinted without commentary as a book, Rados's postcards would be the most devastating published documentation of how music is packaged and received. The extramusical gesture is shown to be indispensable. This is why Rados prefers to "hear" unmediated music—by reading it, holding the score in his lap.

Surely you go too far, I object. What about the late forties, when Otto Klemperer conducted at the Budapest Opera? Was that showmanship? Klemperer was a conductor without affectations, Rados concedes. He even escaped the affectation of humility. But the Mozart operas with which Klemperer gripped the musical public were still fresh repertoire, quite new to Hungary as integrated stage works. And Klemperer had of course had a brain tumor that left him dramatically disabled. This ungainliness, accentuated by his great height, was Klemperer's extramusical prop.

And who is like Klemperer today? Rados continues. The new "market economy"—words he enunciates with a withering precision —dictates that concerts must pay for themselves. A surfeit of "great music" and "great composers" is one result. Hungary is exposed as never before to a chill wind blowing CDs and celebrities, popular culture and music competitions, in which young musicians strive to impress.

Fortuitously, Rados suffers from a chronic hand ailment. He has had to abandon the concert career he once pursued. Not only are his touring days over, he tells me; so are his traveling days. He has seen enough, and everything he has seen looks the same. "Do you mean you'll never again leave Budapest?" I ask him. "Naturally," he replies—and grins.

Rados's fatalism may be unanswerable. But it is also unacceptable, at least for an American like myself. The disunity of Art and Society that he laments is centuries old; not since the 1400s—before the days of "artists"—has music thoroughly complemented the activities of daily life.

Taking stock of the Van Cliburn competition, I find that it holds up a mirror to my own ambivalence. Half of me sides with Rados. The Cliburn seeks and rewards the mediating prop—Alexei Sultanov's kung fu prowess and fearlessness with snakes; his quaking mane and perspiring brow at the keyboard. It epitomizes the cult of the performer. Its cash prizes commodify artists. It mainly endorses the contraction of the repertoire to masterworks of the past, each compared to itself in a dozen barely distinguishable renderings. It espouses a classical music ghetto whose concert rites are anachronistic and redundant; they take no account of the radios, phonographs, and CD players that already spew the *Mephisto* Waltz into our cars and living rooms.

My other half remains an unreconstructed Romantic. In the throes of the concert ritual, in close proximity to an Alexander Shtarkman or a Pedro Burmester, I remain susceptible to the extramusical prop—the tiny and impassive bow, the gold earring; to the drama of the solitary concert hero; to the manic virtuosity and erotic languor of Mephisto's waltz.

The Cliburn competition itself mirrors the ambiguity of the moment. It honors something of the past; it imposes something else of the present. The contradictions produce no cogent synthesis, no vector of transcendence. The best hope—or delusion—I can fabricate is that the Cliburn can achieve truer artistic responsibility without falsifying its surest current truth: its popular appeal.

The expiration of the Leventritt competition was a lesson in the rigors of cultural evolution: its 1977 adaptations rescued the competition from obscurity—only to scorch it to death with the TV lights of a new day. The artistic rescuing the Cliburn needs risks an opposite fate: of a new obscurity, a crippling irrelevance.

It is a pity that the Cliburn asks to be judged by its touted winners. It not only deserves better than Sultanov; in important respects, it is better than any winner. A century ago, when his itinerant orchestra followed the railroad tracks, Theodore Thomas avowed: "A symphony orchestra shows the culture of a community." In Fort Worth today, the Van Cliburn competition shows community culture. More than politics or sports, it inspires a wholesome communal bonding. The city is small enough that there is nothing to eclipse the exciting presence, every four years, of gifted young pianists from around the world. The host families, the volunteer army; Cliburn old-timers like Leon Brachman, newcomers like Gray Mills; the Cliburn Concerts during the off-season—all promote an ongoing municipal identity. The competition instills local pride and lures valued visitors, residents, and businesses. From the standpoint of Tandy Corporation chairman John Roach: "It brings recognition to the city in a different way than the recognition we get for our role in technology, or as a retail center, or for the investments of the Basses." When Tandy recruited Scott Cutler, its vice president for software design, Roach took him to lunch with Andrew Raeburn. An avid amateur pianist, Cutler now sits on the boards of the Fort Worth Opera, Symphony, Youth Orchestra, and Chamber Music Society. At the Cliburn, he designed the computer program used to tabulate the voting. He calls hosting Li Jian, one of 1989's Chinese competitors, "one of the great experiences of my life." Others who have moved to Fort Worth from out of state tell similar stories. A recent advertisement placed in national magazines by the Convention and Visitors Bureau shows Van Cliburn; the headline reads: VAN CLIBURN'S FORT WORTH: BRAHMS TO BRONCOS.

According to Leon Brachman, the Cliburn risks becoming too big for its own good. "What is its purpose? To enhance our life in Fort Worth? To provide a plaything for the jet-setters? To make a career for the winner?" So far, high society has not trampled the foundation's life-enhancing grass roots. But the Cliburn fails to obtain commensurate artistic returns on its multimillion-dollar investments. Some pianists are helped. Some are hurt. The crucial failure is obvious, at least to outsiders: the prime beneficiaries have never been gold medalists. Within the Cliburn community, this failure is blurred: close up, a very big prize looks better than a small one. But two years of hectic concert-giving did not catapult Steven De Groote, André-Michel Schub, or José Feghali into anything like a major career orbit.

The Cliburn should move more decisively toward retiring its ballyhooed gold-medal itinerary. It was a naive inspiration to begin with, a Martha Hyder brainstorm based on happenstance. It burdens young pianists with unfulfillable expectations, and with fatiguing schedules preempting study, reflection, and personal growth. It propels them into venues they cannot be expected to command. The exaggerated praise it generates undermines what it uplifts.

Texas largess breeds a further confusion: that the "best" pianist will excel in concertos and chamber music, études and sonatas, in Bach, Mozart, Chopin, Tchaikovsky. The Cliburn's repertoire requirements are a tangled legacy of Irl Allison, Grace Ward Lankford, Martha Hyder, and Van Cliburn himself. As with so many of the competition's procedures, improvement has been deferred by turnover: a different chairman, a different executive director nearly every time. The Bach and Mozart requirements, especially, are unrealistic; and they penalize the very pianists the competition seeks for its Romantic concertos. Worse: repertoire requirements impinge on artistic prerogatives; a recitalist's program is the first potent statement he makes. For the Cliburn audience, free choice of solo repertoire would reduce the redundancy of ten *Chromatic* Fantasies and nine F minor Ballades, and the attendant focus on trivial disparities in interpretation.*

In a 1989 article on music competitions, the guitarist Eliot Fisk wrote:

> At a time when guitarists should be experimenting and seeking out new ideas in pedagogy, audience development, repertoire . . . competitions continue to behave as if these problems didn't exist. . . . One would think that new ideas might crop up at guitar competitions just as at trade conventions new technology confronts older methods. . . . Applicants are asked to prove basic competence . . . but they are not

---

* The Dublin International Piano Competition, new in 1988, stipulates no required repertoire (other than a commissioned work), so that competitors "may express their individuality." The Kapell competition dispensed with its solo repertoire requirements the same year. Paul Pollei of the Gina Bachauer competition will do away with them as of 1991. Pollei comments: "One thing that changed my mind was hearing Jorge Bolet, at the 1985 Cliburn, say 'I will never judge another competition. The pianists always have to play things they don't really know.' Competitions should show people off at their best." At the opposite extreme, Thomas Beczkiewicz, executive director of Indianapolis's International Violin Competition, misadvises prospective contestants: "Repertory . . . offers one sure sign of a competition's level. If the repertory is broad and complete in its requirements, surveying the highest achievement of the instrument's literature, the competition is serious; and if a significant part of the competition repertory is already an active part of your own, you are probably on the right track." In an article for competitors, in the September 1989 *Musical America*, Beczkiewicz also advises that "serious" competitions have jurors "from every part of the world" and that "other than actually winning the gold, the most exhilarating part of the competition adventure is preparing for it." He warns against "idiosyncrasy" in performance, as well as "bizarre stage dress or behavior." Even losers can benefit from "a career reassessment that will eventually prove more valuable than any other discovery the competition brings to you." The Indianapolis is America's most prominent string competition.

encouraged to seek out new and creative solutions to the critical problems facing the profession.

Pianists, too, face "critical problems": an unreplenished repertoire; a shrinking recital market. The Cliburn mainly addresses the piano's diminishing relevance with a single gesture: the commissioned American work. On balance, this gesture has proved disappointing. The disappointment is not merely that no Cliburn commission has notably enriched the contemporary literature; or even that the Cliburn invariably commissions composers from a dwindling conservative mainstream. The odds are poor that any new work will appeal to a majority of the contestants. A better strategy would be to require each pianist to perform the music of a living composer, and to instruct the jury to make this requirement matter. Instead of twelve performances of *Chester*, the 1989 competition might have featured such potential high points as Alexander Shtarkman playing Schnittke, or Jean-Efflam Bavouzet's Stockhausen. Young pianists should be encouraged to program creatively. Many a featureless New York recital—a little of this, a little of that—can be traced to competition requirements that leave little time for exploring a personalized repertoire. This is one of several areas in which, beyond refining its mission, the Cliburn can undertake a constructive initiative.

"Competitions should include workshops, seminars or master classes, whenever possible," concludes a study by the European String Teachers Association. These, too, can speak to "critical problems facing the profession." The workshops and master classes of the TCU/Cliburn Competition Piano Institute, concurrent with the competition, receive as little attention as they deserve. The recitals, lectures, and classes of the William Kapell competition's "piano festival" are central events. At the 1989 Kapell festival, jurors Roman Vlad and Charles Rosen gave lecture-recitals on the piano music of Stravinsky and Elliott Carter; Carter himself was on hand. The Cliburn can do at least as well.

A final, more drastic revision would seal the logic of these first steps: the Cliburn should not rank its winners. Ranking is false. It sends the wrong message: that artistic achievement is objectifiable, even quantifiable. "Burmester and Shtarkman—they are a world apart," says Philippe Bianconi. So are Alexei Sultanov and José Carlos Cocarelli; the thrill of their manufactured rivalry is as vulgar as the awards "countdown" with its envelopes for sixth, fifth, fourth, third, second, and first place. The idea of "number one" is perniciously seductive; we—and also the pianists, who are sometimes its worst victims—cannot help but think less of "number two." What jury can say who is "best"? No jury can—regardless of its esteemed membership or careful procedures. The jury's role must be understood.* Its judgment, however expert, is subjective. Its service is expedient, not omniscient. It does not reliably "screen" closely matched candidates to find number one. Rather, its verdict creates opportunities for certain pianists. A different jury would produce a different verdict; different pianists would be helped or hindered. What is more: on today's busy competition circuit, with far too many juror slots to fill, obtaining a strong field is much easier than obtaining a strong jury. In any competition, some pianists will play over the heads of some judges. All the more reason that, instead of ranking six finalists, the Cliburn jury should be instructed to choose up to six winners—who would emerge more nearly life-size, rather than bloated with an importance they had not possessed while merely playing.

According to its 1989 program booklet, the Cliburn is "a proven arena from which important careers have developed . . . a leading influence on the world of music." According to the *Fort Worth Star-Telegram*, "strong evidence" exists that the 1989 Cliburn field surpassed "the talent quotient of any other piano competition there has ever been, anywhere." According to subsequent Cliburn literature, the 1989 competition was "a uniquely momentous event" that "left its indelible mark." But if the Cliburn really does make Fort Worth "the center of the music world," its concerto round would utilize a suitable auditorium. It would seek a more stylish, more challenging radio and television image. It would enjoy more privileged relations with the international piano community, promoting access to superior jurors and a jury chairman of more than local eminence. The competition's crowning provincialism, however, is the gold medal and its gaudy trappings. A slate of unranked winners would automatically discourage hyperbolic salesmanship and every other circus aspect.

Van Cliburn, in his speeches, prefers to think of the Van Cliburn International Piano Competition as a "festival." This false description is a true mandate. The final round should be a dignified showcase for gifted young performers—not a competition, but a festival of pianists and piano music.

---

* No competition fosters misunderstanding as explicitly as the Bachauer; its elaborate "audience prizes" are for "audience members who most closely match the choices of the jury for each of the competition rounds."

*   *   *

Other American competitions and auditions handle prizes and programs more sensibly than the Cliburn does. Young Concert Artists and Affiliate Artists do not rank their winners or stipulate elaborate repertoire requirements; as managements, they aim more for modest than for major engagements. The Naumburg competition ranks its top three finishers only, and stipulates no repertoire. Stephen Hough, the remarkable 1983 winner, has enjoyed a smoother, more auspicious career ascent than any Cliburn medalist —thanks partly to Leventritt-style networking undertaken by Lucy and Robert Mann. As had the Leventritts and their circle, the Manns enjoy close contact with leading conductors and impresarios. For that matter, no competition has so proudly repudiated rankings, repertoire lists, or the big, public prize as did the Leventritt. Concomitantly, it repudiated anything like the Cliburn's popular base.

This concomitance summarizes the Cliburn competition's central dilemma. Every refinement of its artistic mission risks jeopardizing its public appeal and community support. Would audiences and sponsors reject unranked winners? Do they insist on the biggest possible prize? The most standardized repertoire? And there is a second constraint: the music business, itself popularized, itself craving one big winner playing the money concertos.

If its popular base is the Cliburn Foundation's outstanding achievement, the music business reduces the Cliburn to the status of symptom or victim. Gone are the days when a private audition or a New York debut could launch a career. Music businessmen find it safer and easier to exploit the young gladiator who comes trailing loud publicity and applause. As never before, they aim for the instant career, quickly begun, quickly expended. "Gifted beginners should not be harassed," Busoni once wrote. "They should give their fresh and promising gifts to the world before a chosen few; a spring festival of the art, a greeting to a bud just coming into bloom, the initiation of a youthful talent, a calm and cheerful ceremony." Even Van Cliburn's Moscow victory brought him fewer engagements than the Cliburn gold medal brought André-Michel Schub. The young Glenn Gould's busiest season was 1956–57, during which he performed forty-four times.

To what extent can the Cliburn competition transcend these popular and commercial pressures? Anthony Phillips, who administered the 1981 competition, regards the obligation to pick a single winner as "a necessary evil. . . . It seems to be the best, almost the only way in which people of influence in the horrible music business can be persuaded to listen to young performers who have not already climbed onto the career ladder or have not made much way up it." Andrew Raeburn also prefers nonranked winners "in principle." "The problem is they would generate much less excitement—not only locally, but also abroad. Particularly for the presenters, the ranking is an important selling point." Richard Rodzinski agrees that ranking "can amount to choosing between apples and oranges"—yet remains mindful that "people want to have a winner." But Paul Pollei, whose Gina Bachauer competition relies on grass-roots support as much as the Cliburn does, is more sanguine about not ranking his six finalists. "It's an idea I've always found attractive. And it would be feasible if I had an unlimited budget. Our present first prize includes a grand piano. If we instead awarded its value in cash, then I would take that $30,000 and do something different. Would it jeopardize our support base? I don't think so. We've always had strong local support. I know there are some people who see the competition as a horse race. But there are lots of others who reject that, who would welcome a less 'competitive' verdict."

If Pollei, with more piano competition experience than Anthony Phillips, Andrew Raeburn, and Richard Rodzinski put together, thinks he could sell unranked winners in Salt Lake City, the Cliburn must be selling itself short. Even the "horrible music business" supports this possibility. As the 1989 Cliburn competition shows, the leading orchestral managers, no longer willing to accept jury rankings, have stopped paying attention. A policy of unranked winners would bring them back. "What is needed is a platform for gifted young artists, before a general audience as well as the most prominent presenters, managers, and impresarios," says the Los Angeles Philharmonic's Ernest Fleischmann. "I think it would be extremely helpful to let the Cliburn pianists play the final round with the pressure of the competition behind them. And speaking for myself, I would be much more likely to engage someone I could hear without the intervention of a jury's verdict." The Chicago Symphony's Henry Fogel says: "I don't think ranking has any artistic validity whatsoever. I would be much more likely to make a commitment if I were given a choice of five or six winners. I'd be much more likely to find a talent I believed in."*

* The Queen Elisabeth competition gives gold medals to both its first- and its second-place finishers. The Rubinstein competition gives gold medals for first, second, and third place. But these are cosmetic touches; they do not influence public perceptions. A more meaningful innovation is at Spain's Santander International Piano Competition, which as of 1990 has dispensed with "numeric classifications" in favor of up to two "grand prizes," up to two "prizes of honor," and a "finalist prize."

Fort Worth enjoys a serious and open-minded piano audience—one that is obviously ready for more contemporary music, that seizes the excitement of an unfamiliar work. And the Cliburn audience has for some time understood, and lamented, the fallibility of the jury. Raeburn himself remarks: "I'm a great believer that you can persuade people of almost anything if you don't wound their egos." Fort Worth egos can be made to appreciate that local claims to cultural sophistication are belied by the Cliburn's blatantly over-valued, overpromoted gold medal.

I belabor this possibility because the audience matters. Music in concert cannot exist without it. The audience stimulates or retards, gratifies or inhibits. As audiences change, so do concerts. Our American audiences are larger, more diverse, less sophisticated than European audiences of a century ago. At the Metropolitan Opera, a huge, complacent audience holds culture hostage to Franco Zef-firelli. In Fort Worth, a dynamic audience stirs with American optimism. It needs help.

The progression from the Leventritt competition to the Cliburn competition charts a sea change in American musical culture: the flourish and decline of an elite enclave; the sweeping ascendance of the populist ideal. This democratization of high culture is the central fact confronting all who arbitrate and debate the fate of classical music.

What used to be classical music is undoubtedly dead, and no amount of handwringing will bring it back. The term itself is already an anachronism, denoting a defunct precinct of high culture. Today's "classical music" is mainly a species of pretentious popular entertainment. Ostensibly raising mass culture, it razes high culture. It is "easy listening" radio stations whose programming strategies reduce Torelli and Mozart to a common denominator. It is Luciano Pavarotti at Madison Square Garden, bellowing Verdi and Puccini into a microphone for a bored, dutiful audience. It is too much music performed for too many people in spaces with too many seats: contradictions ultimately rationalized by marketing strategists adept at creating and maintaining artificial demand. It makes the present moment confused and ambiguous.

My friend Rados turns his back on "post-classical" music, and I understand. But there are other possible responses. There is the possibility of a liberating, post-modern eclecticism, smashing mid-cult's complacency, catalyzing a fusion audience; if we let him, Gidon Kremer may be the one to preside over classical music's rambunctious deconstruction. There is the possibility—in small, high-minded venues—of paring down the audience and of subordinating the performing stars; in New York, the 92nd Street Y's Schubertiade, with its concerts, master classes, lecture-performances, panels, films, and program essays, shows it can be done. There is the creative integration of new music, chamber music, and scholarship into the mainstream symphonic curriculum; the San Francisco Symphony, not so long ago, achieved something of this kind. Odd company for the Van Cliburn International Piano Competition—and yet Fort Worth, too, potentially hosts a meaningful holding action, fortified by a diversified agenda, a refreshed audience, and a capacity to experiment and change.

As a ballyhooed epitome of the popularization movement, the Cliburn wields enormous national influence. It sets standards. It shapes perceptions. I think it defers to the music businessmen more than it needs to. In the skewed world of post-classical music, we are so accustomed to the tail wagging the dog that we have forgotten that this violates the natural order of things.

The Cliburn's challenge is to fine-tune the trade-off between past ideals and present realities, between residual high culture and its democratic diffusion. Is it too late for the dog to wag its tail? Perhaps not. Perhaps.

POSTLUDE:
VAN CLIBURN
REVISITED

Time's 1958 COVER STORY ON VAN CLIBURN BOASTED:

Van's victory dramatically underscored that there is more first-rate native instrumental talent in the U.S. than in the whole of Europe. Moreover, the talent is younger. In Cliburn's generation there are at least nine pianists of equal native ability: Byron Janis, 30, Gary Graffman, 29, Seymour Lipkin, 31, Jacob Lateiner, 30, Claude Frank, 32, John Browning, 24, Eugene Istomin, 32, Leon Fleisher, 31, and Canada's Glenn Gould, 25, who has played widely in the U.S. . . . Some of the Americans are almost sure to step into the shoes of the Backhauses, the Rubinsteins, the Serkins, the Giesekings and Horowitzes.

But none did.*

In retrospect, the surprise of Cliburn's 1978 retirement is less surprising. Even for a pianist, a lifetime of touring is an improbable prospect. Gould once explained his retirement from the stage at thirty-one: "It was never something I wanted to spend my entire life doing. . . . I have pretty well exhausted the [piano] music that interests me." Others let the music exhaust them.

---

* Janis, Graffman, and Fleisher succumbed to hand problems. Gould quit giving concerts. Lipkin turned mainly to conducting, then to teaching and chamber music. Frank, Browning, and Istomin still tour, but not in the giant-size shoes *Time* predicted.

Steven De Groote became a university teacher; Murray Perahia, he predicted, would be the only pianist of his generation to sustain a major solo career into old age. Jeffrey Kahane diversifies: he pursues chamber music, contemporary music, and teaching alongside the Big Career he seeks. Alexander Toradze—scarred in Soviet Russia, marginalized in modern America—recalls a faded species: the heroic virtuoso.

Cliburn kept going for more than twenty years. Santiago Rodriguez once asked him how it felt to play for the last time. "He said, 'The one thing I felt when I got off the stage was: I don't have to do this anymore.' And you know, there's a point to that."

The locus classicus, as ever, is Liszt. He toured tirelessly: to Gibraltar and Lisbon, to Glasgow and Belfast, to Copenhagen and Amsterdam, to Constantinople and Bucharest. Like Cliburn, he conquered Russia: not just St. Petersburg, but Kiev and Odessa. In September 1847, he played in Elisavetgrad and announced his retirement. He would no longer play in public for a fee. He was thirty-five years old.

Liszt had been contemplating quitting for some years. He complained of a "great tiredness of life and a ridiculous need for rest, for languor." Careening from city to city, inwardly driven, pushed and pulled by outward demands, he cried: "Always concerts! Always a valet of the public! What a trade!" He had other trades to ply. He ripened into a great Romantic composer. He turned to conducting, advocating the new music of Wagner, Berlioz, and Schumann. He was an important piano pedagogue. He read voraciously. He lived fully.

Heine said of Liszt: "His intellectual proclivities are quite remarkable; he has a very lively taste for speculation and is less preoccupied with his own artistic interests than with the investigations of the various schools of thought dealing with the great questions of heaven and earth. . . . It is impossible not to praise that indefatigable thirst for enlightenment and divinity which manifests itself in his predilection for sacred and religious matters." Liszt gravitated to France's social philosophers: to the Christian socialism of the Saint-Simonians; to the neo-Catholics Ballanche and Lamennais. For him, art was religion, and the artist's mission included elevating public taste by propagating a more rarefied repertoire—propagating music as an ethical force. Artists are "children of God," he wrote, "predestined, thunderstruck, enthralled men who have carried off the sacred flame from heaven . . . priests of an ineffable, mystical, eternal religion." In later life, he took minor orders toward becoming a Catholic priest.

Liszt's letters prickle with reminders that some things never change. "In our time the public takes the initiative and asks for all the family secrets, all the details of one's private life." "If the truth be told, most artists are not overly offended by the publicity, favorable or not, since it puts their names in circulation for a few days at least." "People never stop repeating that we are living in an age of transition, and that is truer for music than for anything else." "Isn't there . . . an urgent need for the government to [sponsor] an orchestra and a trained chorus for the performance of modern compositions selected by a special committee?" Essentially, however, Liszt was a nineteenth-century Promethean; few who came after him espoused anything like his broad visionary mandate. Meanwhile, the piano, having grown bigger and stronger than any keyboard instrument Mozart or Beethoven knew, stopped evolving. So, after World War I, did its literature. Its once impressive social role all but vanished. The vocation Liszt flaunted and endured as a young adult—the itinerant virtuoso—calcified into custodial routine: a cultural sideshow.

To be sure, modern-day pianists, too, know what Liszt called the "ennobling dream," the "indescribably powerful enchantment" of a public performance "that draws the thoughts and hearts of others to us, that causes other people's souls to . . . shine with . . . mutual enthusiasm." And there are present-day pianists, as well, whose mission includes perpetuating a lineage of repertoire and interpretation, as Rudolf Serkin strives to do in Marlboro; or sponsoring vital new works, as Sviatoslav Richter did for Prokofiev; or more generally espousing progressive cultural and political causes, as Maurizio Pollini does. More typical, however, is the struggling twenty-six-year-old Juilliard graduate and competition winner who tells me that his ambition in later life is to play Beethoven, Chopin, and Liszt "at a higher level" and one hundred times a year. For more thoughtful pianists—pianists like Alexander Toradze, André-Michel Schub, Jeffrey Kahane, José Feghali, William Wolfram, Pedro Burmester, Alexander Shtarkman—the potential rewards of a Big Career are less chimerical. Still, the piano and its literature continue their gradual recession into the past.

In this context the case of Van Cliburn is both typical and anomalous. Typical, because it epitomizes certain twentieth-century syndromes: the instant career, the custodial repertoire. Perhaps it was his hero Rachmaninoff—a distinguished conductor at the Bolshoi Theater before his voluntary exile thrust him toward the career of a touring virtuoso—who once inspired him to do some conducting and composing; essentially, he was and is a pianist only. And yet, more than any of his prominent contemporaries, Cliburn follows Liszt in idealizing Art as Religion. What if Lamartine and the Broadway Baptist Church are continents and centuries apart? Cliburn inspires his church to practice music as a vehicle for communal uplift. His paeans to "timeless" and "eternal" musical values bespeak his belief in music as an ethical force. The Cliburn competition invokes the rhetoric of popularization; Cliburn's remains the rhetoric of an earlier phase of cultural dissemination: sacralization.* Unlike Liszt's more than a century ago, his artistic religiosity is a delimiting oddity, a relic. But it authentically binds him to nineteenth-century ideals of Romantic innocence—ideals in which others can only find cobwebs and clichés.

All this is confirmed and clarified when, in the wake of the Eighth Van Cliburn International Piano Competition, Van Cliburn ends his eleven-year retirement. Predictably, inevitably, it is a journey forward into the past. He has chosen to perform with the Philadelphia Orchestra at its outdoor summer home, the Mann Music Center. The concert, on June 19, is a benefit for the Mann endowment fund; tickets range from $20 to $125. Cliburn plays the Liszt E-flat Concerto and his best-seller: the Tchaikovsky B-flat minor. But first there is a speech. He steps up to a microphone and begins: "This is a very sentimental evening for me—it is an evening of remembrance of two very wonderful friends." Fredric Mann wanted "everybody on the face of the earth to know, . . . to *believe* in classical music"; Mann said: "Classical music is here to stay. It will always have an audience." Eugene Ormandy was born in the same country as Liszt and studied at the Liszt Conservatory. Liszt's pupil Arthur Fried-

---

* As Lawrence Levine (*Highbrow/Lowbrow*, 1988), among others, has argued, the raucous vitality of America's diversified nineteenth-century audiences for theater, concerts, and opera was compromised after the turn of the century when Shakespeare and Verdi were elevated and revered as difficult, unpopular "culture," distinct from popular entertainment. In the American concert milieu, "sacralization" meant the creation of "symphony orchestras," conducted by Germans and serving the high-minded symphonies of Beethoven and other canonized Austro-German masters. The movement's high priests included the conductors Theodore Thomas and Karl Muck, and the critics John Sullivan Dwight and Henry Krehbiel. After World War I, sacralization entered a more popular phase, whose central deities—Beethoven and Arturo Toscanini—were regularly cloaked in religious metaphor; were in fact equated. To the critic Lawrence Gilman, Toscanini was "vicar of the Immortals." But once Toscanini was hired by David Sarnoff's Radio Corporation of America in 1937, and his American constituency grew broader and less elitist, this imagery of aloof, imperious authority grew inappropriate. Toscanini's image was tempered, and Great Music itself was made to seem less specialized and remote. Gradually, but distinctly, popularized sacralization gave way to pure popularization.

heim taught Cliburn's mother, who in turn taught her son. Cliburn's first collaboration with Ormandy and his Philadelphia Orchestra was in the Tchaikovsky concerto. Cliburn concludes with a poem of his own—"Steal not away/O pierced heart"—that he had recited at the Steven De Groote memorial concert in Fort Worth twelve days before. He is such a practiced public personality—he speaks without notes—that he initially looks incongruous seated at the piano, glancing at Stanislaw Skrowaczewski, ready to play. The Liszt, in the grand Cliburn manner, goes off without a hitch. But something is missing, I find. Does Cliburn sound self-conscious, performing with orchestra after an eleven-year hiatus? Or is it that his Romantic innocence disavows Lisztian irony? The Tchaikovsky, the trophy piece, is another matter. I make no conscious effort to remember the story of 1958, but cannot help it: Cliburn even looks like a young man, rocking from the waist, rolling his head to the sky. Then there are encores: four big ones by Rachmaninoff, Debussy, and Chopin, while the orchestra sits and listens. Obviously, Cliburn could play all night. He is a born performer, in love with the crowd.

And yet the crowd is tepid. Attendance is said to be twelve thousand, or "near capacity," but I see many empty seats. Few people stand to applaud when Cliburn appears, or even after he plays. Cliburn's American celebrity, which was never grounded in music, needs freshening. Donal Henahan's review in the *New York Times* is a favorable yawn.*

---

* Weeks later, Cliburn performed the same two concertos in Moscow and Leningrad. Predictably, these concerts were popular triumphs. Concentric police cordons were needed to stem the rush of disappointed ticket-seekers. Onstage, in his hotel room, on the street, Cliburn was showered with bouquets. The Gorbachevs attended the first concert, on July 2. In a speech from the stage, Cliburn said: "I think you know how full my heart is and I think you know that for me this is an important sentimental journey. . . . For thirty-one years I have felt like I had two homes. I will soon be asking permission from your distinguished President Gorbachev to buy an apartment in Moscow. I will be coming for much-needed visits for my music, for my soul, to Russia and to Moscow." Gorbachev promised to help. The apartment—which turned out to be a house—would be named in honor of Rildia Bee; at Cliburn's death, it would become the property of the Moscow Conservatory. Cliburn's first Moscow concert was a benefit for Raisa Gorbachev's Soviet Culture Fund, to which Cliburn himself contributed $10,000. He also gave $5,000 to Moscow's Baptist church and $5,000 to the Moscow Conservatory—which awarded him a Master of Fine Arts degree. According to John Ardoin of the *Dallas Morning News*, who was there: "It was like being with a rock star. The adulation was unbelievable—much more intense than for Vladimir Horowitz in 1986. Crowds of admirers gathered outside Van's hotel room at every hour of the day and night—people with flowers, and with photographs and other memorabilia from 1958. And there was a mob scene every time he left the hotel. The performance itself—of the Tchaikovsky concerto at the first Moscow concert—showed how an audience can work on an artist. Cliburn takes such strength from an audience—if it's there, he will absorb it. As exciting as the Philadelphia performance had been, the Moscow performance was unlike anything I'd ever heard. It was one of the great events of my life." Cliburn's return to Russia attracted scant attention in the New York press, which had lavishly feted him as America's Sputnik thirty-one years before.

My own reaction is intense: Cliburn's performance of the Tchaikovsky concerto is the most memorable in my experience. Like his Rachmaninoff Third, it counteracts conventional wisdom about how to make the piece "work." As in the Rachmaninoff, Vladimir Horowitz's interpretation is conventionally wisest. Horowitz made the concerto a fractured vehicle—it barely holds together—for convulsive athletic prowess. Cliburn makes the concerto more than a vehicle. His tempos are remarkably modest. The first movement's skipping main theme acquires a balletic lilt; Cliburn is the rare pianist for whom the downbeats do not sound like upbeats, coarsening the tune. The second movement, including the *Prestissimo* middle section, is a respite of gentleness and song. Even the boisterous finale sustains a lyric impulse. A Cliburn contestant scheduled to play the Tchaikovsky concerto, had he made it to the last round, confided to me: "I *cannot* get a conception of the work." Cliburn conceives the work as a testament to romantic yearning and loss. In Horowitz's reading, the most telling moment is the octave volcano signaling the last, distended reprise of the finale's big tune. In Cliburn's Philadelphia performance, the most telling moment comes during the first-movement development, where, over a swelling pedal point, piano and orchestra exchange and reiterate an aching four-note phrase for twenty-three measures. The phrase—spanning a descending major third—follows in its rhythmic and melodic profile the hallucinatory cry of Wagner's lusting Tristan: "Ach, Isolde!" *Tristan's* erotic yearning is consummated in death. The Tchaikovsky concerto's yearning theme leads nowhere; *fortissimo* trombones negate it with another idea. For Wagner, the forbidden sexuality of incest and promiscuity expresses Romantic rebellion. For Tchaikovsky, sexual longing—Tatiana's in *Eugene Onegin* (with which the composer confessed he identified); Lisa's in *Queen of Spades*—signifies the neurotic instability of a tender passion from which the storybook bliss of his ballets is the only escape. Tchaikovsky's most popular song sets Goethe's famous formulation of Romantic nostalgia: *"Nur wer die Sehnsucht kennt,/Weiss, was ich leide."** Cliburn's performance fathoms the poignancy of Tchaikovsky's loneliness for the past. No wonder Russia wept in 1958.

Few artists are privileged to live so completely in their dreams. Van Cliburn inhabits the Romantic dream of the piano—the dream the Cliburn competition seeks to recover and cannot.

---

* Only he who knows longing/Knows what I suffer. Tchaikovsky's *Net, tolko tot*, however, is usually translated "None but the lonely heart."

AFTERWORD: THE GILMORE KEYBOARD FESTIVAL

WITHIN TWO YEARS OF THE 1989 VAN CLIBURN INTERNATIONAL Piano Competition, all four major European competitions were held and received remarkably little attention in the United States. The Leeds competition was won by a pianist who got nowhere in the Chopin competition. The Chopin competition, for the first time in its history, named no first prize. The Tchaikovsky competition was riddled by allegations of bribery, by dissatisfaction with the orchestra, by complaints about housing, food, and transportation; the chairman of the organizing committee publicly questioned the feasibility of future Tchaikovsky competitions. The Queen Elisabeth was won by a long-haired twenty-two-year-old who had never previously competed, who was playing with orchestra for the second time in his life, and whose concerto was not the usual blockbuster, but Beethoven's Fourth (which he performed in non-concert garb). A juror remarked: "As far as I can tell, Frank Braley entered this competition on a whim. He's a total outsider. He's also a totally unostentatious player—he completely contradicts the competition-winner type. I think his victory represents an attempt to pick somebody really, really different. I think there was a realization that you simply can't repeat the days when Cliburn won the Tchaikovsky, or when Argerich won the Chopin, or when

Ashkenazy won the Queen Elisabeth. I think people realize that we're not likely to find another young virtuoso who wins a competition and then leaps into the concert world with an enormous splash."

In Warsaw, the highest ranking contestant was Kevin Kenner, who finished second. Kenner also tied for third in Moscow. Previously—as we have seen—he had been an impressive semifinalist in the 1989 Cliburn and had failed to survive the first cut at the 1989 Kapell competition. When I spoke to him in 1991, he declared himself only "a bit disappointed" not to have received the Chopin gold medal. "I feel I've benefited tremendously. In Europe, the Chopin competition is still highly regarded—it's managed to keep a good name. It's enabled me to play virtually any place I want to. I couldn't ask for more than that. And it's such a relief to be able to put competitions behind me. I do hope in the future it will be possible to advance young musicians in a more constructive way."

Meanwhile, in Fort Worth, the Cliburn Foundation was moving toward reducing the rigors of its repertoire requirements and gold medal itinerary. These overdue changes will of course prove welcome. But the Cliburn will have to change fast to keep pace with the newest, most heretical development on the competition circuit: the Irving S. Gilmore International Keyboard Festival.

Irving Gilmore ran Gilmore's Department Store of Kalamazoo, Michigan. He was also an heir to the Upjohn Pharmaceuticals fortune. In Kalamazoo he was well-known as an affable philanthropist as well as an avid amateur pianist. When he died in 1985, he left $88 million to a foundation in his name, and charged it with subsidizing the types of projects he had supported in his lifetime. The foundation elected to initiate an international piano competition, something like the Cliburn competition. David Pocock, a thirty-six-year-old member of the piano faculty at Kalamazoo's Western Michigan University, was hired as a consultant. And yet Pocock did not especially favor piano competitions. After spending two years on the competition circuit, taking notes for the Gilmore, he favored them even less. He reported back that the Gilmore Foundation should forget about starting a piano competition—there were too many already, and their impact was problematic. Instead, he proposed a piano award along the lines of the MacArthur Foundation grants, for which recipients cannot apply.

The format Pocock devised called for a Gilmore Artist to be named every two years. The artist could be of any age, but pianists with established international solo careers would not be eligible. A search would take place, but the nominees would never know they were under surveillance. The winner would be taken by surprise by stipends and engagements worth $250,000. He or she would be feted in the course of a biennial music festival in Kalamazoo. The Gilmore Foundation advanced $1.4 million to implement Pocock's plan. The first Gilmore International Keyboard Festival was scheduled for May 1991.

In the course of two years of study and deliberation beginning in March 1989, the Gilmore's fourteen-member artistic advisory committee—mainly consisting of obscure or well-known pedagogues—heard tapes of fifty nominated pianists, ages sixteen to seventy-six, from twenty-two countries. The field was narrowed to three pianists, all of whom were unobtrusively heard in concert. The committee was unable to reach a consensus. Four more candidates were identified, of whom one was finally chosen. His name was David Owen Norris and he was thirty-seven years old.

Looking for an instrumentalist who was also a rounded musician with something to say, the committee wound up with a Gilmore Artist who violated every known role model for victorious music-competitors. Norris does not even consider himself a pianist. He is a writer and lecturer, an organist, a scholar, a composer, a teacher. He has served as a répétiteur at Covent Garden. He coaches voice at the Royal Conservatory. For the BBC he has presented radio and television documentaries and hosted a weekly music magazine, whose topics ranged from whale music to football songs, singers' accents to Welsh rock music. On a BBC commission he wrote *Die Zabaglione*, a fifteen-minute opera in Mozartean style in which Salieri accidentally poisons himself while trying to murder Mozart. One of his passions is Baroque opera, especially Purcell. His solo keyboard repertoire includes lots of Haydn, Debussy, and Poulenc. His concertos include the Grieg, the Stravinsky, and the Sterndale Bennett. He adores Sting's *Nothing Like the Sun* and considers Joni Mitchell, whose songs he has transcribed for voice and piano, one of his strongest early influences. He calls the piano recital a "funny old idea" and seems well pleased never to have had a manager ("They encourage the artist to think of himself as a neutral element—a flesh-and-blood compact disk"). He lives with his wife and two sons in rural Petworth, in West Sussex, fifty miles southwest of London.

At the Gilmore, Norris was invited to perform with the Kalamazoo Symphony, with the Blair String Quartet, and in recital. He chose the Britten Piano Concerto and the Elgar Piano Quintet.

His solo program consisted of three pieces by William Byrd, Arnold Bax's Second Sonata, and the American premiere of Liszt's transcriptions of twelve songs from Schubert's *Winterreise*—which turn out to form a powerfully integrated cycle. His encores were *Farewell to Stromness* by Peter Maxwell Davies, and a couple of "syncopated pieces" by the late British cocktail pianist Billy Mayerl—into one of which he interpolated "I've Got a Gal in Kalamazoo."

Norris's performances understandably disappointed the piano mavens; he will win no prizes for his études. But, for all save these specialized listeners, his technical shortcomings were obscured by an abundancy of gifts. He is both a born musician and a born performer. With his impetuous energy and round, witty face, he is a brisk, acute presence onstage. His musical intelligence is not only rangy but passionately gregarious. All this yields a rare versatility: Norris proved as conversant with Billy Mayerl's breezy, stride-piano virtuosity as with the Bax sonata's bleak metaphysic. He was the vital nerve center of the Britten and Elgar performances. In the Schubert/Liszt, he was overmatched, yet conveyed the paradoxical convergence of emotional concentration and expansive Romantic rhetoric; his interpretive and emotional risks completed one another.*

The Kalamazoo audience took to Norris at once. Before he had touched the piano, his deft program notes and spoken remarks revealed an irresistible communicative flair. His exotic repertoire was made an adventure, never a chore. Alicia de Larrocha, in performance at the Gilmore Festival, proved by far the more polished executant. But the personal urgency of Norris's musical advocacy made him the festival's clear favorite. In a piano competition, he would have pitted his études, his ballades, his Brahms quintet, his Mozart concerto against the same music as rendered by a dozen others. A jury, pencils and scores in hand, would have sat in solemn judgment. The Gilmore showcase was at all times dignified. It conferred a different kind of imprimatur. People in

---

* Norris contributed a scholarly essay on the Schubert/Liszt *Winterreise* to the September 1985 *Musical Times*. Among his observations: "The importance of the transcriptions lies in the light they shed on the changes in performing practice introduced, it would seem, by Paganini and influentially developed by Liszt. . . . Such is the emotional impetus whipped up by Liszt that Schubert's phrase-lengths and his balanced sections are unable to contain it. Liszt has to add not only ritardandos and pauses but extra bars of interlude between phrases. He sometimes writes the final vocal cadence in notes double Schubert's value, and often adds a coda much longer than Schubert's piano postlude. Experiment quickly proves that these ritardandos and structural additions are not merely decorative; in such an extrovert style of performance, they are essential to the timing of the ebb and flow of emotion."

Kalamazoo understood this. Norris was an esteemed and honored guest. He was nobody's pet.

In fact, the entire nine-day festival proved that neither horse races nor war-horses are needed to produce a popular winner. The program for the opening concert, with the well-drilled and enthusiastic Kalamazoo Symphony, consisted of Copland's *Fanfare for the Common Man*, the Britten concerto, and C. Curtis-Smith's Concerto for the Left Hand—the last a Gilmore commission for Leon Fleisher, who took part as soloist. A second Gilmore commission, again to a local composer, produced Ramon Zupko's *Fluxus No. 9* for Piano and Tape—performed by Abraham Stokman on a program also including *Verticals* for Piano by the recent Pulitzer Prize winner Shulamit Ran. In Kalamazoo and surrounding communities, the Gilmore presented *thirty-four* additional recitals and chamber music events, all featuring piano, fortepiano, organ, or harpsichord, and including complete cycles of the Mozart and Beethoven piano sonatas. There were three concerts with orchestra, eleven master classes, two panel discussions, two lectures, and six lecture-demonstrations. The presiding spirit was enterprising, never opportunistic or perfunctory. The audience responded in kind—and in bewildering numbers. A typical weekday began with a 10 A.M. master class by Aube Tzerko attended by two hundred listeners (the student pianists, both winners of Gilmore Young Artists Awards, were on a higher level than those to be encountered at similar events at the Cliburn and Kapell competitions). At noon Matti Raekallio continued his Beethoven sonata traversal, all eight installments of which filled the two-hundred-seat auditorium of the Kalamazoo Institute of Arts. Overlapping Raekallio, at Western Michigan University, was Harold Schonberg's lecture-demonstration (with recordings) on Romantic piano style. Overlapping Schonberg, back at the arts institute, was Raymond Dudley's lecture-demonstration, with four nineteenth-century pianos and a standing-room-only audience. At 4 P.M., Malcolm Bilson continued his Mozart sonata cycle, on fortepiano, at Kalamazoo College's light-flooded Stetson Chapel. De Larrocha's recital, that evening, filled 2,800 seats in Western Michigan University's Miller Auditorium. Subsequent recitalists and soloists at the festival included Van Cliburn, Igor Kipnis, Chick Corea, Marion McPartland, and George Shearing. The total audience for all nine days surpassed 50,000. The *Kalamazoo Gazette* commented in an editorial:

> We're being regaled with glorious music, some of it familiar, some of it new. Our musical horizons are expanding.

Plus we are meeting some fascinating people from many parts of the globe who have been drawn to blossom-bedecked southwestern Michigan for the festival.

And speaking of fascinating people, Kalamazoo should count itself fortunate indeed to be making the acquaintance of the first Gilmore Keyboard Festival artist, David Owen Norris of Great Britain. . . . What an unforeseen bonus Norris brings along with his unique musical vision! His enjoyment of life, sense of humor and down-to-earth personality make him a delight to get to know. . . .

While he is in Kalamazoo, he appears to be having the time of his life, doing what he most wants to do: playing the music that he loves and bringing his passion for that music to the public.

And in fact Norris *was* having "the time of his life." In a letter to the *Gazette* three days later, he called his two weeks in Kalamazoo "the high spot of my life—so far!" and continued: "What drives me in my music is a vision of art as a necessary part of today's society. It's been a moving experience to see how Kalamazoo's community has provided the right conditions for a Festival that has achieved so much more than anyone could have believed."

While in Kalamazoo, Norris gave a spur-of-the-moment recital at a shopping mall. Equally impromptu, he played for and chatted with a hundred elementary school students who happened by the festival office. At parties, at concerts, in stores, he disarmed the locals with his penchant for impulsive self-revelation. He also addressed a conclave of visiting music critics, and said:

"As the Gilmore Artist I've found myself thrust into a world of the piano of which I am not part. I've become more clearly aware than before of how peripheral I am to it. I'm not a pianist who can swap details of so-and-so's recording of such-and-such a work. I mention these facts because I am uneasily aware that what seems a sort of deliberate iconoclasm can equally appear a symptom of conceit. I come from a fairly basic lower-middle-class country background in which music was something that one did. Music was always an activity rather than an object. And I believe that the salvation of music today lies in its being properly perceived as an activity. In this regard, I think it is the duty of the artist to help create an engaged audience. I think far too many of us assume that being good is all there is to it. I think we should be involved with audiences on the local level, in community action. I've done that all my life. I run a summer festival in Petworth, where I live. When I took it over, it was an elitist affair. The festival brought in players from London and it brought in audiences from London.

There was no local support. That's changed now. For one thing, the out-of-town peformers come for a full week; they establish a personal rapport, which does wonders. Also, we try to engage all the locals who play music. We have a plumber, for instance, who plays the trumpet. I feel that only in this way is music as I understand it going to thrive. Music isn't something you plug into the wall and switch on. This is why I speak of the irrelevance of the piano recital. Recording, too, is a reification of music—it turns it into a thing. In fact, I would restrict the playing of recordings to an occasional hearing over the radio. I would not allow the dangerous hardware into people's homes!"

I cornered Norris afterward and asked him how he became a pianist.

"I've had a lot of false starts. When I was at grammar school, I aspired to become a physicist. Only at Oxford did I begin to think more in terms of music. My ambitions, in turn, were to become a cathedral organist, a general music master in a school, and a scholar of medieval music. When I left Oxford I was a composer. I wrote a lot of music in a style that blended Bax, Shostakovich, and Messiaen. I had worked out a theory to which I composed. Then it was suddenly borne in upon me that I hated it. Mine was the type of music I felt I should write, that I was encouraged to write. But it was manisfestly *not me*. So I stopped. Since then I've developed a compositional style that's quite complicated, but always ingratiating.

"I recall that when I was twenty-three or twenty-four, I made a list of the goals I wanted to achieve by the time I was thirty. These must have been my last goals! One was to become a better pianist—that's still a goal, I think. The second goal was to become fluent in at least one language other than English—and I have become kind of fluent in French. My third goal was a research goal: to have made 'some small corner of musical endeavor on my own.' That's how I expressed it—God, I was naive!

"My most formidable attempt to develop a piano technique came when I was twenty-seven. I spent a lot of time practicing the Cortot exercises. Then, before I got too old to qualify, I decided to enter the 1981 Sydney competition. It was a very great strain. My musical memory is not particularly wonderful, so I made a decision that I would not bother to learn the concertos, because if I did I would surely forget my recital program. The latter included music by William Byrd and Percy Grainger. And to my annoyance, everyone exclaimed, 'Good lord! He must be *eccentric*'—a word I've come to dread. Because everything I do is done because

it seems the obvious thing to do. I mean, it was Grainger's cen-
tennial year, and I was in Australia [where he was born], for God's
sake. Then in the second preliminary round I had to play some
Chopin—which I normally don't play because so many others play
it terribly well. And then there was a required Liszt study, so I
had learned *Mazeppa*, after a fashion. My recital program consisted
of the Bax Second Sonata and the Tippett Third. Apparently I
was doing awfully well at this point, so they thrust me into the
final round, where I was to play a Mozart concerto and the Brahms
D minor. In the Mozart, I had to improvise a cadenza, not having
had the time to learn one. I remember interpolating something
from Bach's B minor Orchestral Suite without any conscious cog-
itation at all. It was at this point that half the jury left the room.
I was actually very close to the nervous breakdown that I had
shortly afterward. The Brahms First seemed a lot to learn in the
space of a week. I was in complete despair. I earnestly begged to
be allowed to withdraw from the competition but was told, 'You
must play it live on TV and from memory.' I then sought an ax
with which to damage my foot. My mind had stepped outside
itself."

In summary: Norris is an original whose guiding premise is not
"eccentric," merely rare. Art, he believes, is a product of society.
Music never exists *in vacuo*, but in relation to an audience. The
audience matters.

One of the panel discussions at the Gilmore Festival was devoted
to the interesting question: "What Happened to the American
Pianists of the Fifties?" Van Cliburn, Leon Fleisher, Byron Janis,
and Gary Graffman were among the artists discussed. None had
sustained a major performing career into middle age. My contribution, as a panelist, was to scrutinize the governing assumption
that a pianist's highest calling, to be pursued decades on end, is
that of performance specialist. Liszt, I pointed out, had virtually
stopped performing at age thirty-five. For the rest of his life he
composed, conducted, taught, and wrote. In fact, the specialization
we take for granted among performing musicians was a late development. Throughout the nineteenth century, such important pianists as Beethoven, Chopin, Mendelssohn, Rubinstein, and Bülow
were important composers and/or conductors. The touring virtuoso
who only plays is essentially a twentieth-century development.

Having said all this, I turned to Leon Fleisher, who was himself a panelist. Fleisher still performs, but only with his left hand. Primarily, he is a leading pedagogue, professor of piano at the Peabody Conservatory and artistic director of the Tanglewood Music Center. He has also conducted extensively since his right hand quit in the 1960s. "Leon," I inquired, "when you were in your thirties, what did you imagine you would be doing in your sixties?" His answer was the one I had hoped for and expected. He had aspired to devote the rest of his life to playing concerts, he said. His hand malady, in retrospect, had rescued him from becoming a "concert fool." It had opened up a world of music and music-making he would not otherwise have discovered.

In fact, the role model once seized by Cliburn, Fleisher, and other fifties' pianists is already musty, and so are the repertoire and formats that support it. Steven De Groote may or may not have been correct in surmising that Murray Perahia could become the only American pianist of his generation to maintain a major career into old age—but De Groote was on the right track, and so was his teacher Horszowski when he said that the "golden age" of touring virtuosos was ending. That David Owen Norris exemplifies a healthier present-day role model is certain. But his fate is not.

Norris himself does not believe in long-range prediction. At the moment, he considers playing the piano "my best chance to do what I want. I look forward to attaining a new degree of technical consistency. This is an opportunity I've never had before."

The Gilmore will manage Norris's international career for at least two years. So far, a 1991–92 American itinerary of some thirty-five engagements has been arranged. Norris will give recitals at such prominent venues as Boston's Jordan Hall, Chicago's Ravinia Festival, UCLA's Royce Hall, and Washington's Kennedy Center. The orchestras on his two-year schedule are the Boise, New Orleans, Rochester (Minnesota), and Syracuse Symphonies, Chicago's Grant Park Orchestra, and the Chicago Symphony at Ravinia. The majority of his engagements are on college and university campuses, where Norris intends to offer two-day residencies including an "educational service." "I'm anxious not to turn into someone who breezes into a city, says, 'Well, this is my dressing room,' and leaves the next day."

He will succeed with audiences. How the music business will react is harder to say. Its cynics and pessimists—who call themselves "realists"—will worry that he is too old, too odd, too intellectual, too erratic, too obscure. Critics and keyboard connoisseurs may prove even harder to convince that how well Norris can play his choice of études is a secondary priority. Norris makes us wonder, what is music for? It is a question seldom asked by those who sponsor, promote, and chronicle concerts.

If Norris will be a tough sell to the businessmen and critics, he may be equally resisted by his colleagues of the keyboard, so many of whom are actual or aspirant "concert fools." Ask them what they hope to do in their sixties, and they may say: "To play Op. 111 better than ever"—an answer demonstrating responsibility to themselves and, after a fashion, to Beethoven, and yet risking irrelevance.

"What advice would you give these fledgling young artists?" an American pianist—and piano juror—was asked at a recent music competition. "How can they be certain what to do in a field so crowded with gifted young performers?" His response: "Ask yourself whether you have something important to say in your playing. If you're really confident, if you're sure in your heart, pursue it." This prescription befits a select few. It also befits another time, when the piano was a more central medium, when its literature was fresher, when its audience was younger and surer. A saner prescription for today would be the David Owen Norris credo that begins, "Ask yourself what you can contribute to the cultural community."

More than timely, the Norris credo is necessary. Norris has a role—a new role—to play. Will he, and others like him, be allowed to play it?

APPENDICES
NOTES ON SOURCES
INDEX

The Cliburn Winners, Jurors, Directors, Rules

1962:
1. Ralph Votapek (US)
2. Nikolai Petrov (USSR)
3. Mikhail Voskresenski (USSR)
4. Cécile Ousset (France)
5. Marilyn Neeley (US)
6. Sergio Varella-Cid (Portugal)
7. Arthur Fennimore (US)
8. Takashi Hironaka (Japan)

Jurors:
Leopold Mannes (US)—chairman
Yara Bernette (Brazil)
Jorge Bolet (US)
Angelo Eagon (US)
Rudolf Ganz (US)
Don Luis Herrera de la Fuente (Mexico)
Motonari Iguchi (Japan)
Milton Katims (US)
Lili Kraus (New Zealand)
Lev Oborin (USSR)
Leonard Pennario (US)
Serge Saxe (US)

Chairman of the Competition:
Mrs. Grace Ward Lankford

1966:

1. Radu Lupu (Romania)
2. Barry Snyder (US)
3. Blanca Uribe (Colombia)
4. Maria Luisa Lopez-Vito (Philippines)
5. Rudolf Buchbinder (Austria)
6. Benedikt Kohlen (W. Germany)

Jurors:

Howard Hanson (US)—chairman
Joseph Benvenuti (France)
Reimar Dahlgrun (W. Germany)
Guillermo Espinosa (Colombia)
Jozsef Gat (Hungary)
Valentin Gheorghiu (Romania)
Arni Kristjansson (Iceland)
Lili Kraus (New Zealand)
Alicia de Larrocha (Spain)
Jean Mahaim (Belgium)
Gerald Moore (UK)
Boyd Neel (Canada)
Ezra Rachlin (US)
Claudette Sorel (US)
Marguerita Trombini-Kazuro (Poland)
Beveridge Webster (US)
Friedrich Wührer (Austria)

Executive Secretary:

Mrs. Grace Ward Lankford

Chairman:

Sam Cantey III

1969:

1. Cristina Ortiz (Brazil)
2. Minoru Nojima (Japan)
3. Mark Westcott (US)
4. Gerald Robbins (US)
5. Diane Walsh (US)
6. Michiko Fujinuma (Japan)

Jurors:

Ezra Rachlin (US)—chairman
Abram Chasins (US)
Leon Fleisher (US)
Peter Frankl (UK)

Nicole Henriot-Schweitzer (France)
Bruce Hungerford (Australia)
Motonari Iguchi (Japan)
Mindru Katz (Israel)
Constance Keene (US)
Lili Kraus (New Zealand)
Leonard Pennario (US)

Executive Secretary:
Mrs. Catherine L. Russell

Chairman:
Richard Lee Brown

1973:
1. Vladimir Viardo (USSR)
2. Christian Zacharias (W. Germany)
3. Michael Houstoun (New Zealand)
4. Alberto Reyes (Uruguay)
5. Evgenii Korolev (USSR)
6. Krassimir Gatev (Bulgaria)

Jurors:
John Giordano (US)—chairman
Abram Chasins (US)
James Dick (US)
Nicole Henriot-Schweitzer (France)
John Hopkins (Australia)
Constance Keene (US)
Lili Kraus (New Zealand)
Fernando Laires (Portugal)
Evgenii Malinin (USSR)
Leonard Pennario (US)
Vlado Perlemuter (France)
Walter Susskind (US)
Luis C. Valencia (Philippines)

Executive Secretary:
Mrs. Catherine L. Russell

Chairman:
Mrs. William M. Fuller

1977:
1. Steven De Groote (S. Africa)
2. Alexander Toradze (USSR)

3. Jeffrey Swann (US)
4. Christian Blackshaw (UK) and Michel Dalberto (France)
5. Ian Hobson (UK) and Alexander Mndoyants (USSR)

Jurors:
John Giordano (US)—chairman
Guido Agosti (Italy)
James Dick (US)
Rudolf Firkusny (US)
Leon Fleisher (US)
Alberto Ginastera (Argentina)
Lucrecia R. Kasilag (Philippines)
Lili Kraus (New Zealand)
Nikita Magaloff (Switzerland)
John Ogdon (UK)
Leonard Pennario (US)
Nicolai Petrov (USSR)
Pierre Sancan (France)
José Serebrier (Uruguay)

Executive Director:
Robert H. Alexander

Chairman:
Mrs. Elton M. Hyder, Jr.

1981:
1. André-Michel Schub (US)
2. Panayis Lyras (US) and Santiago Rodriguez (US)
3. Jeffrey Kahane (US)
4. Christopher O'Riley (US)
5. Daming Zhu (China)

Jurors:
John Giordano (US)—chairman
Marcello Abbado (Italy)
Maurice Abravanel (US)
Abram Chasins (US)
Valentin Gheorghiu (Romania)
Lili Kraus (New Zealand)
Minoru Nojima (Japan)
Leonard Pennario (US)
Vlado Perlemuter (France)
Lucio San Pedro (Philippines)
Earl Wild (US)
Zhou Guang-Ren (China)

Executive Director:
Anthony Phillips

Chairman:
Mrs. Joe A. Tilley, Jr.

1985:
1. José Feghali (Brazil)
2. Philippe Bianconi (France)
3. Barry Douglas (UK)
4. Emma Tahmisian (Bulgaria)
5. Károly Mocsári (Hungary)
6. Hans-Christian Wille (W. Germany)

Jurors:
John Giordano (US)—chairman
Idil Biret (Turkey)
Jorge Bolet (US)
Anton Dikov (Bulgaria)
Malcolm Frager (US)
Arpad Joo (Hungary/US)
Lili Kraus (New Zealand)
Li Mingqiang (China)
Minoru Nojima (Japan)
Cécile Ousset (France)
Harold C. Schonberg (US)
Soulima Stravinsky (US)
Wolfgang Stresemann (US)

Executive Director:
Andrew Raeburn

Chairman:
Mrs. Joe A. Tilley, Jr.

1989:
1. Alexei Sultanov (USSR)
2. José Carlos Cocarelli (Brazil)
3. Benedetto Lupo (Italy)
4. Alexander Shtarkman (USSR)
5. Tian Ying (China)
6. Elisso Bolkvadze (USSR)

Jurors:
John Giordano (US)—chairman
Sergei Dorensky (USSR)

Jan Ekier (Poland)
Nicole Henriot-Schweitzer (France)
John Lill (UK)
Li Mingqiang (China)
Cristina Ortiz (Brazil)
John F. Pfeiffer (US)
György Sándor (US)
Maxim Shostakovich (US)
Abbey Simon (US)
Lawrence Leighton Smith (US)
Takahiro Sonoda (Japan)
Joaquin Soriano (Spain)
Ralph Votapek (US)

Executive Director:
Richard Rodzinski

Chairman:
Mrs. Rice M. Tilley, Jr.

Competitors:
Seizo Azuma (Japan), 27
Jean-Efflam Bavouzet (France), 27
Elisso Bolkvadze (USSR), 22
Kathryn Brown (US), 27
David Buechner (US), 30
Pedro Burmester (Portugal), 26
Angela Cheng (Canada), 30
Angela Cholakyan (US), 30
José Carlos Cocarelli (Brazil), 30
Lora Dimitrova (Bulgaria), 27
Thomas Duis (W. Germany), 30
Konstanze Eickhorst (W. Germany), 28
Seung-Un Ha (US), 23
Eduardus Halim (Indonesia), 28
Jürgen Jakob (W. Germany), 27
Ivo Janssen (Holland), 26
Kevin Kenner (US), 26
Hae-Jung Kim (US), 24
Rita Kinka (Yugoslavia), 27
Leonid Kuzmin (US), 25
Li Jian (China), 24
Lin Hai (China), 20
Benedetto Lupo (Italy), 26
Wolfgang Manz (W. Germany), 29

Kayo Miki (Japan), 29
Károly Mocsári (Hungary), 27
Predrag Muzijevic (Yugoslavia), 26
John Nauman (US), 27
Shari Raynor (US), 27
Veronika Reznikovskaya (USSR), 23
Victor Sangiorgio (Australia), 30
Alexander Shtarkman (USSR), 21
Boris Slutsky (US), 29
Ju Hee Suh (S. Korea), 21
Alexei Sultanov (USSR), 19
Hugh Tinney (Republic of Ireland), 30
Andrew Wilde (UK), 24
Tian Ying (China), 21

REQUIRED REPERTOIRE

PRELIMINARIES PHASE 1

(a) J. S. Bach: any English Suite, partita, toccata, the *Chromatic* Fantasy and Fugue, the *Italian* Concerto.
(b) Haydn: any sonata; Beethoven: any sonata up to and including Op. 31, No. 3.
(c) Chopin: any ballade, any scherzo, the Barcarolle, the Impromptu in F-sharp major, Polonaise in A-flat major, Polonaise in F-sharp minor, Polonaise-Fantaisie.
(d) (1) Chopin: any étude of virtuosity and
(2) any étude of Bartók, Debussy, Liszt, Rachmaninoff, Scriabin, Stravinsky, the Prokofiev Toccata, the Schumann Toccata.

PRELIMINARIES PHASE 2

(a) Mozart: any sonata.
(b) Beethoven: any sonata from the following opus numbers: 53, 57, 81a, 101, 106, 109, 110, 111; any major work of Brahms, Chopin, Grieg, Liszt, MacDowell, Rachmaninoff, Schubert, Schumann, Tchaikovsky.
(c) Any work not longer than 20 minutes in length of Albéniz, Barber, Bartók, Berg, Boulez, Copland, Debussy, Falla, Ginastera, Granados, Hindemith, Messiaen, Prokofiev, Ravel, Schoenberg, Scriabin, Shostakovich, Stockhausen, Stravinsky, Szymanowski, Villa-Lobos, Webern.

SEMIFINALS
    (a) The Piano Quintet of Brahms, Dvořák, Franck, or Schumann, to be performed with the Tokyo String Quartet.
    (b) A recital lasting a total of one hour consisting of works chosen by the competitor, and the especially composed new work by William Schuman: *Chester:* Variations for Piano. The score of this composition was sent to competitors on March 31, 1989.

FINALS
    (a) Mozart: Piano Concerto in C major, K. 467; Piano Concerto in C minor, K. 491; Piano Concerto in F major; Beethoven: Piano Concerto No. 2 in B-flat; or Chopin: Piano Concerto in F minor, to be performed with the Fort Worth Chamber Orchestra, conducted by Stanislaw Skrowaczewski.
    (b) A major piano concerto composed in or after 1800, to be performed with the Fort Worth Symphony Orchestra, conducted by Stanislaw Skrowaczewski.

APPENDIX B:

The Major Winners

A list of first-, second-, and third-prize winners in five international competitions.

1. CHOPIN INTERNATIONAL PIANO COMPETITION (Warsaw)

1927: Lev Oborin (USSR), Stanislav Szpinalski (Poland), Reza Etkin-Moszkowska (Poland)

1932: Alexander Uninsky (France), Imre Ungar (Hungary), Boleslaw Kon (Poland)

1937: Yakov Zak (USSR), Roza Tamarkina (USSR), Witold Malcuzynski (Poland)

1949: Bella Davidovich (USSR) and Halina Czerny-Stefanska (Poland), Barbara Hesse-Bukowska (Poland), Waldemar Maciszewski (Poland)

1955: Adam Harasiewicz (Poland), Vladimir Ashkenazy (USSR), Fou Ts'ong (China)

1960: Maurizio Pollini (Italy), Irna Zaritskaya (USSR), Tania Achot-Haroutounian (Iran)

1965: Martha Argerich (Argentina), Arthur Moreira-Lima (Brazil), Marta Sosinska (Poland)

1970: Garrick Ohlsson (US), Mitsuko Uchida (Japan), Piotr Paleczny (Poland)

1975: Krystian Zimerman (Poland), Dina Yoffe (USSR), Tatyana Fedkina (USSR)

1980: Dang Thai Son (Vietnam), Tatyana Shebanova (USSR), Arutiun Papazian (USSR)

1985: Stanislav Bunin (USSR), Marc Laforet (France), Krzysztof Jablonski (Poland)

2. HARVEYS LEEDS INTERNATIONAL PIANO COMPETITION (Leeds, England)

1963: Michael Roll (UK), Vladimir Krainov (USSR), Sebastien Risler (France)

1966: Rafael Orozco (Spain), Semyon Kruchin (USSR) and Victoria Postnikova (USSR), Alexei Nasedkin (USSR)

1969: Radu Lupu (Romania), Georges Pludermacher (France), Arthur Moreira-Lima (Brazil)

1972: Murray Perahia (US), Craig Sheppard (US), Eugene Indjic (US)

1975: Dmitri Alexeev (USSR), Mitsuko Uchida (Japan), Pascal Devoyan (France) and András Schiff (Hungary)

1978: Michel Dalberto (France), Diana Kacso (Brazil), Lydia Artymiw (US)

1981: Ian Hobson (UK), Wolfgang Manz (W. Germany), Bernard d'Ascoli (France)

1984: Jon Kimura Parker (Canada), Ju Hee Suh (S. Korea), Junko Otake (Japan)

1987: Vladimir Ovchinnikov (USSR), Ian Munro (Australia), Noriko Ogawa (Japan)

3. EDGAR M. LEVENTRITT FOUNDATION INTERNATIONAL COMPETITION (New York City)

(The Leventritt Competition, discontinued after 1976, named "winners" —sometimes one, sometimes two, sometimes none—and "finalists." The following list is for piano years only.)

1940: Sidney Foster
1942: no winner
1943: Eugene Istomin
1944: Jeanne Therrien
1945: Louise Meiszner
1947: Alexis Weissenberg
1948: Jean Graham
1949: Gary Graffman
1950: no winner
1954: Van Cliburn
1955: John Browning
1957: Anton Kuerti
1959: Malcolm Frager
1960: no winner
1962: Michel Block
1965: Tong Il Han
1969: Joseph Kalichstein
1971: no winner
1976: no winner (finalists: Lydia Artymiw, Steven De Groote, Marian Hahn, Santiago Rodriguez, Mitsuko Uchida)

4. QUEEN ELISABETH INTERNATIONAL COMPETITION (Brussels)

(piano winners only)

1938: Emil Gilels (USSR), Moura Lympany (UK), Yakov Fliere (USSR)

1952: Leon Fleisher (US), Karl Engel (Switz.), Maria Tipo (Italy)

1956: Vladimir Ashkenazy (USSR), John Browning (US), Andrei Tchaikovsky (Poland)

1960: Malcolm Frager (US), Ronald Turini (Canada), Lee Luvisi (US)

1964: Evgeny Mogilevsky (USSR), Nikolai Petrov (USSR), Jean-Claude Vanden Eynden (Belgium)

1968: Ekaterina Novitskaya (USSR), Valery Kamyshov (USSR), Jeffrey Siegel (US)

1972: Valery Afanassiev (USSR), Jeffrey Swann (US), Joseph Alfidi (US)

1975: Mikhail Faerman (USSR), Stanislav Igolinski (USSR), Youri Egorov (USSR)

1978: Abdel-Rahman El-Bacha (Lebanon), Gregory Allen (US), Brigitte Engerer (France)

1983: Pierre Volondat (France), Wolfgang Manz (W. Germany), Boyan Vodenitcharov (Bulgaria)

1987: Andrei Nikolsky (stateless), Akira Wakabayashi (Japan), Rolf Plagge (W. Germany)

5. TCHAIKOVSKY INTERNATIONAL COMPETITION (Moscow)

(piano winners only)

1958: Van Cliburn (US), Lu Shi-Koon (China) and Lev Vlasenko (USSR), Naum Shtarkman (USSR)

1962: Vladimir Ashkenazy (USSR) and John Ogdon (UK), Susan Starr (US) and In' Chen-Tszoon (China), Elisso Virsaladze (USSR)

1966: Gregory Sokolov (USSR), Misha Dichter (US), Victor Eresko (USSR)

1970: Vladimir Krainev (USSR) and John Lill (UK), Horacio Gutiérrez (US), Arthur Moreira-Lima (Brazil) and Victoria Postnikova (USSR)

1974: Andrei Gavrilov (USSR), Myung-Whun Chung (US) and Stanislav Igolinsky (USSR), Youri Egorov (USSR)

1978: Michael Pletnev (USSR), Pascal Devoyon (France) and André Laplante (Canada), Nikolai Demidenko (USSR) and Evgeny Rivkin (USSR)

1982: no first place, Peter Donohoe and Vladimir Ovchinnikov, Michie Kayama (Japan)

1986: Barry Douglas (UK), Natalya Trull (USSR), Irina Plotnikova (USSR)

1990–91 Competition Winners

CHOPIN
1990: no first place, Kevin Kenner (US), Yukio Yokoyama (Japan)

LEEDS
1990: Artur Pizarro (Portugal), Lars Vogt (W. Germany), Eric Le Sage (France)

QUEEN ELISABETH
1991: Frank Braley (France), Stephen Prutsman (U.S.), Brian Ganz (U.S.)

TCHAIKOVSKY
1990: Boris Berezovsky (USSR), Vladimir Mishchuk (USSR), third place shared by Kevin Kenner (US), Anton Mordasov (USSR), and Johann Schmidt (Belgium)

Notes on Sources

GIVEN THE RELATIVE PAUCITY OF WRITTEN SOURCES—TO MY KNOWL-
edge, there are no important books about piano competitions—my
sources are mainly oral. All quotations in *The Ivory Trade* are from
discussions and interviews with the author, except as noted below.
Many of those with whom I spoke chose to remain anonymous.

A second component of my research, not indicated below, was
listening to music. Though I did not attend the 1977, 1981, or 1985
Cliburn competitions, they were recorded, and I have listened extensively to the tapes (housed in the library of Texas Christian
University in Fort Worth). I also obtained many tapes from the
pianists themselves. My description of William Wolfram's interpretation of Rachmaninoff's Second Sonata, for instance, is based on
a tape of his performance at the Maryland Competition and on a
New York performance I attended.

INTRODUCTION (PAGES 13 TO 18)

The "survey" showing the proliferation of international piano
competitions is in Gustav A. Alink, *Piano Competitions—A Comprehensive Directory of National and International Piano Competitions* (published in 1988 by the author, P.O. Box 85657, NL 2508 AR, Den
Haag, The Netherlands). For Felix Mendelssohn on music competitions, see his *Letters* as edited by G. Selden-Goth (New York:
Pantheon Books, 1945), p. 290. George Steiner's conviction that we
live in "enormously interesting" times may be found in his *In Blue-
beard's Castle* (New Haven: Yale University Press, 1971), p. 141.
The Tocqueville quote is from *Democracy in America*, volume 2,
chapter 9.

PRELUDE: THE VAN CLIBURN STORY (PAGES 19 TO 37)

Howard Taubman wrote about "new Russian successes" in the June 15, 1952, *New York Times*. Olin Downes hailed Leon Fleisher's victory in the *Times* on June 8, 1952. Olegna Fuschi's story about Cliburn and Rosina Lhévinne has been told many times; one central (but often unreliable) source is Abram Chasins and Villa Stiles, *The Van Cliburn Legend* (Garden City: Doubleday, 1959). Of the many accounts of Cliburn's Moscow success, I draw chiefly on *Time:* April 21, April 28, May 19 (the cover story), June 2, and Oct. 6, 1958; and on *Newsweek*, Aug. 4, 1958, and *Family Weekly*, Jan. 11, 1959. An informative interview with Cliburn appeared in *Contemporary Keyboard*, April 1978. Of newspaper accounts, in addition to the Max Frankel stories, I mainly use the *New York Times*, April 21 (Shostakovich's commentary), May 23, and May 26 (Jack Gould's review), 1958. Mark Schubart's and Howard Taubman's articles appeared in the *Times* on April 20, 1958. With the help of my wife, Agnes Bruneau, I have examined the Russian-language Cliburn clippings of the Music Division of the New York Public Library at Lincoln Center, as well as a book: *Van Cliburn*, by S. Khentova (Moscow: Government Music Press, 1959). And I have interviewed many who knew Van Cliburn in Texas and New York.

For Dwight Macdonald on the "genius act," see "Masscult and Midcult" in his *Against the American Grain* (New York: Da Capo Press, 1983). For how Arturo Toscanini and Vladimir Horowitz were redrawn as "regular guys," see my *Understanding Toscanini: How He Became an American Culture-God and Helped Create a New Audience for Old Music* (New York: Alfred A. Knopf, 1987, and Minneapolis: University of Minnesota Press, 1988). Paul Henry Lang's warnings about Cliburn's future appeared in the *New York Herald Tribune*, April 27, 1958. Abram Chasins's "Will Success Spoil Van Cliburn?" appeared in the *New York Times Magazine*, June 22, 1958. The 1988 interview with Christoph von Dohnányi appeared in the program book of the Cleveland Orchestra and was written by James R. Oestreich.

The critic who suspected Hurok of conserving Cliburn's reputation was Donal Henahan in the Aug. 17, 1986, *New York Times*. Stephen Wigler interviewed Cliburn in the May 17, 1981, *Rochester Sunday Democrat and Chronicle*. Other recent Cliburn interviews of note, in addition to the *Texas Monthly* piece I cite, include Stuart Isacoff's in *Keyboard Classics*, July–Aug. 1985, Michael Fleming's in the *New York Times*, June 9, 1985, John Ardoin's in the Feb. 21, 1988, *Dallas Morning News*, and Isacoff's in *Ovation*, September

1989. The frustrated reviewer of NBC's 1966 "Portrait of Van Cliburn" was Joan Barthel in the Oct. 9, 1966, *New York Times.*

WHERE THE WEST BEGINS (PAGES 41 TO 49)

My portrait of Fort Worth draws on Oliver Knight, *Fort Worth: Outpost on the Trinity* (Norman: University of Oklahoma Press, 1953), Ruby Schmidt, *Fort Worth and Tarrant County: A Historical Guide* (Fort Worth: Texas Christian University Press, 1984), and Leonard Sanders, *How Fort Worth Became the Texasmost City 1849–1920* (Fort Worth: Texas Christian University Press, 1973). On culture, I partly rely on B. McGilvray, *A Brief History of the Development of Music in Fort Worth, Texas, 1849–1972* (an unpublished dissertation, Texas Christian University, 1972). *Newsweek*'s article on Fort Worth appeared Feb. 6, 1989. Also valuable are articles in *Town and Country*, May 1985 (in which Martha Hyder is called "one of this country's great ladies of organized charity") and November 1986. In John Bainbridge's *The Super-Americans* (Garden City: Doubleday, 1961), see especially pp. 150–157 and 365–380. Larry McMurtry's reflections may be found in *In a Narrow Grave* (Albuquerque: University of New Mexico Press, 1968). For Irl Allison on the Cliburn competition, see *Contemporary Keyboard*, March 1978.

HYDERIZATION (PP. 50 TO 58)

The *New York Times* visited Martha Hyder's home Oct. 13, 1977. *Women's Wear Daily* paid her a visit July 5, 1977.

WHERE PIANO COMPETITIONS CAME FROM (PP. 59 TO 69)

On the history of music competitions, the two best sources I know in English are Bob Doerschuk, "Piano Competitions," in the March 1978 *Contemporary Keyboard*, and Eileen T. Cline, *Piano Competitions: An Analysis of Their Structure, Value, and Educational Implications* (an unpublished dissertation, University of Indiana, 1985), which includes a valuable appendix listing winners, judges, and repertoire for the principal competitions. My anecdotes about Bach, Handel, Scarlatti, Mozart, Clementi, Beethoven, Liszt, et al., are well known. Marpurg's story about J. S. Bach may be found in *The Bach Reader*, edited by Hans T. David and Arthur Mendel (New York: Norton, 1966), p. 453. Ries's story about Beethoven may be found in Elliot Forbes (ed.), *Thayer's Life of Beethoven* (Princeton: Princeton University Press, 1949), p. 257. For Arthur Loesser on

Liszt, see his *Men, Women and Pianos* (New York: Simon & Schuster, 1954), p. 367. Arthur Rubinstein's relevant memoirs are in *My Young Years* (New York: Alfred A. Knopf, 1973). *Etude*'s 1948 protest against "contest-itis" appeared in December. The "tally" showing a tenfold increase in international piano competitions is in Alink, cited above. For the democratized "new audience" tutored by music appreciation, and the post–World War II "cultural explosion," see my *Understanding Toscanini*. For Irl Allison's views, see his articles in *The Musician*, March 1934, *Etude*, July 1934, and *Etude*, April 1945. Eileen T. Cline has analyzed the proliferation of aspirant concert pianists after World War II in *The American Music Teacher*, January 1982.

ELITISTS BITE THE DUST (PAGES 70 TO 77)

Of the dozens of people I spoke to about the Leventritt competition, most preferred to remain anonymous. Two who did not were Gary and Naomi Graffman. I also rely on Gary Graffman's *I Really Should Be Practicing* (New York: Avon Books, 1982), and on scrapbooks of Leventritt clippings and press releases belonging to T. Roland Berner. An informative interview with Rosalie Berner appeared in *Contemporary Keyboard*, March 1978. Van Cliburn commented "All they think about is the Leventritt" in John Ardoin's Arts & Leisure article in the *New York Times*, Oct. 9, 1977.

SOME WINNERS AND LOSERS (PAGES 79 TO 142)

Steven De Groote's comments on "burning out" and moving to Tempe appeared in the *Washington Post*, May 29, 1981. John Browning comments on Russian contestants in David Dubal, *Reflections from the Keyboard* (New York: Summit Books, 1984), p. 115. *People* magazine described Alexander Toradze's reunion with his mother on July 4, 1988.

Important accounts of the 1981 Cliburn competition include Lynn Darling's in the *Washington Post* (May 27–June 1), Bob Doerschuk's in *Keyboard* (November 1981), Harold C. Schonberg's in the *New York Times* (May 18–June 1, plus a June 14 interview with André-Michel Schub), and W. L. Taitte's in *Texas Monthly* (August 1981). Steven De Groote talks about "people saying the sort of things I heard last time" in Taitte's piece. My interview with Schub appeared in the July 29, 1979, *New York Times*. Bruno Walter's remarks on Weimar culture may be found in his *Theme and Variations* (New York: Alfred A. Knopf, 1946), p. 268.

Ivan Davis's account of the 1985 Cliburn competition appeared in the June 5 *Dallas Morning News*. Bernard Holland reviewed José Feghali in the Oct. 21, 1985, *New York Times*. Peter G. Davis's Feghali review ran in *New York* magazine on Nov. 4, 1985. Jorge Bolet's conclusions about the 1985 competition are quoted by Stuart Isacoff in *Keyboard Classics*, July–Aug. 1985. Dusty Rhodes's article on William Wolfram appeared in the July 21, 1985, *Dallas Life*. The Holland and Davis reviews of Wolfram's recital were in the Nov. 1, 1987, *New York Times*, and in *New York* magazine, Nov. 6, 1987.

THE EIGHTH VAN CLIBURN INTERNATIONAL PIANO COMPETITION (PAGES 143 TO 242)

György Sándor complains about piano competitions in David Dubal, *Reflections from the Keyboard*, p. 286. Richard Rodzinski's instructions to Peter Rosen, and the comments of the screening jurors, are taken from Cliburn Foundation press releases.

The *Fort Worth Star-Telegram* ran a four-page Cliburn supplement every day of the 1989 competition. Martha Hyder's comments on Steven De Groote's death are from Wayne Gay's article, "Davidovici planning to honor De Groote," in the May 23 *Star-Telegram*. Alexei Sultanov's snake-handling is described in Carol Nuckols's "Notes" on the competition, in the June 6 *Star-Telegram*. Wayne Gay complained about the jury's first cut in "Business as Usual," in the June 2 *Star-Telegram*. Christopher Evans's follow-up, "The choices," appeared the next day. Of the other quoted remarks. I have culled from *Star-Telegram* stories, those not already attributed in my text are Yamaha's Yoji Suzuki on competition pianos, John Nauman's reaction to his elimination, Ralph Votapek defending the first cut, Alexander Shtarkman saying "I don't have any feelings," and Votapek and Abbey Simon on Alexei Sultanov's victory. Maxim Shostakovich's assessment of Sultanov is from the June 12 *Dallas Morning News*. Bernard Holland's periodic pieces on the Cliburn competition—an unusually sophisticated commentary —appeared in the *New York Times* on March 6, March 27, April 17, May 11, May 25, May 27, May 30, June 2, June 7, June 8, June 11, June 12, June 13, and June 28. Beyond those identified in my text, quotations I have used from Holland's stories are from Gary Graffman, on the Asian work ethic, and Tian Ying, on the same topic. Also, it was Holland's May 11 story that gave me the idea of applying C. P. E. Bach's treatise as a standard of musicianship. Lesley Valdez's interviews with John Lill and György Sándor for the *Philadelphia Inquirer* appeared June 5 and June 18.

Charles Edward Russell's reminiscence of Theodore Thomas in his *The American Orchestra and Theodore Thomas* (Garden City: Doubleday, Page, and Co., 1927) may be found on pp. 2–3. My discussion of jury machinations at the 1965 Chopin competition, in "The Jury Speaks," derives from a story in the *New York Times*, March 20, 1965. Daniel Pollack's account of adjudicating the 1986 Tchaikovsky competition appeared in the March 1987 *Musical America*. Liszt's "bitter disgust for art" is from a collection of his letters: *An Artist's Journey*, translated and edited by Charles Suttoni (Chicago: University of Chicago Press, 1989), p. 16. The *Town and Country* quotes are from the issues of May 1985 and November 1986.

Joseph Brodsky's description of Leningrad, in "Aftermath," is from his *Less than One* (New York: Farrar Straus Giroux, 1986), pp. 4–5. The reviews of "Here to Make Music" in the *Los Angeles Herald-Examiner* and *New York Times* appeared on Oct. 15 and Oct. 18, 1989. The reviews of Alexei Sultanov's Pasadena recital appeared on June 24, 1989; Alan Rich's follow-up story appeared July 2 in the *Los Angeles Herald-Examiner*.

CONCLUSION: A BETTER WAY (PAGES 243 TO 255)

Eliot Fisk wrote about music competitions in *Guitar Review*, Spring 1989. The European String Teachers Association study "Music Competitions" may be obtained from the Association at Baron's Keep, Gliddon Rd., London W. 14.

POSTLUDE: VAN CLIBURN REVISITED (PAGES 257 TO 264)

Time's cover story ran May 19, 1958. All the Liszt quotations, and also Heine's remarks on Liszt, are from *An Artist's Journey*, cited above. The sacralization-to-popularization sequence was suggested to me by Kathleen Hulser. Also see my *Understanding Toscanini*, especially pp. 255–69.

Index

About the Author

JOSEPH HOROWITZ WAS BORN IN NEW YORK CITY IN 1948. HE WAS A music critic for the *New York Times* from 1976 to 1980. Since 1981, he has been program editor and principal annotator for the Kaufmann Concert Hall of the 92nd Street Y, one of New York's major concert halls. At the Y, he has hosted a two-year series of Conversations with American Composers, and served as music advisor for the Schubertiade, a landmark comprehensive survey of the music of Franz Schubert. He also directs an annual Schubert symposium, conceived as a meeting ground for scholars and laymen.

Mr. Horowitz is the author of two previous books. *Conversations with Arrau*, currently in print in six languages, won an ASCAP-Deems Taylor award for excellence in writing about music. *Understanding Toscanini—How He Became an American Culture-God and Helped Create a New Audience for Old Music* was named one of the most distinguished books of 1987 by the National Book Critics Circle. He is currently working on a study of America's Wagner cult of the late nineteenth century.

Mr. Horowitz is a member of the faculty of the Mannes College of Music. He lives in New York City with his wife, Agnes, and son, Bernie.